Beware of
This False Doctrine

Of Reciting the Sinners'
Prayer for Salvation

By
NngmingBongle Bapuohyele

Strategic Book Publishing and Rights Co.

Elohiym Edition or FirstFruits (4) Edition
First Revision, January 2015

Strategic Book Publishing and Rights Co., LLC
USA | Singapore
www.sbpra.com

ISBN: 978-1-63135-958-3

This book was first published in Ghana in 2009 of title *You Believed a False Doctrine* and of ISBN 978-9988-1-0360-3. In 2010, it was again published in Ghana under the new title *Beware of This False Doctrine of Reciting the Sinners' Prayer for Salvation* and of ISBN 978-9988-1-3894-3.

Notable Quotes

A life of zeal without knowledge leads to disappointment and disaster. A life of knowledge without zeal lacks fulfillment and joy.

To my knowledge add zeal, and to my zeal, add knowledge of your instruction, oh my Maker.

For true wisdom is the zealous obedience to your instructions.

NngmingBongle Bapuohyele

Courage is what it takes to stand up and speak; courage is also what it takes to sit down and listen.

Winston Churchill

The illiterates of the 21st century will not be those who cannot read and write, but those who cannot learn, unlearn, and relearn.

Alvin Toffler

Table of Contents

Dedication

I dedicate this book to the memory of the first Gentile-convert of African descent to the faith of the *Shlikhim* ("Apostles") of *Yahushua HaMashakhYahu* of the first century—an unnamed minister of treasury under Queen Kandake (Candace?), of ancient Ethiopia. This minister was the first to bring, unadulterated, the doctrine of the *Shlikhim* of *Yahushua HaMashakhYahu* on how one becomes born again, to African soil.

This book is also dedicated to Charles Elikwu, a Nigerian I met in Accra, Ghana, and Charlie Davis my fellow countryman. These two gentlemen, together with others, started me on a course that brought me revelations of Elohiym's Word, the subject of this book.

Charles Elikwu, now resident in London, established a group of enthusiastic seekers of truth in Accra, which was later left in the care of Charlie Davis, now a missionary in Nigeria. I shall forever remain indebted to them, and to Davis in particular, who pursued me persistently and tirelessly in those early days of my contact with them.

Finally, I also dedicate this book to my two lovely daughters, *Naamwindiwgn* and *Naamwinnombo*, who have immortalized in my mind pleasant memories of their paternal grandfathers, Ambrose Amunnabong, John Bongle, and Columbanus Bapuohyele, and of a place called *Saa*.

Chris Bapuohyele

Acknowledgements

My acknowledgements go to all inspired writer-teachers of the New Covenant faith, some of whose books have helped shape my thinking on spiritual issues. Up to today, I zealously study the teachings of such great men of the New Covenant doctrines with a fine comb, imbibing with great delight those teachings which stand in perfect agreement with the *Holy Scriptures*, while rejecting those which do not, by the leading of my spirit. Why would anyone want to eat someone's reared chicken with all its feathers, scales, and entrails, simply because it meets the eye as a well-bred one?

My special acknowledgement goes to Maxwell Y. E. Darteh, Accra, Ghana, for his encouragement and for the precious time he sacrificially spent reading over the manuscript and giving insightful advice on this project at various stages of its advancement.

Though acknowledging his strong sentiments against my disclosure in Chapter Four of this book, my source-teachings on the *"Sinners' Prayer"* practice, as taught in two books authored separately by two of my compatriots, I could not keep their identities from my readers.

I consider it unfair to my readers, and uncharacteristic of such literary work, to keep the identities of authors whose works have been quoted in this teaching silent or unacknowledged. That notwithstanding, I am most grateful to him for his concerns in this regard, which incidentally were not particular to him alone.

I also specially acknowledge all the following persons: Prof. E. Addo Obeng, Prof. Alan S. Duthie, Prof. Witness Add, Dr. Michael Ntumy, Dr. Theophilus Bamfo Dankwa, George Dasaah, James Clottey, Justice Julius Ansah, Douglas Boateng, Nelson Aklamamu, Otis Elis Osei, Eric Darko, Willie Gley, Felix Baddoo, Komodotam Weniamo Moses, Joe Gunney, Peter Koomson, Stephen Wengam, Pilly Preko, Dr. George Osfom-Batsa, Stephen Brafi, Thomas Broni Boahen, Mrs. Georgina Asante, Kanzing Tabariyeng, Hasan Mayaki, Fred O. Addae, and last but not least, Felix Opare.

All these people received from my hand copies of the processed manuscript at various stages of its completion for study of its contents, either in part or in whole. They shall forever remain in my thoughts, during my moments of prayer, for their frank comments, suggestions, expression of doubts, trepidations, worries, reservations, harsh criticisms, misunderstanding of my views to mean an expression of claim to infallibility, etc., which have helped to bring this book to its current state.

I am grateful to the few among them who communicated their thoughts in silence and for those very few who could not say much as they lost the copies of the Word document of the manuscript received from me even before they could read them.

I cannot forget to acknowledge the many other people, so many I lost count of them, who spent valuable time with me as we talked on the salient issues raised in this book. These interactions with them, geared me up tremendously to look critically at all matters raised in this book, and to seek further clarity in the expression of my thoughts. To all you nice people, I am grateful to you for your time and spirit of sharing.

Special mention must be made of the editors at Strategic Book Publishing and Rights Agency (SBPRA) who excellently edited this work, and Ernest Okimba Ebak and Daniel Abugah, who helped put the manuscript into a presentable form for editing. Daniel went beyond what he was supposed to do of the manuscript and finally became my always to cherish consultant-teacher in English grammar. Thanks Daniel, for your frankness about my bad English; it spurred me on to study the language all again.

I also acknowledge the dedication and patience I received from Miss Mary Ama Kwaning, Accra, Ghana, while she worked to produce the Word document from a rather hard-to-decipher handwritten manuscript.

I acknowledge Andy Konah, a dear friend of mine, who painstakingly typeset this work. Thanks Andy, for stretching your patience, tolerance, and dedication beyond limits to fulfill the desires of a hard-to-satisfy friend. I am sure the Almighty will richly bless you for your support of this project.

Finally, mention must be made of "Prof." E. Naamwindiwgn Bapuohyele, my lovely daughter, who edited the *Elohiym* Edition.

While acknowledging the immense and varied contributions all these wonderful people made towards the value of this book, I bear full responsibility for every detail of it and for any of its errors, inaccuracies, and defects. Please, all such must be entirely charged to me.

Chris Bapuohyele

Preface

There are many truths in the *Holy Scriptures* that never come to light, unless you look at them from a specific angle. In this book, I endeavor to closely examine the issue of how one is born again within the context of the salvation of the Most High One which is available only in the name of His only begotten Son, as is revealed in the *Holy Scriptures*.

Much has been taught by people who were sincere and honest about what they were teaching, but which turned out to be out of tune with the doctrines of the *Holy Scriptures*. I have come to know many people, who, in their attempt to teach how the sinner becomes born again into the Kingdom of the Most High One, seemed to be sincere and honest, but who, nonetheless, succeeded only in leading people away from the way of the Most High One, as far as becoming born again is concerned.

You may not call such people false teachers because their intention was not to deceive their pupils. At worst, they could be said to be teachers of a wrong doctrine who did not mean to harm their listeners. That notwithstanding, their teachings have the propensity to deny their listeners the salvation of the Most High One.

The salvation plan of the Most High One for mankind defies human logic. In fact, it is foolishness to the wisdom of the world. But if humanity is to enter the salvation of the Most High One, it must do so according to His doctrines and instructions. There is no other way.

Many people have failed to realize this and, therefore, have developed their own doctrines and instructions about how the sinner can become born again. This they have done by assembling portions of *The Bible* to develop their own logic and practice about how one enters the salvation of the Almighty. Either they have failed to see or they have deliberately ignored the instructions of the Almighty about how man could be born again.

They believe and teach that the sinner is born again through repentance and by saying a prayer, requesting of the Almighty son-ship and salvation. Taking my inspiration from the *Holy Scriptures*, I believe and teach the contrary. I believe that the sinner is born again only through repentance of sin and

13

obedience of the instructions of the Most High One, and not as it were through praying any kind of prayer in pursuit of it.

The thrust of this book is about correcting the error in their teaching on how the sinner takes the first steps into the salvation of the Most High One. In order that the errors inherent in their wrong doctrine would be clearly seen as such, the true way for the sinner to be born again will first be taught in the light of the doctrines of the *Holy Scriptures*.

Also in this book, some rare truths about baptism are taught as a prelude to a specific and detailed teaching on this error of seeking the salvation of the Most High One through prayer.

I will entreat you to read this book with an open mind. Should you have already accepted as genuine the error in doctrine being corrected here, understanding this revealed truth of the Almighty's salvation might be gradual in coming. Nevertheless, that understanding will definitely come, if you read this book open-mindedly and studiously.

For the purpose of teaching, unless otherwise stated, all *The Bible* quotations in this book are from the King James Version (KJV) because of its high popularity among salvation seekers. Readers must, however, be cautioned that the KJV is a translation from a Greek version of the *Holy Scriptures*, which was in itself derived from the original Hebrew texts, and so has lots of errors in it. Readers of these quotations from *The Bible* here in this book must know that there are many hard-lined critics of the KJV who see it as a perversion rather than a version of the *Holy Scriptures*; and though it is referred to as the Authorized Version, they angrily point out that it was never authorized by the Almighty that His Word be translated.

My prayer for you is that you will frequently return to this book until all errors concerning the born again doctrine you might be holding onto are cleared from your mind and replaced with the truth of the salvation of the Most High One. Your understanding and acceptance of the teaching in this book will, no doubt, be of great benefit to you in your pursuit to secure an "Entry Visa" into the Kingdom of the Most High One.

May the Most High One richly bless you as you read on, laboring to understand the issues taught in this book.

Chris Bapuohyele

Preface to this Elohiym Edition

"In the beginning Elohiym created the heavens and the earth". How does this sentence sound to you, dear reader? It may sound strange to you, and that might be due to the word *Elohiym*, which is unpopular to many people. And yet, *Elohiym* is the first known appellation of the Creator who made the universe, as was revealed by Him in the Hebrew language in which He chose to make Himself known to mankind, through the righteous men He inspired to write the *Holy Scriptures* many millennia ago!

For readers who are familiar with the King James Version (KJV) of *The Bible,* they are able to trace and relate the opening sentence in the above paragraph to *Genesis* 1:1. There, in the KJV, and indeed all English versions of *Genesis*, the word *Elohiym* has been deleted and replaced with *God*!

The *Holy Scriptures,* originally written in Hebrew, if ever they were meant to be translated at all, would, however, have had *Genesis* 1:1 translated more appropriately thus: *"In the beginning Elohiym created the heavens and the earth"*.

The question to ask is: Why is *Elohiym*, which is revealed to mankind by the Creator as being His primary description of Himself, lost completely in all the English versions of the *Holy Scriptures*?

Did all those who translated the Hebrew text of the *Holy Scriptures* into English, deliberately, plan and scheme to mislead readers of their versions into believing and accepting that the word *God,* given by them in their translations of *Elohiym,* is an alias to the first known appellation of the Creator of the Universe, and that this is acceptable even to Him as well? Is *God* a nickname coined by man for *Elohiym*; and is it one that He is pleased with?

Supposing that is the case, did these translators intend to make their readers come to believe that both appellations—*Elohiym* and *God*—belong to one and the same being and will produce the same results when either is uttered, and so may be used interchangeably?

But then, let me ask: If the two appellations do indeed mean the same and if their values are also the same, why then was there the need for translators to bring about the second at all? Think about this.

Well, it can not be that whatever errors that are detected in the

15

many translations or versions (or are they rather perversions?) of the English Bible were or are a deliberate ploy by translators to confuse salvation seekers or to even deny them the very salvation they seek in and by the word *God*, which they have given to the Creator, in the stead of *Elohiym* which He has purposely, and for good reason, given to Himself.

For, all translators come out to me as people who love their Creator and are desirous of serving Him in truth and in the best ways they can. Also, they seem to love their fellow men enough to never want to wish or do them any evil, and so, I believe, would not deliberately mislead salvation seekers by their work.

All this notwithstanding, it must be known that no one who has good intentions in trying to please the Most High One, or in seeking to do good service to mankind, will ever be left to himself without the arch enemy of the Almighty—Satan—trying to impede, frustrate, and even pollute his mind in his efforts, as in such work as translation of the *Holy Scriptures.*

The original writers of the Hebrew version of the *Holy Scriptures* were inspired by the Most High One in Hebrew, and were under His direct supervision, as they wrote these scriptures in Hebrew on scrolls of parchment long ago (*Second Timothy* 3:16 and *Second Peter* 1:21). These writers could, therefore, never have made even the minutest of errors in their writings in this language since, one could say, they wrote with the finger of the Most High One.

This perfection, which was characteristic of their work, could not be said to be the same even for the dedicated faithful of the scriptures who, in later years, copied by hand these original Hebraic scriptures onto new and fresh parchments from the aged ones.

Of course, such copyists would do their best in this effort and even plead the leading of *Ruwakh HaKodesh* (the Holy Spirit?) of the Most High One, and so could come up with excellent replicas of the original that would, nonetheless, never be as perfect as the originals.

Obviously, these reproduced copies of the scriptures could never have the same level of purity and perfection as those written by the people who were inspired and closely supervised by the Most High One to write the original scriptures in Hebrew; more so if these copyists worked from manuscripts on faded and, thus, difficult-to-decipher parchments.

Obviously, for those who, centuries later, decided by

themselves, and without the express mandate of the Most High One, to translate the Hebrew version of the *Holy Scriptures* into other languages, insulation from error while they worked could not be guaranteed.

Though they might have sought and determined to do an excellent job, in so far as they did not have the command and mandate of the Most High One to translate His Word into other languages of the world, they were left highly susceptible to error in their work.

The arch enemy of the Most High One is able to infiltrate the minds of any people who may be zealous to His cause and so could ultimately render their work fraught with errors, inaccuracies, untruths and outright pollutions.

Sadly, many translators are very often ignorant of such devices and trickery of the devil, while trying to execute their self-appointed tasks without Elohiym's mandate.

The English and other versions of *The Bible* must therefore be read with lots of careful and deep thoughtful consideration, and not be taken as *"Thus sayeth the Most High One"* in every word, verse, and chapter, of any of its books from *Genesis* to *Revelation.*

It would be very dangerous for any salvation seekers to read any translated versions of the Hebrew *Holy Scriptures* without the mind and thought that there may be human faults within these versions.

Readers must look out for any errors, inaccuracies in expression of thought, untruths, and outright pollutions, which, although translators never deliberately intended to mislead readers of their versions of the *Holy Scriptures* into, have, nonetheless, been found to occur in their work.

In our search for truth from the *Holy Scriptures* we must understand that names and titles of people are unique words that give identity to these people. Names and titles are the embodiment of those who bear them—the whole identity and persona of a person are revealed in his or her name and title.

Names are essentially sounds meant to be responded to by those who bear them when pronounced by other people. And so, names of people must always be properly uttered to bring into manifestation the desired attention and effect.

So then, would the word *God* have the same effect as *Elohiym* when uttered? I doubt this can ever be so. Of course, in sound, the word *God* is very much the same as the name *god* used in reference to idols made by humans for use as mediums of worship. Clearly, when the words *God* and *god* are written, they show a difference, but not when pronounced.

And so, because the name of a person is essentially a sound, meant to be responded to when properly pronounced, one can imagine the resulting confusion anytime and wherever either *God* or *god* is uttered to the hearing of the two beings that man has named as such.

Another question to ask is: Do the appellations, *God* and *god,* put the two beings, called as such by mankind, in the same class? Is the Creator in the same class as idols, with the only difference between them being that the Creator is the superior one, because, He is omniscient, omnipotent, and omnipresent? How could one ever think in such a manner at all?

According to the *New Strong's Exhaustive Concordance of the Bible* (Red letter ed.) the words *God, goddess, Godhead, godliness, godly, God's, gods* (idols), and *God-ward,* appear in the King James Version of *The Bible* as many as over forty-seven hundred times!

So then, by the time one is through with one complete reading of the King James Version of *The Bible,* one's spirit and mind become programed with the word *God,* as being a proper appellation of the Creator of the universe.

That being so, just think of the permanence and seeming indelibility of this programing in the spirits and minds of those who dedicatedly read *The Bible* several times in their lifetime!

The effect of this on readers of *The Bible* becomes the same as that which was forced upon people under Nazi propaganda. Nazi propagandist, Joseph Goebbels (1897-1945), is quoted to have said: *"If you tell a lie big enough and keep repeating it, people will eventually come to believe it."*—www.quotationspage.com/quote/35298.html.

And so, when salvation seekers, in their many readings of *The Bible,* are repeatedly informed that *God* is a holy appellation of the Creator of the Universe, they come to accept it as truth.

In fact, the sacredness attached to all English versions of *The Bible* by almost all its readers, supposing it to be the unblemished Word of the Most High One written verbatim by people who heard Him speak these very words, makes their acceptance of this lie—that *God* is the Creator of the Universe—even more thorough, far reaching, and eternally damaging.

As the return of the Savior to judge the world now seems imminent, salvation seekers must begin asking themselves questions in relation to many of the things they have believed and acted on in faith.

One question of importance would be to know whether, indeed, *Elohiym* and *God* do mean the same and, thus, do have the same effect when uttered with the intent of addressing the Creator of the Universe.

Another common name in all English versions of *The Bible* is *Jesus*. This name and its possessive pronoun, *Jesus'*, together, appear 981 times in the King James Version.

Every bible student knows that *Jesus* is a name of Greek origin. And yet, bible readers have come to consider the name *Jesus* to be appropriate for the Savior of the world, who was of Hebrew descent and who, in his days in *Yisroel,* was called by a Hebrew name by all Hebrew people of his day.

Sadly, by the time that the name *Jesus* is encountered by readers of the English versions of *The Bible* in as many times as it appears there, their minds and spirits would have become programed into believing and accepting that this name of Greek origin is what was given by the Most High One, Himself, to His only begotten Son and Savior of the world.

The effect of this in the minds of salvation seekers is that the Most High One has purposefully and willingly permitted that, His Son, the Hebrew-born Savior—*Yahushua*—now becomes savior to Greek-minded and other Gentile people of the world, in and by the name *Jesus*!

It is sad to note that even many of today's Hebrews calling themselves "Messianic Jews" are comfortable believing in the name *Jesus,* and seem to think that it is accepted by the Most High One as being the name of the Savior of the world!

Before the coming of the Savior to the world, however, it was prophesied to Hebrews in particular and to all Gentiles in general, that he would not only bring salvation to mankind, but also that his name would mean **Salvation**. The Savior was thus known by the name *Yahushua*, which means *"Yahuwah Is Salvation"* or *"Yahuwah Gives Salvation"* in Hebrew, when he sojourned this earth. The Savior was never called *Jesus* in *Yisroel* or by any children of *Yisroel*, anywhere else.

And so, in as much as all names are of eternal value, being spirit in nature and power, the name *Yahushua* is no doubt what name the Savior is forever known by, by the Most High

One and His holy angels in *Shamayim* (Heaven). The Most High One gave this name to His Son so that he would live and manifest its relevance in fulfillment of prophecy in all three worlds—whether on the earth, in the heavens above, or in the deeps below the earth.

Here, also, the question to ask is: Do the two names— *Yahushua* and *Jesus*—get the same response and have the same effect when uttered?

More curious to me is that, if the name *Yahushua* is what has been given by the Creator to His only begotten Son, and if it is in and by this name that He ordained for men to believe and accept in order to receive His salvation (cf. *Acts* 4:10-12), then would the name *Jesus* do same?

If it is only in the name *Yahushua* that the salvation of the Most High One must be obtained, what then can the name *Jesus* (a man-made alias or nickname to *Yahushua*?) do in mankind's quest for salvation? In any case, would it be true to say that it was *Jesus* who ascended to *Gulgotha*, or was it *Yahushua* rather who did?

For me, the most serious error committed by bible translators lies in their translation of names and titles of people they found in the Hebrew texts of the *Holy Scriptures*. While names of biblical locations and landmarks have remained essentially the same in English versions, albeit in corrupted pronunciations, as they are in the Hebrew text from which English versions are made, such great titles and names as *Elohiym* and *Yahushua*, and other human names, have been translated into English! This is not only ridiculous but completely unacceptable.

All titles and names the world over, despite whatever cultures they emanate from, must remain the same. They must never be translated. They should only be transliterated.

And so, the name *Bapuohyele* must remain same in all the cultures of the world—Chinese, Indian, European, American, Fulani, Xhosa. All people of other cultures outside Bapuohyele's *Dagaaba* culture must be taught how to properly pronounce the name *Bapuohyele* to good effect.

So then, why would English translators of *The Bible* treat differently the title *Elohiym* and the name *Yahushua*, which are meant to give unique meaning, value and power to any people who believe in them, by translating them? Why are these typically Hebrew names translated, and not rather transliterated?

For me, salvation seekers of all non-Hebrew culture ought to have been taught the meaning, value, and power in *Elohiym* and *Yahushua*, so they may properly utter them and do so in faith for their intended purposes and results.

Just before the publication of the previous edition of this book, I had a very strong and frequently recurring urge to meditate on the titles *Elohiym* and *HaMashakhYahu*, and the name *Yahushua*, all of which convey deep and special meanings that only Hebrew spirituality and thought have.

Within Hebrew thought and spirituality, these titles and name are not only relevant, but are also indispensable in mankind's quest for the salvation of the Holy One.

The title, *HaMashakhYahu*, which means *The Anointed One of Yahuwah*, belongs to only *Yahushua* for ever and ever, and for good reason. This title is conferred by *Elohiym* upon His only begotten Son, *Yahushua*, and upon no other person.

The title *HaMashakhYahu* must, therefore, be accepted by salvation seekers the world over—speakers of Hebrew and non-speakers alike—if they are to obtain the salvation of the Most High One.

The political titles—president, king, or emperor—when mentioned, connote a certain kind of authority exercised and displayed in how peoples of particular nations are ruled. These titles also uniquely describe the political heads bearing them—in their power, authority, splendor, and glory. They also define the type of state that is governed by these rulers. Just because all who bear these titles are heads of states, it does not mean that these titles may be ascribed anyhow to any head of state!

The Most High One has purposefully conferred the title *HaMashakhYahu* upon His only begotten Son for good reason. It will be wrong, offensive and unacceptable to Him for this title to be corrupted to "Messiah", as has been done by English translators of the *Holy Scriptures*!

Well, we do know the meaning of *"HaMashakhYahu"* to be *"The Anointed One of Yahuwah"* because the Almighty has told us so; but what does "Messiah" mean? It might seem to man that the English word "Messiah" means "The Anointed One of Yahuwah" in much the same way that *"HaMashakhYahu"* in Hebrew does. But then, that would be man telling himself so; and not the Most High One telling man so at all!

It is only the Most High One who gives revelation knowledge to man, and since he has not done so in man's understanding of

"Messiah" to mean "The Anointed One of *Yahuwah*", man could be living in delusion as a result of his belief. At the end of it all, man's beliefs in this would yield him no benefits but rather woes.

I consider it dangerous for salvation seekers to use words coined by man, such as *God, Jesus,* and *Messiah,* which are unknown to the Most High One, in seeking to enter His salvation and kingdom.

It is in the light of all these thoughts that I deem it needful to write another preface—*Preface to this Elohiym Edition*—to this book of mine. All through this current edition, *Elohiym, Yahushua,* and *HaMashakhYahu* have featured prominently. These are all further explained in the Glossary at the end of this teaching.

The red letter edition of *The Bible,* with all its many quotations relating to the Savior, his *talmidim* ("disciples"), and angels of *Elohiym,* seems to me to emphasize more falsehood than truth. The Savior, his *talmidim,* and holy angels, are quoted to have said words they never did.

Listen to these quotations that English bible translators attribute to the Savior: ***"Ought not CHRIST to have suffered these things, and to enter his glory?" (Luke 24:26, KJV); "For GOD so loved the world, that, he gave his only begotten son, that whosoever believeth in him should not perish, but have everlasting life" (John 3:16, KJV);*** and ***"I am JESUS, whom thou persecutest:" (Acts 9:5, KJV); caps mine.***

In *Matthew* 1:20-25, bible translators would like to have salvation seekers believe that the holy angel of *Elohiym* who was sent to *Yosef* (Joseph?), emphatically gave him the name JESUS and that, indeed, *Yosef* named the Savior as such when he was born! Is that not ridiculous and incredible?

Read the following statement that is attributed to *Shimon Kefa*: ***"Then Peter (Kefa) said unto them, Repent, and be baptized every one of you in the name of JESUS CHRIST for the remission of sins, and ye shall receive the gift of the Holy Ghost"—Acts 2:38, KJV, caps and word in parenthesis are mine.***

I can say with all the certainty given to me by the leading and unction of *Ruwakh HaKodesh* (the Holy Spirit?) of the Most High One who dwells in my spirit that neither the Savior, nor any angels of *Elohiym,* nor *Shimon Kefa,* ever uttered any of the words—God, Christ, and Jesus—they are quoted to have said in the above quotations and many others attributed to them!

I am certain in my claims simply because these words—God, Jesus, and Christ—never existed in *Shamayim* (Heaven) for angels to be instructed to utter, and neither did they exist in the vocabulary of *Yahushua* while he was on earth, nor of that of *Shimon Kefa*, or any Hebrew in the days of the Son of Man, and hence were never uttered by anyone in *Yisroel*. Why then do translators attribute these words to them in direct quotes? Is this done in error or mischief?

One may ask: How about these same words—Jesus, Christ, and God—that are found in the very popular so-called *Apostles Creed*, that is recited on daily basis by many people who claim to be followers of the Savior; are they not words which came out of the mouths of the *Shlikhim* of *Yahushua HaMashakhYahu*?

No, they are not. The so-called *Apostles Creed* was formulated, in the name of the *Shlikhim* of the Savior, long after they were laid to rest in their sepulchers. Someone decided to formulate this creed in their name and, by that, aimed to convince the world that it was good to exercise belief and faith in it, since it is supposed to carry the blessings of the *Shlikhim* of the Savior.

Was some supernatural being involved in this ploy to get the entire world within his grips, and to be deceived and taken away from the true way of entering into the salvation of the Most High One? I dare say this is so.

The fourth and last beast in Daniel's prophecy in the book of *Daniel* is responsible for all this deception of the salvation seeker. And he seems to have been extremely successful in his efforts as *Daniel* 7:15-25 foretold he would!

Salvation seekers, somehow, seem to have taken their eyes off the ball and, by this, have given the devil the chance to deceive even the elect of the Most High One!

And all this work of the fourth beast in *Daniel* is linked to the Great Falling Away that salvation seekers have been warned of in *Second Thessalonians* 2:3-4. Contrary to the thinking of many salvation seekers that the great falling away is yet to come, it hit our world a long time ago.

This falling away was, in effect, brought about in and by the preaching of false names for salvation by the devil and those he managed to take to his side.

Therefore, let salvation seekers beware of names and titles they have believed in their quest for the salvation of the Almighty since it is in the one and only one name—*Yahushua HaMashakhYahu*—that the Most High One has vested His wisdom, power, will, and glory into, by which sinners can find deliverance from their enslavement to sin.

In order to make the teaching of this book easily understood by its targeted Christian readership, certain jargons of their faith, which have come from Greek sources, have been maintained in this teaching. The words "apostles", "disciples", "baptism", and others, all of which are derived from Greek, are used rather reluctantly in this teaching, just because of their popularity with the target audience of this book.

On the other hand, even though "Holy Spirit" is a popular jargon among Christians and is deemed by them to mean the Spirit of *Elohiym* given as a gift to dwell in all genuinely born again people, the Hebrew name *"Ruwakh HaKodesh"* is rather used throughout this book because I consider it wrong to translate names.

I hope this second preface and the entire revelations of this book will bring you, dear reader, to the true way of the salvation of the Most High One—a salvation that is designed by Him to come to mankind in and by the name *Yahushua HaMashakhYahu* and through one's exercise of faith in this name, in a manner absolutely devoid of any so-called *Sinners' Prayer* or *Prayer for Salvation* recitals.

May the Most High One, bless you richly for your humility and patience in accepting the teachings in this book. *Shalom.*

Chris Bapuohyele
Dated this 7th day of September, 2013
Accra, Ghana.

PS: In this *First Revision* of the *Elohiym Edition* of this book, I sought to give readers a feel of the days of *Yahushua HaMashakhYahu* in the Holy Land of *Yisroel* of the first century, by bringing into it many ingredients of Hebrew culture of that time, aimed at restoring flavors of that past into our faith and salvation discourses today.

This, I have done by bringing into this teaching the Hebrew names and titles of people—Scripture writers and their book-titles inclusive—and of places, feasts of *Elohiym*, etc., revealed in the Hebrew *Holy Scriptures*, to replace those of English origins found in *The Bible*, simply because names must never be translated. Wherever I have done this, the anglicized names are placed in parenthesis to avoid confusing my readers.

Doing this, I found *The Jewish Orthodox Bible* by Dr. Phillip E. Goble, an invaluable source and aid.

I also feel urged in my spirit to suggest to readers how the English word "Messiah" came about as the unholy derivative of *HaMashakhYahu*! It may seem obvious to many that the title *"HaMashakhYahu"* underwent a process of shortening and slanging in its transliteration to evolve to finally become the English word *"Messiah"*, all without the involvement of *Elohiym*!!

Clearly, *HaMashakhYahu* can be broken down to yield three words—*Ha* (The), *Mashakh* (Anointed*)* and *Yahu*, a short form of *Yahuwah* (Name of the Almighty).

And so, *HaMashakhYahu* in its first shortening was made to sound as *HaMashakhyah*, and from thence to sound as *HaMashayah*, and to *HaMasayah*; finally becoming *"the Messiah"* in and by the work done by English bible translators without the mandate of *Elohiym*.

It is therefore sad that the word *"Messiah"* has, today, found world-wide acceptance and preeminence over *HaMashakhYahu*, as if it is rather the more genuine Hebrew title conferred on the Savior by *Elohiym*!!

Finally, while talking about name changes, let me inform readers about my own official name-change from *Chris* to *NngmingBongle*, which strongly reflects my *Dagaaba* roots and culture. May you fall in love with it! Once again, *Shalom Aleikhem.*

NngmingBongle Bapuohyele
Dated this 7th day of January, 2015
Accra, Ghana

Chapter One
A Hidden Problem Laid Bare

As to how to enter the salvation of *Elohiym* prepared for mankind, which is available only in *Yahushua HaMashakhYahu*, one must go by the Word of *Elohiym* and not that of men. Going by the instructions of men could lead one to err, and into the delusion of being saved. The salvation of *Elohiym* in *Yahushua HaMashakhYahu* is of such great value that, in trying to enter it, one must be mindful and cautious of what one hears, believes, accepts, and acts on, so as to avoid being deceived.

Anyone who enters Elohiym's salvation becomes blessed with His gift of *Chayyei Olam* (Everlasting Life)—the very type of Life in *Elohiym*—to dwell in his/her body.

Entering Elohiym's salvation means entering the *Malchut HaElohiym* (Kingdom of *Elohiym*), being clothed in *Yahushua HaMashakhYahu* or becoming born again, meaning receiving a new birth.

No doubt, these various terms of salvation are familiar to many people who profess to be devout followers of *The Bible*. As we read along, we should keep these terms in mind and should understand them to mean the same.

For many people who belong to the numerous Bible-related religious denominations, the word of their leaders is often taken without question. Insofar as the word of their leaders is the Word of *Elohiym*, they are safe in their beliefs and practices.

Unfortunately, the word of many preachers is oftentimes not the Word of *Elohiym*. As a result, people have believed, accepted, and acted on wrong doctrines postulated by man. The sad thing is that these people are unaware that they have believed wrong doctrines taught by their leaders.

One of the oldest and most widespread doctrines of some denominations seeking the salvation of the Most High One is that of praying the so-called *"Sinners' Prayer"* or *"Prayer for Salvation"* for one to be born again. These denominations teach sinners, who desire to enter the salvation of *Elohiym* or to become born again, to pray this prayer to ask Him for the forgiveness of their sins and to request for "Jesus Christ" (*Yahushua HaMashakhYahu?*) to come and stay in their hearts, ostensibly to take control of their lives.

For many years, extending beyond decades into centuries, these denominations have taught this doctrine in their attempt to lead people into the salvation of *Elohiym* in *Yahushua HaMashakhYahu*. They teach that if one would repent of one's sins, say a prayer to *Elohiym* asking for the forgiveness of one's sins, and further request for "Jesus Christ" (*Yahushua HaMashakhYahu?*) to come into one's heart and life, this would result in one becoming born again, securing one's entry into Elohiym's Kingdom, and enabling one to become a child of *Elohiym*.

Chapter Four of this book gives details of this doctrine by which people are taught that they can become born again by reciting special prayers. For now, however, let me say that this doctrine draws its strengths from some passages of the scriptures; the most notable among them are *Romans* 3:23, 6:23, 10:9-10, *Ivriim (Hebrews)* 9:27 and *Hisgalus (Revelation)* 3:20.

A message is developed with these verses at the centre and taught at meetings or services of these denominations. Those who accept the message are invited forward to receive "Jesus Christ" (*Yahushua HaMashakhYahu?*) as *"their Lord and Savior"*, an invitation popularly known to many as *"altar call"*.

Upon responding to the *"altar call"*, the salvation seekers are led to pray, reciting after the preacher the so-called *Sinners' Prayer*. Thereafter, the preacher prays to thank the Most High One for supposedly granting salvation to those who responded to his invitation by coming forward to say the *Sinners' Prayer* after him, asking Him to make them born again!

Having gone through this process, the salvation seekers return to their places in the congregation: their faith and satisfaction being the same as the preacher's own, that, they have become born again and are in the *Malchut HaElohiym* (Kingdom of *Elohiym*)! The salvation seekers could hold this belief of the preacher the rest of their lives: that they have become born again, saved, and are in "Jesus Christ" (*Yahushua HaMashakhYahu*, the true Savior?), through their response to the *"altar call"* and the saying of the *Sinners' Prayer*!

This teaching is contrary to Elohiym's Word on the issue of how the sinner is born again. The fact that this erroneous doctrine has been around for a very long period of time and has therefore become accepted by a great number of people makes them believe it is genuine.

In fact, many people have become comfortable with it, unaware that it is wrong. As a result, it is not easy for such people to see it as such. Nevertheless, it cannot stand the strength and evidence of Elohiym's Word which exposes it as being wrong. With the evidence of Elohiym's Word, this error in doctrine will come to be seen by all salvation seekers as such.

It is sad that many people who want to gain the salvation of *Elohiym* seem to be too lazy to read the *Holy Scriptures* and compare them with what their teachers instruct them to do. The issue of salvation is so important that one must be sure that one's faith is indeed based on and founded on the Word of *Elohiym*, and not, as it were, on the word of some preachers.

Those who believe they have entered the salvation of *Elohiym* in *Yahushua HaMashakhYahu*, based on some kind of prayers, should ask themselves, **"Did I do as those saved in the accounts of *Acts* did for salvation?"** Did you do as they did? This is the question you need to answer, if you believe you have an assurance of salvation.

Today, many people who believe they are saved do not do as the crowd of Hebrew Diaspora returnees did for their salvation on the day *Ruwakh HaKodesh* (the Holy Spirit?) was outpoured on the *Shlikhim* of *Yahushua HaMashakhYahu* (Pentecost?), in *Yerushalayim* (Jerusalem). Many people today do not do as the Ethiopian eunuch did, under the ministration of *Philippos* (Philip), for his salvation. Do we do as Cornelius and his household did for their salvation? Do we do for our salvation as many others have done in *Acts* including *Sha'ul* (Saul), a *Shliakh* (emissary or "apostle") of *Yahushua HaMashakhYahu* to the Gentiles?

Our generation is gullible when it comes to spiritual issues. A great many of us are always looking out for a quick fix to man's numerous spiritual, mental, physical, and socio-economic problems. This attitude makes us open to deception, prey to counterfeiting, and victims of outright fraud, particularly in spiritual and religious issues.

In Christianity, there is so much misinterpretation of the Word of *Elohiym*. There is also a high amount of deception and fraud in the propagation of the Word of *Elohiym* among people by others who claim to have been called by *Elohiym* to do His business.

Because such people call themselves "men of God", their followers take their word to be the real truth and seek very little or no reconciliation at all of it with the teachings of the *Holy Scriptures*. Nobody who has an idea of the blessings of *Elohiym* available to the saved should be so naive as to accept the word of man without question.

The fast-growing denominations in my part of the world, which claim to believe the *Holy Scriptures*, seem to house the people who are in this error in doctrine. While there is yet time before the return to earth of *Yahushua HaMashakhYahu*, we must look back at what we have done as a people and as individuals for our salvation and make amends if need be.

In our attempt to make changes to any conflicting or contrary beliefs we may hold on the born again doctrine, we have to get the humble spirit of Apollos, who, when yet in error of faith, met to have a fellowship with Aquila and Priscilla (cf. *Acts* 18:24-28), and that of the twelve *"talmidim"* that *Sha'ul* met at Ephesus (cf. *Acts* 19:1-7). They all accepted correction from their errors and, therefore, found the true salvation of *Elohiym*.

We read in the accounts of *Acts* 17:10-12 about the people of Berea, who earnestly sought through the scriptures, with the desire to reconcile them with whatever *Sha'ul* taught them. This attitude of the Bereans was recorded as an example for us to follow today.

Anybody who seeks the salvation of the Most High One must be as serious-minded as the people of Berea were, but alas, our generation has an attitude far from that of those noble Bereans. We believe what we hear, without any investigation, especially when it comes from people who take delight in calling themselves "men of God".

From the first two chapters of *Galatians* (particularly, 1:15-2:9), we read of how *Sha'ul*, a *Shliakh* of *Yahushua HaMashakhYahu*, questioned himself concerning his beliefs. This is serious thinking. *Sha'ul*, after holding onto the faith of the first century followers of the Savior for about seventeen years, finds time to investigate his beliefs about the *Besuras HaGeulah* (Good News of Redemption) and salvation.

It is almost unbelievable that *Sha'ul* could be doing this. This is the man who heard, loud and clear, the voice of *Yahushua HaMashakhYahu* call him from *Shamayim* (Heaven) as he was about to enter Damascus on some glorious day—cf. *Acts* 9:4-6; 22:7-10; 26:14-18. This is the man whom *Elohiym* used to perform many miracles of healing the sick (cf. *Acts* 14:10; 19:12), raising the dead (cf. *Acts* 20:9-10), and preaching *Yahushua HaMashakhYahu* among the Gentiles, and yet found it prudent to examine himself with regard to his beliefs and practices in the New Covenant faith.

Elohiym delivered *Sha'ul* from death by stoning, attacks of wild beasts, snake bites, ship wrecks, hunger, the vagaries of the weather, treacherous brethren, imprisonment—cf. *Second Corinthians* 11:23-27, etc. This man would simply not die because he lived in the perfect will of *Elohiym*, and yet he saw the need to reexamine his doctrine and his teaching on the *Besuras HaGeulah* he preached.

Sha'ul could hear *Yahushua HaMashakhYahu* speak to him directly on many occasions. *Yahushua HaMashakhYahu* told *Sha'ul* to continue to speak of him in Corinth (cf. *Acts* 18:9-10); to immediately flee *Yerushalayim* (cf. *Acts* 22:18, 21); to prepare himself to witness of him in Rome (cf. *Acts* 23:11); to not bother about the thorn in his flesh (cf. *Second Corinthians* 12:7-9), etc.

But he saw the need to reexamine his faith and to properly define his confines. *Sha'ul* seemed to be living in the very bosom of the Almighty, and yet he was worried about whether he was running the race of faith in *Yahushua HaMashakhYahu* in vain.

Sha'ul had the privilege of being transported miraculously on two occasions to the presence of *Elohiym*, first to *HaShlishi HaShamayim* (the Third Heaven) and later to *Gan Eden* (Garden of Eden, Paradise), where he heard and saw things mortals are not able to see, hear, or speak of—cf. *Second Corinthians* 12:1-4. These experiences notwithstanding, *Sha'ul* found the need and time for self-examination of his faith, beliefs, doctrines, and teachings against the faith and teachings of the followers of *Yahushua HaMashakhYahu* who were called before him—and all this, after seventeen long years of ministry!

You see, you could have all these experiences of *Sha'ul* and still not have your name written in *HaSefer HaChayyim* (the Book of Life). You do not enter the *Malchut HaElohiym* by your experiences but by your faith in Him and your obedience to His Word for your salvation. That is why it is very dangerous to teach people based on your experiences rather than on the Word of *Elohiym*.

One problem of Christianity is that most people teach their personal experiences instead of the doctrines of *Yahushua HaMashakhYahu*. By preaching their experiences, they preach self and, by that, attract their followers to themselves, rather than to *Yahushua HaMashakhYahu* who is the Savior.

Some words I never expected to hear got to me from the mouth of a bishop of a Christian denomination. Talking about his experience of salvation, I was shocked when the bishop mentioned that he was born again first and then baptized later on, presumably after some days of preparation. I wished he did not teach on the born again doctrine altogether, since his experience of it was different from the teachings of the *Holy Scriptures*, concerning how to be born again and to enter the *Malchut HaElohiym*.

The bishop sought to call people through his experience and have them go through the same manner of entering his so-called salvation, which, in actual fact, did not bring him to the salvation of *Elohiym* in *Yahushua HaMashakhYahu*, when put against the scrutiny of Elohiym's Word. This bishop obviously missed the import of what is in **Markos (Mark) 16:16: "He that believeth and is baptized shall be saved."**

Well, the bishop said he was saved and then later baptized! For such a bishop, this verse should be rewritten to read, "He that believeth and is **(not)** baptized shall be saved." One cannot but feel sad for such a bishop, in his ignorance and confusion, and for his many followers whom he has so wrongly taught.

Investigating himself on his beliefs and practices against the faiths of the other *Shlikhim* of *Yahushua HaMashakhYahu* called before him, *Sha'ul* makes a long trip to *Yerushalayim* and gives a report of his work among the Gentiles to see, if in so doing, he might find correction to his faith by the *Shlikhim* of *Yahushua HaMashakhYahu* who were called before him. He did not want to die while believing and acting on a false version of the message of the *Besuras HaGeulah* (Good News of Redemption) and thereby not able to enter into *Shamayim* (Heaven).

But *Sha'ul* was on the right path to *Shamayim*, insofar as his faith and practices in *Yahushua HaMashakhYahu* were concerned, and he returned from *Yerushalayim* with the peace of mind needed for his work to the Gentiles.

Why are people of today not zealous enough to investigate their beliefs against Elohiym's Holy Word? My prayer for you, dear reader, is that you obtain Sha'ul's kind of humility and desire, investigate your faith in the born again doctrine and your experience of it, and make the necessary amends, if the need be, before you depart from this world.

I am sure, if you seek to have this like-mindedness and desire to do right in your obedience to Elohiym's Word for your salvation, *Sha'ul* will be your next-door neighbor on "Faith Avenue" in *Shamayim*, at the end of Time. And you will both relish daily the joy in the wisdom of such self-examination on your parts when you were both still mortals on earth.

The *Holy Scriptures* warns us in *Romans* 10:2-3 to let knowledge drive our zeal. This is because zeal without knowledge can be destructive. It is, therefore, with little wonder that *Sha'ul* goes to great lengths to investigate his beliefs and practices in his faith in *Yahushua HaMashakhYahu*.

This is somebody who, when living the Hebrew religion in its strictest sect of *Perushim* (Pharisees), had so much zeal to persecute Elohiym's chosen people, ignorant that he did so contrary to His will. *Sha'ul*, at the time, had a zeal for *Elohiym* and yet did not have knowledge of what He wanted him to do.

This was somebody who was zealous to please *Elohiym* and so called himself to a ministry, which turned out to be antagonistic to Elohiym's plan and His people. Such was a sad situation indeed.

This book will lead you to the truth of *Elohiym* concerning the salvation process of the sinner. As I share these revelations of Elohiym's Word with you, it is my hope that you would go back and make the right decisions for your salvation before you depart from this world.

I entreat you to do this, to avert disappointment on *Yom HaDin* (the Day of Judgment) because you believed a counterfeit version of the *Besuras HaGeulah* and a wrong name of the Savior. May *Elohiym* forbid that this be your fate.

Chapter Two

Elohiym's Salvation Laid Bare

Elohiym masterminded a foolproof way for the sinner to enter His salvation. The salvation of *Elohiym* for the sinner is available only in *Yahushua HaMashakhYahu*. This salvation in *Yahushua HaMashakhYahu* brings sinful men into a covenant relationship with *Elohiym*.

The terms of this covenant are in the *Holy Scriptures*. Therein, the terms are spelled out as to what *Elohiym* will do and what sinful men should do to stay within this covenant, celebrating it in the marriage to His Son, *Yahushua HaMashakhYahu*, in *Shamayim* at the end of time.

Everything man has to do to enter this salvation is detailed in the **Beyrit Chadasha** (New Covenant) teachings of the *Holy Scriptures*. It is absolutely important for anyone desiring to enter the salvation of *Elohiym* in *Yahushua HaMashakhYahu* to do as *Elohiym* instructs him in these scriptures to do. Any other way would be contrary to the will of *Elohiym* and will not bring about the desired results.

If man chooses to disobey the detailed instructions of the **Beyrit Chadasha** teachings to enter this salvation, he does so to his own peril, disappointment and doom. He should not blame *Elohiym*.

If any man decides to do something else, no matter how very similar it is to what *Elohiym* designed for him to do, he should be ready to accept the consequences. He should not expect to recieve what *Elohiym* has promised, if he has not obeyed His instructions to the letter.

The *Holy Scriptures* tell us that we would bear full responsibility for what we believe. We shall also be judged by what we believe. We must therefore be careful what we hear and believe about salvation or the born again experience, as we cannot blame anyone for our disappointments regarding Elohiym's salvation.

In this chapter, the right way, according to the revelation of the *Holy Scriptures*, on how the sinner can get to enter the salvation of *Elohiym*, which is only available in *Yahushua HaMashakhYahu*, is taught. This is done by looking at the issue from four different standpoints:

(1) Atonement, forgiveness, and remission of sins

(2) Baptism into life

(3) The Great Commission instructions

(4) The Good News (*Besuras*) and the response to it

Each of these standpoints leads us to a definite instruction of *Elohiym* for our salvation in *Yahushua HaMashakhYahu*. That one instruction of *Elohiym* is His command to us to repent of our sins and be baptized in the name of His Son, *Yahushua HaMashakhYahu*. Any of these four standpoints will lead us to our entry into the born again experience in a way devoid of prayer.

Beyond these issues, in their relationship to how one is born again, we shall also look at the accounts in *Acts*, where on two occasions people who were ignorant of the baptism in the name of *Yahushua HaMashakhYahu* went astray from the salvation of *Elohiym*.

Then we shall move on to look at three classic salvation accounts, also, in *Acts*. These accounts should bring illumination to our understanding of how, in the age of the *Shlikhim* of *Yahushua HaMashakhYahu*, people were led to receive or enter the salvation of *Elohiym*.

(1) Atonement, Forgiveness, and Remission of Sins

Let us look at how *Elohiym* deals with sin in the lives of men. *Elohiym* deals with sin in the lives of men in three distinct ways. These ways are described by the words atonement, forgiveness, and remission.

Under the Old Covenant, the spiritual, political, social, and economic life of *Yisroel* was regulated by many stringent laws. These laws were so far-reaching, dealing with issues of personal hygiene, environmental care, sanitation, kindness to animals, feast days, *Shabbat* (Sabbaths) of rest, consecration of first-born males, etc. These laws touched on every aspect of the lives of the people of *Yisroel*.

The *Tanakh* (Old Covenant Holy Hebrew Scriptures) in *Shemot (Exodus)*, *Vayikra (Levticus)*, *Bamidbar (Numbers)*, and *Devarim (Deuteronomy)* has all the details of these laws. Any infringement of them constituted a sin against *Elohiym* that brought punishment. Also found in these four books are Elohiym's detailed instructions as to how to deal with any sin situation arising from the infringement of these laws. These instructions were aimed at taking sin from among the people by, as it were, covering the sin from the sight of *Elohiym*, and thereby averting its consequences.

Elohiym instituted various ordinances and rituals to be performed by duly anointed priests, aimed at covering the sin of the people from His sight. These involved the offering of sacrifices, almost all of which were blood sacrifices involving bulls, sheep, goats, and fowls. Other sacrifices, to a lesser extent, were made by offering grain, flour, unleavened bread, oil, fruits, wine, or incense. We can read more about these in *Vayikra (Leviticus)* 1:2, 10, 14, 2:1 and 6:15.

Every sin that was committed had its prescribed sacrifice meant to cover it and, thereby, avert its consequences from coming upon the people. The one who committed the sin was to provide the sacrificial items for the priest, duly ordained by *Elohiym*, to offer them on behalf of the sinner to Him. Depending on one's leadership position, politically or spiritually, within the house of *Yisroel*, the demands on the provision of sacrificial items could be different for the same sin. We can read more on this in *Vayikra (Leviticus)* 4:13-35.

At the end of the day, the sacrifice which was offered in strict compliance with the instructions of *Elohiym* by the priest covered the sin of the people from His sight. This covering of sins through the offering of blood sacrifices was known as atonement of sin or *kapporah* in the *Torah*. Actually, the word atonement means a "covering."

Once *kapporah* was obtained for any sin committed, it averted the consequences of the sin that would have come upon the individual, his entire house, or the whole house of *Yisroel*. The sacrificed animal took the death sentence, as it were, which the sinner's sin brought about.

It should be noted that, *kapporah* in itself could never take away sins. Also, Elohiym's acceptance of one's sacrifice for *kapporah* could not, and did not take away the sin nature alive and active within the spirit of the sinner. Atonement of sin only concealed the sin and its horror from the sight of *Elohiym*, and thereby forestalled His anger and wrath from coming on the sinner.

Sacrifices for atonement of sin were demanded of *Yisroel* by *Elohiym* on a daily basis. These daily sacrifices notwithstanding, *Elohiym* instituted a compulsory annual sacrifice for sin for the entirety of *Yisroel* on *Yom Kippur* (Day of Atonement). This was a day fixed by *Elohiym* in the calendar year in which the whole house of *Yisroel*—though, in fact, a convocation of male adults and male family heads—gathered in solemn assembly to have the sins of the nation committed in the course of the year atoned for.

As part of these rituals and ceremonies, the *kohen gadol* (high priest) of *Yisroel* would take the blood of a sacrificed bull and sprinkle it on the people who had gathered. This was an act of purification from sin meant to affect the entire population of *Yisroel*.

Another part or aspect of the rituals of *Yom Kippur*, also meant to take away sin from the people, involved a confession by the mouth of the *kohen gadol*. All the sins the house of *Yisroel* committed in the year were confessed by the *kohen gadol* upon the head of a goat—the so-called scapegoat (*sa'ir l'Azazel*).

The *sa'ir l'Azazel* (scapegoat of Azazel), as it were, was made to bear all the sins committed by the people of *Yisroel* in the year and was sent by a vibrant, strong, and youthful man into the wilderness, far away from human habitation, to be left there to its fate, under the burden of the sins of the people—cf. *Vayikra (Leviticus)* 16:10, 21-22.

Yom Kippur was Yisroel's most hallowed, most revered, and most solemn day. It was a day for fasting, reflection, spiritual renewal, cleansing from sin, and becoming closer to *Elohiym*. No servile work was permitted on this day; it was labor holiday for man and all beasts of burden. It was also a day dreaded by many, as any *kohen gadol* coming under the wrath of *Elohiym* got killed in the process of offering to Him the blood of sacrifice for the *kapporah*—cf. *Vayikra (Leviticus)* 23:26-32.

By and large, *kapporah* took the effects of sin away from the people. *Kapporah* covered the sin from Elohiym's sight, so that the sin lost its power to provoke His wrath. It also averted all other consequences that every sin attracted. It kept at bay the fierce anger of *Elohiym* and forestalled His wrath—cf. *Tehillim (Psalms)* 78:38; 85:2-3.

In addition to the ritual of animal sacrifices for *kapporah* of the sins of the people, another dimension to the issue of Elohiym's prescription against the effects of sin involved confession of the offence, restitution, reparation, and reconciliation. This aspect of Elohiym's instructions to the people of *Yisroel* to deal with their sin problems involved any issues that existed among themselves that tended towards injustice, bitterness, disharmony, and lack of affection.

The person who committed the sin was obliged to confess it to *Elohiym* and to the wronged member of the house of *Yisroel*. Forgiveness and pardon were sought from *Elohiym* for the sin, while at the same time reconciliation was sought by the wrongdoer from the one wronged through dialogue, restitution, and reparation—cf. *Bamidbar (Numbers)* 5:5-8.

When *Yisroel* was in exile from the land of their forefathers, having been taken captive by heathen nations, they could not keep the ordinances and rituals of sacrifices for *kapporah*. In such situations, they were to verbally confess their sins and the sins of their fathers in seeking Elohiym's forgiveness.

It seems to me that *Elohiym* made a norm for their sins to be atoned for or covered when they were in exile by verbal confession. You may, please, read more on this in *Vayikra (Leviticus)* 26:40-42, *Nechemyahu (Nehemiah)* 1:4-11 and *Daniel* 9:3-20.

Under the *Torah, Elohiym* dealt with the sin of *Yisroel* through these two ways: offering of sacrifices for *kapporah* and confession of sins for forgiveness. *Yisroel* remained in covenant relationship with *Elohiym*, as long as he observed Elohiym's instructions for *kapporah* and reconciliation, pardon, or forgiveness of sins.

Any person who did not obey Elohiym's instructions for *kapporah* and for forgiveness of sin was cut off from his people. He lost his membership to the house of *Yisroel* and his spiritual connections with *Elohiym* were severed; that person was stoned to death.

The yearly atonement of sin with the blood of lambs was, however, a shadow, or a pointer, to the ultimate *Yom Kippur* to come under the *Beyrit Chadasha* by the sacrifice of *Yahushua HaMashakhYahu. Yahushua HaMashakhYahu* became the perfect, sinless, flawless *Seh* (Lamb), provided by *Elohiym* Himself, who was slain to bring about this perfect *kapporah* of sin. The atoning-blood of *Yahushua HaMashakhYahu* was not meant to cover the sins of *Yisroel* alone, but that of the whole of mankind forever.

The single sacrifice of *Yahushua HaMashakhYahu* provided the blood-covering over the sins of mankind once and for all. Because the blood of *Yahushua HaMashakhYahu* has provided this cover over the sins, or has made *kapporah* for the sins of mankind, every sinner now has a legal right to call out to *Elohiym* from under this blood-covering and be heard of Him.

As the sinner cries out to *Elohiym* for any need, He looks down on Earth and sees the blood of His beloved Son, *Yahushua HaMashakhYahu*, as it were, covering the entire world. That blood, which *Yahushua HaMashakhYahu* shed when he took the place of the sinner, to die in his stead, is seen to make *kapporah* for or a covering over all the sins of the world including, of course, those of the wailing sinner.

While *Elohiym* looks down upon the helpless sinner, for whom His only begotten Son shed his blood and died, his potential *Kohen Gadol* (High Priest), *Yahushua HaMashakhYahu*, pleads with the Most High One to provide the sinner's need since he died to meet His Justice for the sins of the wailing sinner.

The sinner's greatest need is salvation: that is, deliverance from the dominion and enslaving power of the devil. The sinner's need is to be made a child of *Elohiym*, so he can together with others call Him *"Avinu"*, (our Father), be set on a pilgrimage to *Shamayim*, be made Ambassador of *Shamayim* to Earth, and so he can qualify to inherit the riches of the Amighty.

The atoning-sacrifice of *Yahushua HaMashakhYahu* provides the legal framework for every salvation seeker to come into all these situations. This legal framework, in itself, is not an end to salvation for the salvation seeker but a means by which he obtains it. Within this legal framework of Yahushua's sacrifice for *kapporah* are the specifics as to how one may enter the salvation of *Elohiym* and remain within it.

These specifics are described by the terms **remission of sin,** for entry into this salvation, and **forgiveness of sin,** for one to regain fellowship with *Elohiym* and His family on earth, should one commit any sin after coming into His salvation. Remission of sin grants one the entry into the salvation of *Elohiym* in *Yahushua HaMashakhYahu*, while forgiveness of sin provides a means to remain in it. Subsequent discourses in this book will provide the distinction between remission and forgiveness of sin and teach how *Elohiym* has used these two means to deal with the sin of mankind since the resurrection of *Yahushua HaMashakhYahu*.

At a point in time, close to the coming of *Yahushua HaMashakhYahu*, a prophecy was given through *Zecharyahu* (Zacharias), the father of *YahuChanan* (John the Baptist), by which the word **remission** was introduced in connection to Elohiym's salvation for mankind for the first time in the *Holy Scriptures*. *Zecharyahu* prophesied of his son *YahuChanan* that he

(*YahuChanan*) would be a teacher of *Yisroel*, bringing to *Yisroel* **knowledge of salvation by the remission of their sins.** This prophecy reads:

"And thou, child, shalt be called the prophet of the Highest: for thou shalt go before the face of the Lord to prepare his ways, to give knowledge of salvation unto his people by the remission of their sins..."—Lukas (Luke) 1: 76-77, KJV.

By this prophecy of *Zecharyahu*, man was given Elohiym's Word and notice that a time was coming when man would receive His salvation by a certain means or process known as **remission of sin.** In the fullness of time, no salvation would come to man by any other means except through the remission of sins. We had better know this and seek to know when and how this would come about.

It was thus important for man to know everything about this salvation that was coming, so he could put himself in the right position to receive it. *Yisroel* himself would no longer have salvation on the basis of his election and obedience to the *Torah*. *Yisroel* would have access to this incoming salvation of *Elohiym* through the remission of his sins.

The *Holy Scriptures* say that *YahuChanan* came as a messenger of *Elohiym* to prepare the way for *Yahushua HaMashakhYahu*. *YahuChanan* was Elohiym's appointed ambassador to teach *Yisroel*, and for that matter humanity, about the coming of *Yahushua HaMashakhYahu*. It was YahuChanan's responsibility to teach a thorough understanding of the salvation of *Elohiym*, which was soon to come through the remission of sins by the sacrifice of *Yahushua HaMashakhYahu*.

And this he did creditably in the wilderness of the countryside about *Yarden* (Jordan), earning the commendation and praise of *Yahushua HaMashakhYahu* later on. The commitment of *YahuChanan* to the business of *Elohiym*, and the perfection with which he carried out his assignment, earned him a status that is above every *navi* ("prophet") born of woman. To fully understand the ministry of *YahuChanan ben Zecharyahu*, the "Baptist", we have to look at it from two angles.

First, we see *YahuChanan ben Zecharyahu* calling the people of *Yisroel* to repentance, since the expectation of *HaMashakhYahu* was at hand. He warned *Yisroel* about the axe of *Elohiym*, which was about to strike down any tree that did not bear good fruit. All the people of *Yisroel* were therefore demanded to repent of their sins to avert the wrath of *Elohiym* from being visited on them as a result of their sins.

Those who heeded his warning message accepted YahuChanan's person and mission as coming from *Elohiym*. They responded by receiving baptism in his name. This act of baptism in his name was to testify or bear witness that the one who was baptized had repented of all his sins, ceremonially washed them away and also identified with what *YahuChanan* stood for, believed, and preached.

The baptized was now lost in the *persona* of *YahuChanan*, who himself was lost in Elohiym's will. The baptized became a true and loyal disciple, ready to imbibe and live by the teachings and faith of his master, *YahuChanan*. Since *YahuChanan* stood on the side of *Elohiym*, everyone that stood with him in his baptism stood with *Elohiym* and was therefore separated unto Him.

We can read more about this account of *YahuChanan ben Zecharyahu* from *Mattityahu (Matthew)*:

"In those days came John (YahuChanan) the Baptist, preaching in the wilderness of Judæa, and saying, Repent ye: for the kingdom of heaven (Shamayim) is at hand. For this is he that was spoken of by the prophet Esaias, saying, The voice of one crying in the wildernesss, Prepare ye the way of the Lord, make his paths straight. And the same John (YahuChanan) had his raiment of camel's hair, and a leathern girdle about his loins; and his meat was locusts and wild honey. Then went out to him all Jerusalem (Yerushalayim), and all Judæa (Yahudah), and all the region round about Jordan (Yarden), And were baptized of him in Jordan (Yarden), confessing their sins. But when he saw the Pharisees (Perushim) and Sadducees (Tzedukim) come to his baptism, he said unto them, O generation of vipers, who hath warned you to flee from the wrath to come? Bring forth therefore fruits meet for repentance: And think not to say to yourselves, We have Abraham (Avraham) to our father: for I say unto you, that God (Elohiym) is able of these stones to raise up children unto Abraham (Avraham). And now also the axe is laid unto the root of the trees: therefore every tree which bringeth not forth good fruit is hewn down and cast into the fire."—Mattityahu (Matthew) 3:1-10, KJV; words in parenthesis are mine.

Again, we read the following about *YahuChanan* and his ministry in *Markos (Mark)*:

"The voice of one crying in the wilderness, Prepare ye the way of the Lord, make his paths straight. John (YahuChanan) did baptize in the wilderness, and preach the baptism of repentance for the remission of sins. And there went out to him all the land of Judæa, and they of Jerusalem (Yerushalayim), and were all baptized of him in the river Jordan (Yarden), confessing their sins"—Markos (Mark) 1: 3-5, KJV; words in parenthesis are mine.

The third chapter of *Lukas (Luke)* also bears testimony to the above references (of *Mattityahu* and *Markos*). Please read *Lukas (Luke)* 3:4-14 for the complete fill in.

These accounts formed one aspect of the ministry of *YahuChanan ben Zecharyahu*. They introduced him, his mission, and his baptism of repentance to *Yisroel*. As his followers accepted him and his faith, by receiving baptism in his name as a sign of their repentance from sin, they were ready to take more revelation about the impending brand-new salvation of the Most High One.

The second part of YahuChanan's work in the wilderness of *Yarden* involved his teaching ministry about the impending salvation of *Elohiym* that would be made possible by, and received through, remission of sins. *YahuChanan ben Zecharyahu* preached about *HaMashakhYahu* dying a sacrificial death for sinful man, by and through which payment of all the sins committed by the entire human race in the past, present, and future would be made possible.

He preached about how, in due time, mankind would have *HaSeh HaElohiym* (the Lamb of *Elohiym*) die to take away his sins. Much of what he taught in this light was a reechoing of prophecy awaiting fulfillment, which was now imminent.

YahuChanan ben Zecharyahu would have been teaching how man would enter the state of remission of sin by a baptism of fire into the name of the one above him, and from above, whose sandal thong he (*YahuChanan*) was not qualified to untie. And when he had the opportunity, he pointed out to *Yisroel* who *HaSeh HaElohiym* was; the only begotten Son of *HaAv* (the Father), who had manifested to take away the sin of the world.

YahuChanan ben Zecharyahu first linked remission of sins to baptism in *Markos (Mark)*. The account of this linkage between remission of sin and baptism reads:

43

"John (YahuChanan) did baptize in the wilderness, and preach the baptism of repentance for the remission of sins"— Markos (Mark) 1:4, KJV; word in parenthesis is mine.

Let us add this verse to one other in *Lukas: "And he came into all the country about Jordan (Yarden), preaching the remission of sins."—Lukas (Luke) 3:3, KJV; word in parenthesis is mine.*

From a linkup of these verses, we understand *YahuChanan* taught that remission of sin comes about in baptism. Is that right? Well, I do not know of any other way to understand these verses. Baptism brings one into the state of remission of sin. To access remission of sin is to receive baptism in the name of *Yahushua HaMashakhYahu.*

We, however, must understand that the baptism of repentance for the remission of sins, which *YahuChanan* preached, was not the same as was received by his *talmidim* in his name. YahuChanan's baptism, which he administered, was simply a show of repentance of the baptized. It was not meant for remission of sin: remission of sin being, in effect, payment for sin. Baptism for the remission of sins was to come later in the name of *Yahushua HaMashakhYahu.*

Though the remission of sins was to be obtained in baptism into the name of *Yahushua HaMashakhYahu*, it could only be given or received after his death and resurrection. By teaching in the manner of these verses of *Markos* and *Lukas, YahuChanan ben Zecharyahu* was simply working in fulfillment of the prophecy of his father, mentioned in *Lukas* 1:77, as to bring knowledge of the salvation of *Elohiym* by the remission of their sins to his generation.

We should never confuse our faith by the way *Markos (Mark)* 1:3-5 stands to believe that the baptism *YahuChanan ben Zecharyahu* ministered to repentant Hebrews was for remission of sin. It was not. We should keep in remembrance that *Yahushua HaMashakhYahu* was Elohiym's choice of a worthy sacrificial lamb to die in payment for the sins of mankind and was, therefore, the only person whose death made it possible for mankind to obtain remission of sin.

Is it not absurd to think that *YahuChanan ben Zecharyahu* baptized *Yahushua HaMashakhYahu* so *Elohiym* would grant him remission of sin, when it is only in Yahushua's death that remission of sin can be made available to any person who exercises genuine faith for it? YahuChanan's baptism was not to bring remission of sin to anybody. If it was, then remission of sin would have also been given to *Yahushua HaMashakhYahu* in the baptism he received at YahuChanan's hand.

YahuChanan ben Zecharyahu simply taught the Hebrews of his day, and mankind for that matter, remission of sin was to be made available to every sinner after the unblemished *Seh HaElohiym* (Lamb of *Elohiym*) was slain, through the knowledge of repentance and baptism. The task to teach this truth to mankind kept *YahuChanan ben Zecharyahu* crying in the wilderness until he was shut in prison.

Moving a little from *YahuChanan ben Zecharyahu*, let us look at the earthly ministry of *Yahushua HaMashakhYahu*. Evidence abounds in the *Holy Scriptures* of *Yahushua HaMashakhYahu* granting people forgiveness of their sins before his sacrficial death at *Mekom HaGulgolet* (or simply *Gulgotha*, which means the Place of the Skull)—cf. *Markos* 15:22, *Lukas* 23:33 and *YahuChanan (John)* 19:17. On many occasions, before *Yahushua HaMashakhYahu* went to *Gulgotha*, he forgave the sins of the sick so they would be healed. He even forgave the sins of those who mocked him, including those who hanged him.

He also taught his *talmidim* to forgive each other of their faults, even as they sought to obtain forgiveness of sin from *Elohiym*. They were to forgive one another their sins in order to qualify to obtain Elohiym's forgiveness for their own. The fact is, before *Yahushua HaMashakhYahu* went to *Gulgotha*, forgiveness of sin was receivable by man from *Elohiym*. Forgiveness of sin was obtainable from *Elohiym* through repentance and confession.

In what has come to be known among Christians as *"the Lord's Prayer"* (*Lukas* 11:9-13), *Yahushua HaMashakhYahu* before going to *Gulgotha* taught his *talmidim* to ask and to receive Elohiym's forgiveness of sin by confession. *Yahushua HaMashakhYahu*, through his own word, also pronounced people's sins forgiven much to the chagrin of his enemy critics before he sacrificed himself.

There are many references in the *Holy Scriptures* to support these assertions. However, a few of them are listed here for readers to discover for themselves and study. These are *Mattityahu (Matthew)* 6:14-15 and 9:2; *Markos (Mark)* 2:5 and 11:25; *Lukas (Luke)* 5:20-24, 7:47-48, 11:4, 17:4 and 23:34.

We have to fathom the depth of the Savior's love for sinners by what he did for us. He went a step further beyond pronouncing sins forgiven so that people could be healed of any infirmities in their physical bodies. Before walking to *Gulgotha*, he further gave us another dose of power against all sicknesses affecting our mortal bodies—he bared his back and took thirty-nine lashes of the cruel, multi-stringed Roman-Hebrew whip.

By doing this, *Yahushua HaMashakhYahu* took our place to receive Elohiym's punishment due to us for our sins, which he did not take part in committing. He did this so we would not have to suffer the consequences of our sins—notably, sickness and disease—cf. *Devarim (Deuteronomy)* 28:15-65. Through those lashes, he took our sickness away and brought healing.

We must believe and accept that he took our sickness away by doing this because it was foretold by *Yeshayahu* (Isaiah) the *navi* that he would—cf. *Yeshayahau (Isaiah)* 53:4-5. It was also confirmed by *Shimon Kefa* (Simon Peter), a *Shliakh* of *Yahushua HaMashakhYahu*, in the **Beyrit Chadasha** teaching on our rights, privileges, status, etc., and in fact, of all what we become in *Yahushua HaMashakhYahu*, that this prophecy of *Yeshayahu* (Isaiah) had become real, in his suffering and scourging with whips, as a prelude to the actual sacrifice of himself at *Gulgotha*—cf. *Kefa Alef (First Peter)* 2:24.

So whenever we picture the bruised body of our loving Savior as he walked to *Gulgotha*, the Place of the Skull, and the wretchedness of that bloodied body as it hung there, discerning the meaning and power behind that horrible spectacle of our Savior, we can claim instant healing from *Elohiym* for our mortal bodies.

When you understand that the Savior took all this suffering upon himself, for your sake, so you will not have to go through it, sickness can no longer have any power over your mortal body. And we can receive all these blessings before the greater and more glorious ones of salvation, adoption, son-ship, impartation of the divine nature, ordination as royal priests, etc., that come to us in exercising genuine faith in his death, burial, and resurrection.

Anyone of the house of *Yisroel* who was bitten by a snake in the wilderness journey looked just once at the bronze serpent that *Moshe* hung on a pole and got healed instantly—cf. *Bamidbar (Numbers)* 21:8-9. That was the shadow of our healing, coming through our discernment of the bruised body of our Savior as it hung on a pole at *Gulgotha*.

We are blessed by the truths of *Elohiym* that we know and accept by faith. We are likewise doomed by what we do not know or by our ignorance of Elohiym's truths and our faithlessness. How true *Hoshea (Hosea)* 4:6 then becomes for many of us: **"*My people*** *are destroyed for lack of knowledge."* Forgiveness of sin for the healing of the physical body is what *Yahushua HaMashakhYahu* made available for mankind before he died at *Gulgotha.*

We can therefore say that *Yahushua HaMashakhYahu* did not go to *Gulgotha* to necessarily bring about forgiveness of sin to man from *Elohiym.* The question then is this: What did *Yahushua HaMashakhYahu* accomplish for man when he went to *Gulgotha?*

As far as the solution to the sin problem of man and his salvation were concerned, *Yahushua HaMashakhYahu* went to *Gulgotha* to take away the sin of the world. He went to *Gulgotha* to break the power of sin over the lives of men by dealing with sin at its roots. *Yahushua HaMashakhYahu* went to *Gulgotha* to perform the needed spiritual surgical operation to remove the cancer of sin from our human spirits to enable us stop sinning.

The sacrificial death of *Yahushua HaMashakhYahu* was the ransom price he had to pay to *Elohiym* in order to rescue man from the tyranny of the devil and to send him (man), completely cleansed from sin, back to *Elohiym.* He could not do this anywhere else but at *Gulgotha!* In other words, the Savior's pronouncement of peoples' sins as being forgiven, before he went to *Gulgotha,* could not bring about any of these blessings to them.

Yahushua HaMashakhYahu went to *Gulgotha* to pay the price for our redemption. This payment of the price for sin makes it possible for every sinner to enter the state of remission of sin by faith and understanding of what one must do.

It is when one enters the state of remission of sin that one can be born again, gain entry into the *Malchut HaElohiym,* receive deliverance from the power and dominion of sin, and obtain the divine nature of *Elohiym* imputed to his spirit.

On the receipt of remission of sins, however, one automatically enjoys forgiveness of sin. This is because when you have had your sins paid for, you will, as a matter of cause, have them forgiven. Forgiveness of sin can be found within remission of sin or in payment for sin. However, remission of sin cannot be found in forgiveness of sin.

For anybody who can rightly divide *HaDavar HaEmes* (the Word of Truth), he is able to see forgiveness of sin within remission of sin but not vice versa.

What this means is that you may receive forgiveness of sin and still not become born again by that act of forgiveness from *Elohiym.*

You cannot receive remission of sin or become born again, however, and not be forgiven of your sins.

In much the same way, you could receive healing from *Elohiym* for your bodily infirmities and yet not be born again. But you cannot be born again, or become a new creature in a new birth, have *Ruwakh HaKodesh* of *Elohiym* who raised *Yahushua HaMashakhYahu* from death dwell within you—cf. *YahuChanan (John)* 3:5, *Second Corinthians* 5:17 and *Romans* 8:11—and not be healed of all your bodily infirmities.

Therefore, we have to understand what remission of sin is and how mankind can obtain it according to the doctrines of the *Holy Scriptures*, if we are to enter Elohiym's salvation in *Yahushua HaMashakhYahu*.

It is only when we understand what remission of sin is, and obey Elohiym's instruction as to how to receive it through baptism in the name of *Yahushua HaMashakhYahu*, that the power and wisdom of *Elohiym* are unleashed towards us, bringing to our inner beings the born again experience.

While we seek to understand what remission of sin is and how we can obtain it, we have to accept that *Elohiym* did not simply ordain our entry into His Kingdom by forgiveness of sin. If *Elohiym* had ordained man to enter His salvation simply through forgiveness of sin, He would have taught us how to do so. He would then have made it plain in His instructions to us to seek forgiveness of sin, orally, when we desire to enter the *Malchut HaElohiym*.

Then it might have been appropriate to pray some *Sinners' Prayer* of confession and request forgiveness of sin to secure that entry into the *Malchut HaElohiym*. Even if a so-called *Sinners' Prayer* of confession of sin and request for entry could bring us into the salvation of *Elohiym*, He would have had such a prayer made available to be said by all seeking His salvation in *Yahushua HaMashakhYahu* in the same words.

In fact, if by asking *Elohiym* in prayer for His salvation one could gain it, in much the same way as one obtained healing by asking the Savior for it, then *Yahushua HaMashakhYahu* would have simply pronounced man **saved,** by forgiving his sins, without going to *Gulgotha*, just as he had on many occasions pronounced man's sick and diseased body **healed,** by forgiving his sins. However, Yahushua's sacrificial death did remain necessary, even after he forgave men's sins on those many occasions before *Gulgotha*.

This is because *Elohiym* ordained that the salvation of man was to be accessed through remission of sin. This fact is what *Elohiym* sought to inform mankind about, when *YahuChanan ben Zecharyahu* was thrust onto the spiritual scene of *Yisroel*.

I do not know how much clearer, and more forcefully, to teach the fact that man does not enter the born again experience simply by obtaining forgiveness of his sins from *Elohiym*. Whether man obtains forgiveness of sins from *Elohiym* by asking for it or by being pronounced forgiven by *Yahushua HaMashakhYahu* himself, it does not, or better still, cannot, bring man the new birth and into the *Malchut HaElohiym*.

If the receipt of the pronouncement of one's sins as being forgiven could ever bring any sinner unto the new birth, then those who spat on *Yahushua HaMashakhYahu*, slapped and insulted him, forced a crown of thorns on his head, and finally hanged him, would have also had the new birth since he asked *HaAv* (the Good Father) to forgive all of them their sins.

It seems to me that these were the kind of sinners who had the most urgent need to be born again into the *Malchut HaElohiym*, and yet, did not get born again by Yahushua's prayer for their forgiveness.

Forgiveness of sin alone does not, and cannot, bring the sinner into Elohiym's Kingdom or make him become born again. This truth of *Elohiym*, we must know and accept.

Anytime *Yahushua HaMashakhYahu* pronounced people's sins forgiven or asked *HaAv* to forgive people of their sins, he meant any one of two things: either that the suffering people went through as a consequence of their sins should be taken off them, or that all the evil consequences that were bound to come upon these sinners should be stayed by Elohiym's mercies.

Yahushua HaMashakhYahu never meant for sinners to become born again through these acts of forgiveness of sin. He never meant that people would be delivered from the power of committing sin in these ways because, in some of these cases, he went to great lengths to warn them not to sin anymore, for a worse fate could befall them. Forgiveness of sin is, therefore, not what you should seek in your pursuit to become born again.

As I mentioned earlier on in this book, the doctrine on remission of sin makes its first entry into the *Holy Scriptures* in the *Beyrit Chadasha* teachings. The absence of this doctrine in the *Tanakh* should not be considered strange, however, since this doctrine is linked exclusively to the work of *Yahushua HaMashakhYahu* in his sacrificial death at *Gulgotha*.

Elohiym brought remission of sin into being so as to enable humanity to obtain a unique blessing by the sacrifice of *Yahushua HaMashakhYahu*, which neither an atonement nor the forgiveness of sin could bring to the sinner under the Old Covenant.

The issues of remission of sin, therefore, hold key to our understanding of the value of the sacrifice of *Yahushua HaMashakhYahu* and how we may enter Elohiym's salvation. In fact, none of the blessings due man, through the sacrifice of *Yahushua HaMashakhYahu*, can be received without an understanding of the value and meaning of the doctrine of remission of sin. Remission of sins brings such great spiritual power and blessing that the human mind is not able to fully comprehend it.

Remission of sin is Elohiym's wisdom to deal with any imperfections, inadequacies, deficiencies, weaknesses in efficacy, short-term limits, etc., that the ordinances of animal sacrifices had. Remission of sin was meant to stem the repetitive nature of animal sacrifices that were monotonously offered day by day or year by year, and which lacked the needed efficacy or potency to deal with sin at its roots.

The wisdom of *Elohiym* in remission of sin also sought to recreate a better human being, one better than any biological son of *Yisroel*, with whom He could establish a better relationship and fellowship than He hitherto had with *Yisroel*.

Many teachers of the *Holy Scriptures* have made a devastating mistake by equating remission to forgiveness. It is a devastating mistake because such a posture robs mankind of all the blessings intended for him but hidden in the word "remission".

Some publishers of *The Bible* have not helped in this matter either. The publishers of the *Good News Bible*, the *New International Version Bible*, the *New Living Translation Bible*, the *New American Standard Bible*, and many others, have not considered the word at all and so have used in its place "forgiveness", as if we could equate "remission" to "forgiveness"!!

Miraculously, however, the translators of the King James Version of *The Bible* drew a distinction between remission and forgiveness. It is rather unfortunate that they were also drawn into the same error of interchanging remission with forgiveness in some parts of their work as other translators have done.

To me, the most powerful word in the *English Bible* is *"remission"*. This is one particular word that teaches us a great deal on the value of the sacrifice of *Yahushua HaMashakhYahu* and the blessing to mankind that this sacrifice brings.

The New Covenant not only evolved through this word, but it also revolves around it. Yet this word is missing in many versions of *The Bible*! It is sad that translators have been misled to take it out of many versions of *The Bible*. What is *The Bible* then, without this word **"remission"**?

YahuChanan ben Zecharyahu was born to teach remission of sin—cf. *Lukas (Luke)* 1:77—and died in the course of this service. *Yahushua HaMashakhYahu* was sent by *Elohiym* to this world to make it possible for mankind to secure remission of sin. Remission of sin sent him to his sacrificial death at *Gulgotha* where he died for mankind. He announced at the "Last Supper" with twelve of his *talmidim* that he was going to die to shed his blood for the remission of sin—cf. *Mattityahu (Matthew)* 26:28.

All the *Shlikhim ("Apostles")* of *Yahushua HaMashakhYahu* lived their lives after his resurrection as witnesses of the fact that remission of sin was forever made available to mankind due to his sacrifice at *Gulgotha*. They were taught and instructed by the Master to teach others how to receive it, all their lives on earth, after his resurrection. They all died while teaching to bring to mankind knowledge of remission of sin and how one could secure it.

The Master told us—you and I, our generation—in the Great Commission to go out and preach repentance and remission of sin to bring his salvation to sinners—cf. *Lukas (Luke)* 24: 46-48. We have been misled to believe that when the Master said **"remission"**, he meant **"forgiveness"**.

Because we mistakenly believe forgiveness of sin is crucial for salvation, we teach people to pray to *Elohiym* asking for it, instead of leading them to the obedience of Elohiym's instruction for repentance and baptism as the way into His salvation.

Many people acknowledge *Yahushua HaMashakhYahu* took away our sins through his death. They, however, do not make a distinction between what he did about sin in the lives of men, in, and by, his death, and what he did while alive. We should seek to make this distinction in order to reap the benefits of the Savior's sacrifice.

In my view, many students of the *Holy Scriptures* have not been able to make this distinction due to inherent problems of translation of what is commonly available and popularly known *Greek New*

Testament texts, from which all English language versions are derived. These problems arise, in part, from inaccuracies in the rendering of certain words of the Greek texts into English. Even from my position as a novice of the *Greek New Testament*, this problem of translation is a very serious and disturbing one that calls for critical examination and resolution.

I suppose it might be beneficial for all readers of the *Holy Scriptures* to look at the usage of certain Greek words used in the *Greek New Testament* to describe the concepts of atonement, forgiveness, and remission of sin. From my point of focus on what is termed *"New Testament Greek"*, I can see about fourteen words used in the definition of the concepts of how *Elohiym* deals with sin in the lives of men.

These words, and their frequencies of usage in the *Greek New Testament* put in parenthesis are as follows: **aphesis (17X), aphiemi (146X); apolutrosis (10X), apoluo (69X); charizomai (28X), charis (156X); hilaskomai (2X), hilasmos (2X), hilasterion (2X); paresis (1X); lutron (2X), lutrosis (3X), lutrotes (2X); and epikalupto (1X).**

Altogether these words make some 440 appearances in the Greek texts that demand accurate rendering into any of the three possible English words—namely atonement, forgiveness, or remission—anytime any of them appear in the Greek texts.

Let me state at this point that, contrary to the wrong view held by many theologians and Christian clergymen, the New Covenant scriptures were not inspired by or written in Greek! This book is not, to me, the appropriate medium to debunk the assertion held by bible translators, theologians and Christian clergymen that the New Covenant scriptures were of Greek origin.

The point must, however, be made here that *Elohiym* never speaks any language but Hebrew, in and outside of *Shamayim*!! Well, fact is, all of Elohiym's *neviim* ("prophets") from *Avraham* are Hebrew; the last of them being His Son, *Yahushua HaMashakhYahu*, the most renown of Hebrews (cf. *Hebrews* 1:1-2). And so, *Elohiym* speaks Hebrew to all His *neviim*!

When *Elohiym* sends His holy angels to deliver His messages to Earth, He speaks Hebrew to them; these angels then act as His linguists, with neither the right of option nor worthiness to paraphrase, add to or translate His Word, and neither is there the need for them to do so, since all the people *Elohiym* ever sends His angels to are Hebrew or speak Hebrew anyway!

So then, obviously, the New Covenant scriptures were inspired by *Elohiym* in Hebrew, to be written in Hebrew by Hebrew men He chose Himself even before their birth, and for, principally, Hebrews to believe and obey; just as He did with the Old Covenant scriptures!

The *Greek New Testament* available in the world today must, therefore, be a translation from an original Hebrew text. You may call the *Greek New Testament*, the *Textus Receptus (Received Text)* as theologians do, or by any other name, yet its descent from Hebrew cannot be doubted! The *Greek New Testament* following very closely on the heels of the inspired Hebrew text may seem to be better in meaning, value, and richness than its much later English derivative, but is still seen to be clearly and woefully unathentic when studied in comparison with the Hebrew text written under the guidance and inspiration of *Ruwakh HaKodesh*.

There is therefore a great danger to mankind's salvation when the *Besuras HaGeulah*—the message for mankind's redemption—is taught as if it was inspired by *Elohiym* and initially received by mankind in Greek. Salvation seekers ought to be warned of this!

The Hebrew New Covenant scriptures were written against a background of a popular cultural relationship between slaves, slave owners, and slave dealers. At the core of that relationship, or culture, were the freedoms of the slave.

Under what conditions could a slave be liberated or receive pardon for an offence? When and how could a slave be transferred or sold to another master or owner?

Could slaves act in their own capacity to gain their freedom, pardon, or transfer? When could the slave's master or owner, or some other person, act for and on behalf of a slave to bring him or her freedom? Many legal issues evolved within that culture to define the rights of slaves to freedom or liberties of any kind.

These legal issues had to be clearly defined so as to be unambiguous with regards to how slaves could relate to their masters or owners and how they could obtain certain rights, liberties, or freedoms—not just how, but also when, where, and by whom, or by what means. When were the freedoms granted to slaves meant to be temporal or timeless? All these involved legal matters and these words dealt with them clearly and adequately.

The translators of the *Greek New Testament* knew a lot of this Hebrew slave-master culture because they lived in it and felt its heart throb. Therefore, they easily took their vocabulary from that culture to describe the state of the sinner in the manner of his enslavement to sin and the devil, before and after the sacrifice of *Yahushua HaMashakhYahu.*

Translators who later translated the *Greek New Testament* into the many English versions available, however, did not live in this powerful, dehumanizing slave-master culture, and for that reason they were, and still are, unable to feel the strong emotions that the slaves and their masters went through under these conditions, as captured by these Greek words. Besides, it might seem difficult, if not a handicap, to render appropriately this large basket of Greek words with the rather limited English vocabulary of just three words.

The difficulties encountered in these tasks are compounded when we come to understand that these Greek words have very close or double meanings. However, the meanings of atonement, remission, and forgiveness are not as closely related; that could, in itself, pose further difficulties in their rendering into English.

Within the context of their usage in the *Greek New Testament*, all these words describe or deal with processes whose end-results are to take sin away, break the power of sin over the slave-sinner, and cause sin's consequences to disappear or to prevent them from coming about at all. Even though they all act in such a way as to bring about end-results that are similar to each other, are the various processes involved in the eradication of the sin, or its effects and consequences, the same?

Are the end results or their benefits the same? Do these results and benefits exist in the same time frame? Obviously not, and these further add a headache to translators in their work in this regard.

Let us pause briefly to look at what benefits Yahushua's sacrifice gave to man. His sacrifice covers the sins of mankind; therefore, it makes atonement for man. It brings back Elohiym's favor to man; therefore, it propitiates. It also brings pardon from *Elohiym*; meaning, it forgives. It brings liberty from sin and the dominion of the devil; meaning, it liberates. The sacrifice of *Yahushua HaMashakhYahu* also pays for the consequences of sin and forestalls them from coming upon the liberated sinner. Yet still, the sacrifice of *Yahushua HaMashakhYahu* pays a ransom: it redeems or buys back man from the ownership of the devil.

The value of the sacrifice of *Yahushua HaMashakhYahu* to man is so great that it embodies all the three English words used to describe how *Elohiym* deals with sin in the lives of men—namely, atonement, forgiveness, and remission. It is a one-off sacrifice that was executed in order to bring to man complete freedom from sin's power, snare, and consequences, and whose efficacy goes to the farthest past and future one can imagine.

With this understanding of the value of the sacrifice of *Yahushua HaMashakhYahu* in our minds, let us now look at this large basket of Greek words to determine the one that best fits the all-encompassing liberation from sin, its dominion and effects, which the sacrifice of *Yahushua HaMashakhYahu* brings to the salvation seeker.

The Greek word **aphesis**, rendered **remission** by the King James Version translators, seems to be the most appropriate word of all the fourteen listed, describing in an encompassing detail, the manner, means, value, and benefits of the sacrifice of *Yahushua HaMashakhYahu.*

This word denotes the payment of a ransom or debt with blood or life. It suggests liberation from bondage, a pardon, or a grant of freedom. It is correctly translated in *Mattityahu (Matthew)* 26:28; *Markos (Mark)* 1:4; *Lukas (Luke)* 1:77, 3:3, and 24:47; *Acts* 2:38 and 10:43; *Romans* 3:25; and *Ivriim (Hebrews)* 9:22 and 10:18 as **remission** since the context of these verses mean a sacrifice of Yahushua's life for the liberation of man from sin and its consequences and from the controller of sin, the devil.

Sadly, however, in *Acts* 5:31, 13:38, and 26:18; *Ephesians* 1:7; and *Colossians* 1:14, where the context of these verses mean the offer in sacrifice of the life-blood of *Yahushua HaMashakhYahu* to bring liberation and freedom from the power and dominion of sin and its consequences, **aphesis** is rendered as **forgiveness**. This gives the impression of liberation from a situation by oral pronouncement or by a wave of the hand, so to speak, without the payment of a bloody ransom or any other ransom for that matter.

I think readers and students of the English versions of the *Holy Scriptures* would have been better helped by the King James Version translators to get a stronger feel of the power and spirit of their work if **aphesis** were rendered as **remission** in these five important verses. To me, this would have brought consistency and added a little more value to their work.

This need for consistency should have left no options at all for the translators to erroneously render **aphesis** as **forgiveness** when the context of its usage relates unambiguously to the shedding of

Yahushua's blood to bring redemption to mankind. English bible translators ought to have been consistent, firm and bold in translating *aphesis* as *remission* in *Acts* 5:31, 13:38, and 26:18; *Ephesians* 1:7; and *Colossians* 1:14, in all of their Bibles.

In many other places, *aphesis* is translated as *forgiveness*. In all such instances, there is no difficulty in understanding that what was done to bring about the forgiveness was a verbal pronouncement, a written declaration of pardon, and or the payment of a ransom or price that did not involve the performing of a blood-sacrifice.

This double-meaning or dual usage of *aphesis* places a responsibility on all translators of the Greek texts to be extremely careful in their work. In fact, I would have wished the translators of the King James Version of *The Bible* were more circumspect in this regard than they had been.

The words *apoluo, charizomai* and *charis* denote pardon, forgiveness, granting of liberty, etc., by oral pronouncement or by payment of a debt by a means other than by blood-sacrifice. They are all, therefore, adequately rendered in various places of the English New Covenant scriptures as **forgiveness.**

Where *apolutrosis* is used, it is translated in the context of redemption, which is in agreement with its Greek meaning and usage. This we see in its rendering in *Romans* 8:23, *First Corinthians* 1:30, and *Ephesians* 4:30.

Rare words, such as *epikalupto, paresis, lutron, lutrosis, lutrotes, hilaskomai, hilasmos,* and *hilasterion,* all invariably relate to the sacrifice of *Yahushua HaMashakhYahu*: the purity of the sacrificed item, its meaning, redemptive power, reconciliatory effect, efficacy to go back and forth in time, etc. They do not pose serious problems in their translation into English, since what they mean are always clear.

We must be always guided by the spirit of the entire revelation of the *Holy Scriptures* to enable us to determine how we could safely render these various Greek words into English. Indeed, we need this guidance so as to be able to capture and portray the meanings of these words in their relation to the work of *Yahushua HaMashakhYahu* in dealing with mankind's sin problem before, at or after his death. This, we should aim to do, so that even the casual reader of the *Holy Scriptures* can easily understand what was involved in the sacrifice of *Yahushua HaMashakhYahu* and how, in, by and through it, the sins of the world and their consequences are forever taken away.

The word remission carries a legal connotation. It is not uncommon for a judge in a court trial to pronounce verdict in favor of an accused who had a debt charge against him. The judge gives verdict for the cancellation of the debt without giving any punishment to the accused.

The accused is then discharged or released from the obligation or penalty. The reasons for such a verdict could be many, but one of the hard-to-come-by reasons is that the plaintiff himself turned round and paid the debt on behalf of the indebted, accused person. According to **Black's Law Dictionary**, when this happens it is said that a remission of the debt has been made.

Why would the plaintiff pay off the debt owed to him by the person he dragged to court? The plaintiff may have had mercy and compassion stirred up within him when he saw the pathetic defense and miserable state of the accused as the case progressed in court.

He might have seen, as the case progressed in court, the inability and hopelessness of the accused in paying back what was owed him. He may have, then, out of sympathy desire to relieve him from the obligation of payment and write-off the debt.

To relieve the accused of payment would mean to withdraw the case from court. That is to tell the court that he, the plaintiff, is no longer interested in the case and wants the court to stop its processes of prosecuting the accused. If the plaintiff takes this course of action, however, it would not be pleasantly received by the court. The court would certainly determine its time has been wasted.

The court would stop the processes of prosecuting the accused but, at the same time, adjudicate costs against the plaintiff for wasting its precious time. The plaintiff then loses money on two fronts: court fines and the debt owed by the accused. The smaller loss to the plaintiff would be for him to pay on behalf of the accused the debt he owes, if the plaintiff has the capacity to liquidate the debt.

In the court of *Elohiym* in *Shamayim*, before the sacrifice of *Yahushua HaMashakhYahu*, everybody stood accused of committing sin and nobody could be freed. This was because mankind sinned, and came short of the Glory of *Elohiym* (*Romans* 3:23).

We are told in the *Holy Scriptures* that death is earned as the wages of sin (*Romans* 6:23). Man could only put up a porous, pathetic, and miserable defense for his sins. Condemnation to death for sin was, therefore, what awaited mankind before the sacrifice of *Yahushua HaMashakhYahu*.

When *Elohiym* sees the helplessness of His creation in defending himself from the consequences of his sins, His compassion and mercy are stirred up on man's behalf. He then works a plan to rescue sinful man from his misery and wretchedness that resulted from his sins.

Elohiym is the only one with the capacity to liquidate this debt of sin. *Elohiym*, however, cannot do this Himself; therefore, He gives His only begotten Son the power to payoff this debt of sin and break its power over man. *Yahushua HaMashakhYahu*, to this end, brings to the sinner remission of sin in his sacrifice. *Elohiym*, in *Yahushua HaMashakhYahu*, demonstrates His love for the pathetic sinner in paying off his debts to sin through Yahushua's sacrifice.

So you see *Yahushua HaMashakhYahu* does far more than forgiving us our sins; he pays for them. This is what remission of sin is about. How we have not understood this for so long a time puzzles me. In his sacrifice at *Gulgotha*, *Yahushua HaMashakhYahu* paid the penalty of our sins. He took man's place, receiving the death sentence for man's sins.

When a man receives the remission of sin, it brings him into the position or state where all his sins have been paid for, in and by the sacrifice of *Yahushua HaMashakhYahu*. *Elohiym* no longer executes punishment on that man for the sins he committed before coming to *Yahushua HaMashakhYahu*, the Savior. Never will *Elohiym* demand that any man in the state of remission of sin be punished.

This is because *Yahushua HaMashakhYahu*, *HaGo'el* (the Redeemer), has paid that debt to enable that man to be pronounced "not guilty" in the courtroom of *Elohiym*. There is, therefore, no condemnation for them that are in *Yahushua HaMashakhYahu* (*Romans* 8:1) or those who have received remission of sin.

Remission of sin is a blessing of *Elohiym* that one can access or enter into only **once** in a lifetime. Remission of sin brings to us the new birth. Because it is a single-transaction payment for sin, we can easily understand it is a one-time event in the life of any sinner. Just as we are born once, and our particular debt to someone is also paid in full only once, so is remission of sin obtained once in one's lifetime.

This is what *Romans* says about remission of sin: ***"Whom God (Elohiym) hath set forth to be a propitiation through faith in his*** *blood, to declare his righteousness for the remission of sins that are past, through the forbearance of God (Elohiym)"—Romans 3:25, KJV; words in parenthesis are mine.*

This fact that remission of sins is a once-in-a-life-time blessing of *Elohiym* greatly contrasts it from forgiveness of sin. Forgiveness of sin is obtainable many times in a lifetime. In the words of *Yahushua HaMashakhYahu*, forgiveness of sin can be obtained as many times as *"seventy times seven"* from one wronged person alone, or from *Elohiym*, and possibly in one day.

The requirement for true and genuine repentance would, however, not permit us to seek forgiveness for as many as "seventy times seven" times from *Elohiym*, or an individual, in a given day. That would simply render our repentance absurd, insincere, and without any spiritual benefits.

Furthermore, because remission of sin is a blessing bestowed on the sinner by *Elohiym* alone, it distinguishes it from forgiveness of sin. Forgiveness of sin can be rendered by a man to his fellow man, but man cannot render remission of sin to another man. Sinful man does not have the capacity to pay for the sins of others since he himself needs someone to pay for his sins.

In the remission of sin, the spirit of the salvation seeker is brought into contact with the shed blood of *Yahushua HaMashakhYahu*. As in the days of the *Law*, when a man's physical body came in contact with the sprinkled blood of bulls bringing a cleansing from sin to his body, one's spirit in contact with the blood of *Yahushua* brings one into the state of remission of sin, where one's sins are washed away.

Nobody gets into contact physically with the shed blood of *Yahushua HaMashakhYahu*. One contacts the blood of *Yahushua HaMashakhYahu* by faith. Contact and union are made between the human spirit and the Spirit of *Yahushua HaMashakhYahu* when they agree, based on the understanding of Elohiym's Word.

This agreement of spirits in faith ignites salvation. You must have the faith of *Elohiym* to become born again. Your faith is in your obedience to the instructions of *Elohiym* in His Word, which is how you can get in contact with Yahushua's blood.

You do not express faith in Elohiym's Word if you ask through a particular kind of prayer that the shed blood of *Yahushua HaMashakhYahu* touch you, enabling you be cleansed. You do not act in faith by a prayer of such kind since nowhere in the Word of *Elohiym* are we taught to do this.

Faith, we are told, comes from hearing Elohiym's Word—cf. *Romans* 10:17. Where do we hear *Elohiym* speak to us, to pray asking for cleansing from sin that will enable us to become born again? Were you not misled and or deceived by somebody to do this?

Please check your doctrine before it leads you to disappointment and doom. Do not even think or believe that by asking *Elohiym* in prayer to touch your spirit, with the blood of *Yahushua HaMashakhYahu* that was shed at *Gulgotha*, He will do for you what your expectations are in the born again experience.

This is because Elohiym's Word has not instructed you to pray for this or like that. You pray amiss if you do. You could have prayed fervently and zealously and still have prayed amiss, because you did not pray according to the will and instructions of *Elohiym*.

This is one type of prayer that can never be answered no matter how many days you fasted in this regard to back your request. Your human spirit only gets in touch with the blood of *Yahushua HaMashakhYahu* in the waters of baptism and in your obedience to the baptism of repentance in the name of *Yahushua HaMashakhYahu* for the remission of sin, as instructed by Him for you to do in order to gain salvation.

Let us try to go further in the remission of sin business by looking at the following scripture:

"And almost all things are by the law purged with blood and without the shedding of blood is no remission"—Ivriim (Hebrews) 9:22, KJV.

Under the *Torah*, the carrying out of the instructions of *Elohiym* by priests was very important. For example, in the offering of blood for cleansing of instruments of worship and of people from sin, the type of blood—that is, of goat, sheep, bull, or bird—was always specified. Sprinkling of the blood was specified to be done with the aid of a hyssop, scarlet wool, or the finger of the priest. The number of times the sprinkling was to be done was also specified.

The priests, acting in the place of *Elohiym*, had these strict instructions to comply with to bring about the cleansing from dirt sought under the *Law*. The priest had no choice but to carry out the instructions of *Elohiym* to the letter.

In regards to our obedience of Elohiym's instructions in the New Covenant, the same commitment of the Old Covenant *kohenim* (priests) ought to be maintained. Their strict compliance to the instructions of *Elohiym* should be our example.

Because the New Covenant priesthood is of a better order than the defunct Levitical one, our obedience of the instructions of our *Kohen Gadol* (High Priest)—*Yahushua HaMashakhYahu*—must be perfect. We must exhibit perfection in our obedience to *Elohiym* compared to that of the priests under the Old Covenant.

The actors of the New Covenant salvation enjoy more Grace from *Elohiym* than the Old Covenant priests. The Grace of *Elohiym* very often keeps at bay His anger and wrath due us because of our disobedience to His instructions.

Unfortunately, as *Elohiym* has sought to show His love to us under the New Covenant, it has brought about mediocrity in our commitment to Him. This has led to all manner of people teaching all manner of doctrines, claiming to do so in the name of the Most High One.

We elect ourselves as messengers of *Elohiym* because of some theological schooling we have received. We go to people with this claim, teaching them all manner of doctrine and claiming it is the doctrine of *Elohiym* and His Son *Yahushua HaMashakhYahu*. We do all manner of miracles, claiming we act in the name of the Savior, yet many of us do not know him.

It is time for all people professing the name of *Yahushua HaMashakhYahu* (Jesus Christ?) to act according to his clear and simple instruction meant to lead sinners into his salvation, by teaching repentance and remission of sin.

We must stop preaching *Sinners' Prayer* recitals to salvation seekers if, truly, we are professing the Name of the Master. *Yahushua HaMashakhYahu*, the Master, did not teach anybody to recite a *Sinners' Prayer* to become born again. Let us, therefore, not bring his name into the *Sinners' Prayer* practice.

To have your sins purged by the shed blood of *Yahushua HaMashakhYahu* is to respond to the instructions of Elohiym's Word to repent from sin and accept baptism in the name of the Savior. For the sinner to get a touch of the blood of the Savior shed at *Gulgotha*, he must express his faith in the name of *Yahushua HaMashakhYahu* by obeying his simple instructions.

It is by obeying Yahushua's instruction to be baptized in his name in deep and drowning living waters that one's spirit can get a touch of his blood and be cleansed from sin. The blood of *Yahushua HaMashakhYahu*, with all its cleansing powers, meets the sinner in the waters of baptism to remove the roots of sin from his spirit.

Let us continue our study of remission of sin by looking at the verses of *Ivriim (Hebrews)* 10:17-18:

"And their sins and iniquities will I remember no more. Now where remission of these is, there is no more offering for sin"— *Ivriim (Hebrews) 10:17-18, KJV.*

The sacrifice of *Yahushua HaMashakhYahu* which brought remission of sin also brought an end to all blood sacrifices of animals for atonement or for forgiveness. The spirit of the sinner, who has been able to access remission of sin, is in constant touch with the shed blood of *Yahushua HaMashakhYahu* as long as he walks in the light, or lives in the faith, of Elohiym's Word. The shed blood of *Yahushua HaMashakhYahu* constantly works as a cleansing from sin in the life of any believer that has gained entry into the new birth by remission of sin. That is why the end of blood sacrifices for cleansing from sin has come.

Forgiveness of sin, for those who are in the salvation of *Elohiym*, no longer involves the offering of blood sacrifices of any kind. In fact, as mentioned earlier, the offering of blood sacrifices to deal with the effects of any manner of sin came to an end with the sacrifice of *Yahushua HaMashakhYahu.*

Under the *Beyrit Chadasha*, forgiveness of sin is received purely in dialogue, restitution, and reconciliation. Forgiveness of sin is obtained through repentance and confession. When we speak with *Elohiym*, we tell Him we are sorry for committing the sin and seek His forgiveness. This same approach is adopted for reconciliation among the children of *Elohiym* on earth who have problems living together in harmony.

The *Beyrit Chadasha* doctrines teach that we enter the new life through repentance and faith in baptism into the name of *Yahushua HaMashakhYahu*. By expressing that faith, we obtain remission of our sins and the gift of *Ruwakh HaKodesh* to dwell within our hearts. If, afterwards, we sin and want forgiveness of our sins, we repent and confess those sins, and ask for Elohiym's pardon.

When we understand that forgiveness and remission of sins are not the same, we can reap the blessings *Elohiym* intends for us to receive in these regards. The spirit of the *Beyrit Chadasha* teaches remission of sin as different from forgiveness of sin. Oversimplified versions of *The Bible* seek to equate them. This is completely wrong.

In *Ivriim (Hebrews)* 9:22 of the King James Version of *The Bible*, the word **remission** cannot be replaced with the word **forgiveness**.

That would render the entire verse flawed. This is because even before Yahushua's blood was shed in his sacrifice for the remission of sins, man could receive Elohiym's forgiveness. And so, for those producers of English bibles which have the word *forgiveness* in place of *remission* in *Ivriim (Hebrew)* 9:22, I hope they see their glaring error.

We must also note that *Ivriim (Hebrews)* 9:22 talks about the purging of nonhuman and inanimate objects with blood of animals that have been offered in sacrifice. To put the word forgiveness in place of remission in this verse would mean to suggest that inanimate objects can be forgiven, which in this case would be ridiculous. Remission of sin **cannot be** the same as forgiveness of sin.

Shimon Kefa, a *Shliakh* (one sent, emissary, "apostle") of *Yahushua HaMashakhYahu*, knew the truth about how the salvation of *Elohiym* would be received in remission of sin after the sacrifice of the Savior. He had been taught this and was compelled to teach the same.

When he had the singular duty to lead Hebrews who had come home on a visit from the then Hebrew Diaspora into the salvation of *Elohiym, Shimon Kefa* led them to repent of their sins and to receive baptism in the name of *Yahushua HaMashakhYahu*. He taught his listeners to do these two things with understanding, faith, and sincerity, so as to receive the remission of sins and the seal of *Ruwakh HaKodesh* as children of *Elohiym*—cf. *Ma'asim (Acts)* 2:38.

Remission of sin therefore provides the key into Elohiym's salvation in *Yahushua HaMashakhYahu* and hence into the *Malchut HaElohiym*. The demands of *Elohiym* for our sins are met through the remission of our sins.

However, even though the demands of Justice have been met on your behalf by *Yahushua HaMashakhYahu* providing the key to the door which opens into the Grace of *Elohiym*—cf. *YahuChanan (John)* 10:7-9,—your ignorance of how to enter Elohiym's justice by means of the remission of sins can keep you in bondage perpetually. This could cause you to suffer from many things *Elohiym* intended you to be delivered from through His plan and scheme in Yahushua's sacrifice. You need to possess the knowledge of how to use this key to open the door into the *Malchut HaElohiym*.

Our knowledge of remission of sin, and how to obtain it in baptism into *Yahushua HaMashakhYahu*, will open the door for us to enter into the salvation of *Elohiym*. Without proper understanding of remission of sin, we would at best only get to the door of the *Malchut HaElohiym* and just keep standing there.

Since the days of *YahuChanan ben Zecharyahu, Yahushua HaMashakhYahu, Shimon Kefa* and *Sha'ul*, all of whom have, at various times, taught us about remission of sin and its crucial and indispensable role regarding our salvation, we have come to acquire so much knowledge as to how to enter the salvation of *Elohiym*.

The *Shlikhim* (sent ones, emissaries, messengers, "apostles") of *Yahushua HaMashakhYahu* have clearly taught us that remission of sin comes to the sinner in his baptism into *Yahushua HaMashakhYahu* and that we are born again through this baptism. We cannot, therefore, provide any explanation why we do anything to the contrary, like the praying of *Sinners' Prayers*, in our pursuit to become born again and to enter the salvation of *Elohiym*.

In summary, let me reiterate that sin is dealt with by *Elohiym* in three ways. These ways are atonement, forgiveness, and remission. None of these are given out automatically, even though they are made available to mankind today by virtue of Yahushua's sacrificial death on behalf of humanity. You can only access them by understanding Elohiym's instructions and responding to those instructions in the right manner.

Do you want to enter the salvation of *Elohiym*? Then you need remission of your sins, and you can only obtain remission of sins by repenting of your past sins and accepting baptism into the name of *Yahushua HaMashakhYahu*.

The wisdom of *Ruwakh HaKodesh* of *Elohiym* in directing the salvation seeker into His salvation in *Yahushua HaMashakhYahu*, on the Day of the Outpouring of *Ruwakh HaKodesh* (Pentecost?) in *Yerushalayim*, instructed for him to repent of his sins and be baptized into the name of *Yahushua HaMashakhYahu*—cf. *Acts* 2:38-39. This was to bring him remission of sin and the gift of *Ruwakh HaKodesh* to dwell in his heart, therefore, enabling him to enter the Kingdom of the Most High One.

This is the only method and means by which any sinner can enter the salvation of *Elohiym* until *Yahushua HaMashakhYahu* comes back to earth.

Do you want forgiveness for your sins? You must confess the sin and ask Elohiym's pardon after showing repentance in your heart. Forgiveness of sin is primarily designed by *Elohiym* to deal with any sin problem or situation of those who are in *Yahushua HaMashakhYahu.*

The person who is in *Yahushua HaMashakhYahu* must not sin. The recreation of his spirit in the new birth gives him power over sin—cf. *YahuChanan Alef (First John)* 3:8-9. This power over sin must constantly be exercised in the faith of the believer. Any believer who lives in this exercise of faith is able to overcome the works of the devil.

If, by chance, the devil gains the better part of the person who is in *Yahushua HaMashakhYahu* by causing him to sin, however, such a person will suffer broken fellowship. His fellowship with *Elohiym* and His family of all people born of water and *Ruwakh HaKodesh* on earth is disturbed, or troubled, in his state of sin.

The hedge of protection of *Elohiym* around any of His children in a state of sin is broken, and the rights, privileges, and responsibilities due him as a member of the *Beyrit Chadasha* family are also withheld.

He does not lose membership to, or contact with, the True Vine though. He remains, however, a diseased and an ineffective branch of the True Vine, because a fiery dart of the devil has hit him. In his state of suffering, the entire vine suffers with him.

The way to get out of this suffering, which is a result of the consequences of his sin and broken fellowship, is to quickly obtain the forgiveness of *Elohiym* and the *Beyrit Chadasha* family.

Genuine repentance and confession of the sin to *Elohiym* and to any members of His family on earth will restore the rights, privileges, and responsibilities of the *Beyrit Chadasha* family to him.

The Parable of the Prodigal Son clearly reveals this truth. Please read it in *Lukas (Luke)* 15:11-32. The prodigal son remained a son of the good father even in his sinful and self-willed state, which cost him his peace of mind and comfort. The confession of his sin to *Elohiym* and to his earthly father restored to him all his rights and privileges as a son.

When we as *Beyrit Chadasha* folks confess our sins, it restores to us all that we are entitled to in the family of *Elohiym, HaAv.* Confession of sin and obtaining forgiveness for it does not deal with the manner and means of our adoption as Elohiym's children, but restores us to the family we lost fellowship with temporarily.

We read the following verse from *YahuChanan Alef (First John)* which is meant for instruction of the born again person, who finds himself in a sinful situation, and not for the sinner who wants to become born again: *"If we confess our sins, he is faithful and just to forgive us our sins, and to cleanse us from all unrighteousness"—YahuChanan Alef (First John) 1:9, KJV.*

Understanding and obedience of this verse should restore the born again person who has sinned, into the rights and privileges due all members of the family of *Elohiym*, and also reenlist him for service and duty.

However, if you have not yet become a child of *Elohiym*, because you are not as yet born of water and of *Ruwakh HaKodesh* in water baptism, and somehow you get to know you are suffering because of sin, you could confess the sin to *Elohiym* and ask Him for forgiveness.

Though *Elohiym* will hear and attend to you by delivering you from the consequences of the sin, you will remain outside the family of *Elohiym*—unsaved—until you receive remission of your sins.

You will need to go beyond the confession of your sins by obeying Elohiym's instructions to enable you receive the new birth and adoption as a child of the Most High One.

Forgiveness of sin deals with the issues of sin in man before and after the Savior's death, while remission of sin deals with issues of sin in his death. Both cases have their unique processes of how they can be appropriated and accessed.

For forgiveness of sin, you need to repent of the sin and confess it to *Elohiym* and the person or persons you have wronged.

For remission of sin, you have to repent of the sin and be baptized in the name of *Yahushua HaMashakhYahu* to appropriate and access the blessing it accords from the work he has done for humanity in his death.

We must know these truths of *Elohiym* and accept them in faith—in obedience to His Word—to be able to receive their blessings.

Do you want to benefit from the atonement of sins made by *Yahushua HaMashakhYahu*? Cry out to *Elohiym* for deliverance from any danger, or for such need. *Elohiym* will hear and respond to you because of the work of *Yahushua HaMashakhYahu* done in his death on your behalf.

Because there is *kapporah* of sin for the sinner arising from the blood shed by *Yahushua HaMashakhYahu* in his sacrifice, he can cry out to *Elohiym* and be heard. Even though the sinner might not have entered the family of *Elohiym* on earth yet, *Elohiym* will hear him if he cries out to Him in distress for help.

This is because when *Elohiym* looks down on earth, as if to make out who is calling out to Him in distress, He sees the blood of atonement shed by *Yahushua HaMashakhYahu* covering the sin of the earth and also over this sinner in need. Because the atoning blood of *Yahushua HaMashakhYahu* has come over this sinner, *Elohiym* sees the blood over him—but not his sins—and so will help him out. *HalleluYahu!*

(2) Baptism into Life

The *Holy Scriptures* of the Old Covenant, tell us of how the people of *Elohiym* were saved by water on at least two occasions. These accounts in the *Holy Scriptures* of the Old Covenant about how Elohiym's people were saved through water were shadows pointing to our baptism into *Yahushua HaMashakhYahu* today.

This revelation came to us later in the New Covenant teachings. In fact, if not for these revelations in the New Covenant teachings, we would never have been able to link these Old Covenant events to such an enormously important ordinance as baptism in the name of *Yahushua HaMashakhYahu.*

Our understanding and appreciation of the New Covenant command to baptize and be baptized in the name of *Yahushua HaMashakhYahu,* so as to obtain remission of our sins, has been very much boosted, enriched, and made the more urgent by the record of these shadows of baptism into *Yahushua HaMashakhYahu* in the Old Covenant.

In *Kefa Alef (First Peter)* 3:20-21, we read that *Noach* and his family were saved through water as a shadow or a forward pointer to baptism in living waters in the name of *Yahushua HaMashakhYahu,* which **now saves us today**. This means that baptism unto *Noach,* as it were, brought salvation to *Noach* and his household. These verses read:

"Which sometimes were disobedient, when once the long-suffering of God [Elohiym] waited in the days of Noah [Noach], while the ark was a preparing, wherein few, that is, eight souls were saved by water. The like figure whereunto even baptism doth also now save us (not the putting away of the filth of the

flesh, but the answer of a good conscience toward God [Elohiym]) by the resurrection of Jesus Christ [Yahushua HaMashakhYahu]"—Kefa Alef (First Peter) 3:20-21, KJV; words in square brackets are mine.

Then also in *First Corinthians* 10:1-2, we are told of how the children of *Yisroel*, in their crossing of the Red sea from *Mitzrayim* (Egypt), were baptized unto *Moshe* (Moses) in the sea. Baptism unto *Moshe* brought life and salvation unto the children of *Yisroel* who heeded Moshe's message, which he carried from *Elohiym*, and obeyed it by following him out of *Mitzrayim*. Let us read this:

"Moreover, brethren, I would not that ye should be ignorant, how that our fathers were under the cloud, and all passed through the sea; and were all baptized unto Moses (Moshe) in the cloud and in the sea"—First Corinthians 10:1-2, KJV; word in parenthesis is mine.

This scriptural quotation says that the children of *Yisroel* who crossed the Red sea were baptized **unto** *Moshe*. Baptism unto or in the name of any spiritual leader is a separation or setting apart of the baptized unto the person, values, beliefs, will, authority, etc., of the master unto whom the one is being baptized.

Baptism into any person's name is an act of identification with, dedication to, acceptance of, and an expression of faith in the whole personality of the one into whose name that act of baptism is being received. Baptism puts the baptized not only onto the side, but also into the very being of the one in whose name one is baptized. It grants the baptized the opportunity to be tied to the spiritual destiny of the one in whose name the act of baptism is received.

In *The New Strong's Expanded Exhaustive Concordance of the Bible*, Dr. James Strong could not have put these facts of baptism more succinctly. In entry **No. 907** of his **Greek Dictionary of the New Testament**, this is what this teacher of the New Covenant doctrines says: *"...the baptized person was closely bound to, or became the property of, the one into whose name he was baptized."* I am particularly thrilled by this thought on baptism of such a renowned commentator on the *Holy Scriptures*, and of modern history.

Maybe, like the baptism unto *Moshe*, we can also talk of a baptism unto *Yehoshua (Joshua)*. In the manner of crossing the *Yarden* (Jordan) by the children of *Yisroel* from *Mitzrayim* to Canaan, we are told of the similarity of this event to that in the Red Sea. Let us read it from *Yehoshua (Joshua)* thus:

68

"Then ye shall let your children know, saying, Israel (Yisroel) came over this Jordan (Yarden) on dry land. For the Lord your God (Elohiym) dried up the waters of the Jordan (Yarden) from before you, until ye were passed over, as the Lord your God (Elohiym) did to the Red sea, which he dried up from before us, until we were gone over"—Yehoshua (Joshua) 4:22-23, KJV; words in parenthesis are mine.

Beyond the physical similarities of the crossings of the Red Sea and the *Yarden* are the significances of these experiences in the lives of the children of *Yisroel*. By virtue of the significances of the flood of *Noach* and the crossing of the Red Sea, it seems to me that the crossing of the *Yarden* by the children of *Yisroel* under *Yehoshua (Joshua)* was a third occasion in the Old Covenant scriptures, where Elohiym's people went through experiences that were shadows pointing to the baptism into *Yahushua HaMashakhYahu* of New Covenant folks.

The *Holy Scriptures* make us understand that the *Yarden* was crossed by those children of *Yisroel* who were too young to be spiritually accountable, or had not been born at all, at the time of the Red Sea crossing. This is to say, those who crossed the *Yarden* were not part of those who were baptized unto *Moshe* in the sea.

The entire generations of mature, able-bodied, war-suited, male children of *Yisroel*, who departed *Mitzrayim* under the leadership of *Moshe* and subsequently crossed the Red Sea, died in the desert while heading for the Promised Land. It was the generation of *Yisroel* who were born not long before their departure from *Mitzrayim*, and those born in the wilderness, that had to cross the *Yarden* under the leadership of *Yehoshua*. Let us read this account from *Yehoshua (Joshua)* 5:4-7:

"And this is the cause why Joshua (Yehoshua) did circumcise: all the people that came out of Egypt (Mitzrayim), that were males, even all the men of war, died in the wilderness by the way, after they came out of Egypt (Mitzrayim). Now all the people that came out were circumcised: but all the people that were born in the wilderness by the way as they came forth out of Egypt (Mitzrayim), them they had not circumcised. For the children of Israel (Yisroel) walked forty years in the wilderness, till all the people that were men of war, which came out of Egypt (Mitzrayim), were consumed, because they obeyed not the voice of the Lord: unto whom the Lord sware that he would not shew them the land, which the Lord sware unto their fathers that he

would give us, a land that floweth with milk and honey. And their children, whom he raised up to their stead, them Joshua (Yehoshua) circumcised: for they were uncircumcised, because they had not circumcised them by the way"—Yehoshua (Joshua) 5:4-7, KJV; words in parenthesis are mine.

Since these people had no taste of the baptism in the Red Sea, it seems to me that *Elohiym* designed for them to experience baptism unto *Yehoshua* before they could enter Canaan. This they did by crossing the *Yarden* just as the Red Sea had been crossed by the preceding generation of *Yisroel*. The fact of genuine baptism being a once-in-a-life-time experience probably made it impossible for any of those baptized unto *Moshe* in the sea to go through the rite a second time in the crossing of the *Yarden*, except for *Yehoshua* and Caleb who acted as leaders at this crossing.

Did you ever consider why the children of *Yisroel* were made to cross the *Yarden* from the east bank to enter Canaan? Since *Mitzrayim* was to the western side of the *Yarden*, the children of *Yisroel* traveling from *Mitzrayim* to Canaan could have entered it without crossing the *Yarden*. Has it been of any interest to you why the children of *Yisroel* had to cross the *Yarden* to enter their Promised Land? While thinking of answers to these questions let me lead you further on in this thought.

From *Bamidbar (Numbers)* 32:1-42, *Yehoshua (Joshua)* 1:12-18 and 22:1-6, we read very interesting accounts of the partitioning of the Promised Land among the twelve non-priestly Tribes of *Yisroel*.

When the children of *Yisroel* got to the east bank of the *Yarden* on their journey from *Mitzrayim*, the tribes of *Reuven* (Reuben) and Gad made a seemingly hurried request to *Moshe*. These tribes had more livestock than all the other tribes of *Yisroel*, and when they saw the very fertile lands of the east bank, they considered them very suitable for their animal-rearing enterprises.

Even before they could see other parts of Canaan to ascertain whether these east bank lands were indeed best suited to their vocation, they made a formal request to *Moshe* that these lands be given to them as their inheritance. This way they would not have to cross over to the lands on the west bank of the *Yarden*, where Canaan actually was located, along with the other tribes.

Before his death, *Moshe* granted their request in full on one condition—that all the men of these two tribes of *Yisroel* would have to cross to the west bank of the *Yarden* and go with all *Yisroel* throughout the Promised Land until all the other tribes had also entered and settled in their inheritances that the Most High One was giving them.

In fact, the men of these two tribes were to act as infantry soldiers, going ahead of all the other tribes to conquer the land. Half the tribe of *Menasheh* (Manasseh) was also to join the tribes of *Reuven* and Gad, in the execution of this task. For this, *Moshe* gave this half tribe of *Menasheh* an inheritance on the east bank of the *Yarden*, of the lands of *Gil'ad* (Gilead), *Chavot Ya'ir* (Havoth-jair) and *Novach* (Nobah).

Consequently, on the day of the crossing of the *Yarden*, all the men of *Reuven*, Gad, and half *Menasheh* left their wives, little ones, and livestock on the east bank to join *Yisroel* by crossing the River *Yarden* to the west bank. All *Yisroel*, therefore, crossed the *Yarden* under the leadership of *Yehoshua*, in similar manner as all their fathers crossed the Red Sea under *Moshe*.

Could there have been any spiritual significance to this crossing of the *Yarden* by this new generation of wandering children of *Yisroel*, in the same manner that their fathers crossed the Red Sea? Looking at the close similarities of the two events, I believe that there was.

I hope you appreciate that, at this point in the history of *Yisroel* and in the spirit of *Yehoshua (Joshua)* 5:4-7, only men of the military and spiritually accountable age of twenty—cf. *Bamidbar (Numbers)* 1:2-3, 26:2, 32:11—and those who were heads of families constituted the nation of *Yisroel*. All wives and children, including those yet unborn and in the loins of their fathers, were tied spiritually to their husbands and fathers, respectively, and were not regarded as separate individuals.

It is obviously the case from the effects of the misdeeds of *Korach* (Korah), *Datan* (Dathan), and *Aviram* (Abiram), who, acting in a group in *Bamidbar (Numbers)* 16:23-33, and Achan in *Yehoshua (Joshua)* 7:1-5, 11-13, 24-25 & 20:22, and Gehazi in *Melechim Bais (Second Kings)* 5:25-27, all of who either perished with all their seed or were placed under a perpetual curse together with their present and future offspring.

Similarly, the good deeds of *Caleb* in *Bamidbar (Numbers)* 14:24, *Pinchas* (Phinehas) in *Bamidbar (Numbers)* 25:13, and *Boaz* in *Ruth* 4:13 brought to all these men blessings from *Elohiym* individually, and which were also extended to all their seed forever.

The crossing of *Yarden* by all the mature men of *Yisroel*, therefore, meant that the entire nation of *Yisroel* in existence then, and all his future generations, had successfully crossed into Canaan.

We can say, in view of this fact, that whatever blessings *Elohiym* dispensed to these mature men of *Yisroel* in the act of baptism in the *Yarden* were also received by their family members, including those who did not form part of the convoy that crossed the river. All those who were left on the east bank of the *Yarden*, and those yet to be born to those matured men who crossed, were qualified to receive all the blessings bestowed by *Elohiym* to these men in this baptism. Whenever any children of *Yisroel* came of age, they entered into full spiritual blessings of this baptism of their fathers and became eligible, automatically, for any services to *Elohiym*.

In all of these shadow baptisms, we see that those who were baptized had the opportunity to start a new-lifestyle, as it were, which came from a new birth. The old life was left behind them as they faced the new.

When *Noach* and his family came out from the flood, they walked in new-life experiences. They faced a vast expanse of water and watched it gradually recede, uncovering the face of the earth slowly.

The development of vegetable life came about gradually, and *Noach* and family had to watch a lifeless earth go through a process of re-vegetation. The diet of *Noach* and his family was to change as a result of the temporary absence of vegetative life-forms on the earth. *Elohiym* permitted man, for the first time ever, to eat the flesh of any ritually clean animal. He was told by *Elohiym*, however, to be careful not to eat the meat with any blood in it—*Bereshis (Genesis)* 9:3-4.

Coming out of the deluge, which was a shadow baptism to that of ours in *Yahushua HaMashakhYahu* today, Noach's appreciation, comprehension, and commitments to the things of *Elohiym* took on new dimensions. Think about the higher kind of worship of *Elohiym* he had come to develop, exemplified in the immediate and spontaneous sacrifice of clean animals to Him, as soon as he touched earth again—cf. *Bereshis (Genesis)* 8:20-22.

After the flood, one of the most refreshing new-life experiences for righteous *Noach* and his family, although short-lived, was the absence of wickedness and violence from their environment, which before was the cause of Elohiym's wrath being visited on the earth.

After the flood, *Elohiym* restored to *Noach* one of His most glorious blessings to man, which had been lost in the *Gan Eden* (Garden of Eden). *Elohiym* restored the supremacy and dominion of man over all of His creation to *Noach*. *Elohiym* also established a covenant with man, in *Noach,* with the rainbow as a sign. We can read more about this in *Bereshis (Genesis)* 9:1-17.

The children of *Yisroel,* as they fled *Mitzrayim* under the pursuit of Pharaoh, made a clean escape by crossing the Red Sea. Upon reaching the eastern side of the Red Sea, a completely new life of signs and wonders from *Elohiym* awaited them. It was a new life with new values, demanding a closer relationship with *Elohiym.*

They experienced the presence and influence of *Elohiym* at levels which, up to this time had been unknown. They saw a canopy of clouds over their heads by day and pillar of fire in front of and behind them by night, as they made their journey. They enjoyed in a new way the commitment of *Elohiym* to a people of promise in the supply of manna, quails, and drinking water from a rock.

No doubt, the result of all of their experiences, including their clothing not getting worn-out after extensive wear, and their feet not swelling during many years of walking, was intended for them to develop an awesome awareness of *Elohiym,* as a higher kind of worship of Him.

Once they crossed the Red Sea, a new covenant or law between *Elohiym* and the children of *Yisroel* known as *Aseres HaDevarim* (The Ten Commandments), sealed by *Elohiym* on tablets of stone, was established for them to live by while on their journey, and, forever, in the new land. The crossing of the Red Sea by the children of *Yisroel,* which was a manifestation of their baptism unto *Moshe,* brought them into all these new-life experiences.

Similarly, the crossing of *Yarden* under the leadership of *Yehoshua,* the son of Nun, after the demise of *Moshe,* brought a new generation of wandering children of *Yisroel* into a new life. Beyond *Yarden,* new-life experiences of war victories, and miracles of collapsing kingdoms, were to inform *Yisroel* in their worship of and dependence on *Elohiym,* the only One who had been worshipped by their forefathers for centuries.

As the children of *Yisroel* entered the fertile lands of promise, with all the fruit trees, milk, and honey, as it were, at their disposal, it was an experience of a new life, a break from the desert kind of lifestyle. The crossing of the *Yarden* into the Promised Land brought about the withdrawal of desert privileges of cloud canopies, directing and protecting pillars of fire, wear proof clothing, manna, quails, and the supply of drinking water from rocks.

All these accounts are intended to portray the picture of an old way of life that gave way to a new one, based on baptism unto some spiritual leader. In these cases of baptism unto *Noach*, unto *Moshe*, or unto *Yehoshua*, a new life awaited those who entered them. Baptism in the name of these spiritual leaders brought to their followers the initiation or induction into a new life.

This new life through baptism is also the experience of all New Covenant folks who have entered into the spiritual Body of *Yahushua HaMashakhYahu*. The baptism into the name of *Yahushua HaMashakhYahu*, which all would-be followers of the Master are commanded by him to accept and receive, brings to them the new birth. This new birth brings them the opportunity and power to start the new life. Through baptism in the name of *Yahushua HaMashakhYahu*, we are born to live a new life of faith, righteousness and holiness unto *Elohiym*.

In *Galatians* 3:27, we are told that it is when we have received baptism into the name of *Yahushua HaMashakhYahu* for the remission of our sins that we are clothed with him. Baptism into the name of *Yahushua HaMashakhYahu* causes us to wear the *persona* of the Savior as one wears a spacesuit or any dress for that matter. We are in *Yahushua HaMashakhYahu* only through baptism into his name. Let us read on this here:

"For as many of you as have been baptized into Christ (Yahushua HaMashakhYahu) have put on Christ (Yahushua HaMashakhYahu)"—Galatians 3:27, KJV; words in parenthesis are mine.

We are in *Yahushua HaMashakhYahu*, surrounded or enveloped by him, only in our baptism into his name. It is when we put on *Yahushua HaMashakhYahu* in our baptism into his name that we can say we are *"in Yahushua HaMashakhYahu"*. It is only those who are *"in Yahushua HaMashakhYahu"* who are *"new creatures,"* as we are told in *Second Corinthians* 5:17. The fact is *"...old things are passed away; behold all things are become new,"* only when we are *"in Yahushua HaMashakhYahu"*, and we are *"in Yahushua HaMashakhYahu"* only in our baptism into him. This is the plain truth. We are not *"in Yahushua HaMashakhYahu"* when we pray to *Elohiym* in the manner of *Sinners' Prayer* or *Prayer for Salvation* recitals, requesting to be put into "Jesus Christ".

Let us take the issue of baptism into the name of *Yahushua HaMashakhYahu* a step further by looking at the substance of *Romans* 6:3-7 and *Colossians* 2:12:

"Know ye not, that so many of us as were baptized into Jesus Christ (Yahushua HaMashakhYahu) were baptized into his death? Therefore we are buried with him by baptism into death:

that like as Christ (Yahushua HaMashakhYahu) was raised up from the dead by the glory of the Father, even so we also should walk in newness of life. For if we have been planted together in the likeness of his death, we shall be also in the likeness of his resurrection: Knowing this that our old man is crucified with him, that the body of sin might be destroyed, that henceforth we should not serve sin. For he that is dead is free from sin"—Romans 6:3-7, KJV, words in parenthesis are mine.

"Buried with him in baptism, wherein also you are risen with him through faith of the operation of God (Elohiym), who hath raised him from the dead"—Colossians 2:12, KJV, word in parenthesis is mine.

From the above readings, we understand that we die with *Yahushua HaMashakhYahu* in our baptism into him. We are also buried with him, in and by baptism.

We are brought to newness of life by resurrecting with him, in and by our baptism into him. We die to sin, in and by baptism. We are also made new creatures, in and by our baptism into *Yahushua HaMashakhYahu.*

From this revelation of *Romans* 6, we cannot remain ignorant of the value and significance of our baptism into *Yahushua HaMashakhYahu.*

We must appreciate the indispensable role of baptism in the name of *Yahushua HaMashakhYahu* to our receipt of Elohiym's salvation. *Colossians* 2:12 emphasizes what *Romans* 6:3-7 says about our dying with *Yahushua HaMashakhYahu* in baptism and rising to the new life after being buried in water, momentarily, in and by baptism into his name.

Do you want to die to self and sin? If your answer is "yes", then you need to understand the baptism into *Yahushua HaMashakhYahu* and to receive it. Do you want to be buried to the past life of sin? If again your answer is "yes", then you need the baptism into *Yahushua HaMashakhYahu.*

Do you want to rise into a brand-new life of victory over sin and its consequences? If you do, then you must be baptized into the name of *Yahushua HaMashakhYahu.* Baptism into the name of *Yahushua HaMashakhYahu* is, simply, indispensable to our entry into Elohiym's salvation.

From *First Corinthians* 12:13, we read: **"For by one Spirit (Ruwakh HaKodesh) are we all baptized into one body, whether** *we be Jews (Hebrews) or Gentiles, whether we be bond or free, and have been all made to drink into one Spirit" (words in parenthesis are mine).*

By this verse, we receive the revelation of *Elohiym* that our union with *Yahushua HaMashakhYahu* is made possible only in our baptism into his name.

The Hebrew and Gentile, alike, join the mystical Body of *Yahushua HaMashakhYahu*, the body of sanctified people, through baptism. We become grafted into *HaGefen HaAmittit* (the True Vine) in our baptism into *Yahushua HaMashakhYahu*.

It is in baptism into *Yahushua HaMashakhYahu* that we enter the *Malchut HaElohiym*, become citizens and ambassadors of *Shamayim* to Earth, and have the righteousness and holiness of *Elohiym* imputed to our spirits, which enables us to walk as *Yahushua HaMashakhYahu* walked on earth. Let nobody teach you some other way, as that would be tantamount to falsehood and deception.

All the accounts, in *Ma'asim (Acts)* regarding the salvation of any persons, hinge on baptism in the name of *Yahushua HaMashakhYahu*. Baptism into the name of *Yahushua* brings one into the legal rights of using his name. Not only that, but it is also in baptism into the name of *Yahushua* that remission of sins is obtained. It is also in baptism that *Ruwakh HaKodesh* is given as a gift to dwell within the believer.

It must be taught that there is only one baptism. Some people teach what is contrary to the Word of *Elohiym*; that there are two or even more baptisms. They teach a baptism of—or in—water and a baptism of—or in—the "Holy Spirit" as two separate baptisms that must be experienced at two different times by every salvation seeker! This is contrary to the revelation of *Elohiym*, as recorded in *Ephesians*.

In *Ephesians* 4:4-6, we read of the seven-fold platform for unity among true and genuine followers of *Yahushua HaMashakhYahu*. We believe what we read there that there is one body, one Spirit (*Ruwakh HaKodesh*), one hope, one Lord, one faith, **one baptism**, and one Creator (*Elohiym*), but yet we cannot believe in the same vein that there is only one baptism? There is only one baptism; this is Elohiym's revelation for you to accept in simple faith, if you say truly that you believe His Word.

The one baptism mentioned in *Ephesians* is for remission of sin. That one baptism is for the receipt of the gift of *Ruwakh HaKodesh*

(Holy Spirit?). That one baptism is executed in water, by immersion. That one baptism establishes all believers in one faith—one common and divinely-given doctrine—demands of all who subscribe to it be obedient to and serve one Master, gives them one hope of calling, and knits all of them together firmly into one body where each part feels the pains and partakes in the joys of all the other parts, all the time and everywhere! That one baptism excludes any other that man's imaginations have conceptualized, developed, and erroneously taught.

The fact of our faith in baptism into *Yahushua HaMashakhYahu*, leading us to the salvation of *Elohiym* cannot be overemphasized. All our glorious new life realities are available to us only when we are in *Yahushua HaMashakhYahu*.

It is only when we can be found inside of *Yahushua HaMashakhYahu* that we can say, for example, that we are seated with him in *Shamayim* far above all principalities and powers.

We can only get to be in *Yahushua HaMashakhYahu* when we are baptized into him. We are not in *Yahushua HaMashakhYahu* through the recital of a so-called *Sinners' Prayer*, when any pastor or general overseer of some denomination determines it.

The devil has cunningly led us from the significance and indispensability of baptism in the name of *Yahushua HaMashakhYahu* to the salvation of *Elohiym*, into wallowing in theologies that do not benefit us in our quest to obtain the salvation of the Most High One.

It is surprising that we could be so easily deceived by the devil, when there is so much evidence about the indispensable role of baptism in the name of *Yahushua HaMashakhYahu* in leading us into the salvation of *Elohiym*.

Nobody becomes born again by saying a prayer to *Elohiym* requesting to be born again while, at the same time, willfully or unwittingly ignoring His instructions on how one becomes born again.

When people teach that repentant sinners can become born again by saying a prayer, it contradicts the New Covenant teachings. It is this teaching on reciting prayers for one to become born again that all salvation seekers should reject!

My dear reader, you would do yourself a lot of good if you stopped to ask yourself this question, which I would like you to keep in mind throughout your reading of this book: **Did you, in the course of praying the *Sinners' Prayer* in your quest to get born** again, do as those who were saved in the accounts of *Ma'asim (Acts)* did for their salvation?

If those who were saved in the narratives of *Ma'asim (Acts)* did anything other than praying to get born again, then you must do the same to be sure of your salvation.

We are told in the *Holy Scriptures* that we are born again of water and of *Ruwakh HaKodesh*. Let nobody teach you that we can be born again by or of prayer.

Today, sinners can only enter the salvation of *Elohiym* in repentance from sin and in the baptism they receive in and into the name *Yahushua HaMashakhYahu*.

(3) The Great Commission Instructions

Yahushua HaMashakhYahu, the First-born Son of *Elohiym*, came into our world so that through his sacrificial death, which was in accordance with the plan of *Elohiym*, he would purchase a people fit for His Kingdom. Being sent by *Elohiym*, *Yahushua HaMashakhYahu* came to do His will and to carry out His express instructions.

All of the commandments, teachings, and doctrines that *Yahushua HaMashakhYahu* taught his followers were not his own but of *Elohiym*, *HaAv* (the Father). He himself bore testimony of this in many instances. Let us look at two of these in *YahuChanan (John)*:

"Jesus (Yahushua HaMashakhYahu) answered them, and said, my doctrine is not mine, but his that sent me"—YahuChanan (John) 7: 16, KJV; words in parenthesis are mine.

"For I have not spoken of myself; but the father (HaAv) which sent me, he gave me a commandment, what I should say, and what I should speak. And I know that his commandment is life everlasting: whatsoever I speak therefore, even as the father said unto me, so I speak"—YahuChanan (John) 12:49-50, KJV; word in parenthesis is mine.

By these teachings, *Yahushua HaMashakhYahu* portrayed to his *talmidim* that he could be successful only if he depended on the commandments, instructions, and doctrines of *HaAv (The Father)*. He sought to teach his *talmidim* how their own successes as his instruments in soul-winning would depend solely on their obedience of his instructions to them, which, in fact, were those of *HaAv*. Thus, they would succeed only if their obedience to his instructions was absolute and to the letter.

When *Yahushua HaMashakhYahu* accomplished his mission to earth, he had to return to *HaAv* to give a report of the work of salvation for mankind that he had been sent to execute. Before leaving, he gathered his *talmidim* together and gave them the mandate of leading sinners into the blessings of his redemptive work done at *Gulgotha* for mankind.

He further gave specific and detailed instructions about how they were to go about this mission of bringing sinners into his salvation. His instructions to his *talmidim* were, and still are, clear and simple. We find this in the *Holy Scriptures*—the books of *Mattityahu (Matthew)* and *Markos (Mark)*—in what has come to be known as the Great Commission.

Prior to giving these instructions, *Yahushua HaMashakhYahu* told his *talmidim* he is the one and only way to *Elohiym*. Being **"The Way"**, he is the only one who is qualified and has the knowledge to show the way to *Elohiym*—cf. *YahuChanan (John)* 14:6.

In these instructions of the Great Commission, *Yahushua HaMashakhYahu*, showed the *talmidim* the only manner they could ever lead sinners to a genuine entry into the salvation of *Elohiym*. Let us read *Mattityahu (Matthew)* 28:18-20 and *Markos (Mark)* 16:15-16:

"And Jesus (Yahushua HaMashakhYahu) came and spoke unto them, saying, All power is given unto me in Heaven (Shamayim) and in earth, go ye therefore, and teach all nations, baptizing them in the name of the Father (HaAv), and of the Son (HaBen), and of the Holy Spirit (Ruwakh HaKodesh): teaching them to observe all things whatsoever I have commanded you: and, lo, I am with you always, even unto the end of the world. Amen"—Mattityahu (Matthew) 28:18-20, KJV; words in parenthesis are mine.

"And he said unto them, go ye into the entire world, and preach the gospel to every creature. He that believeth and is baptized shall be saved; but he that believeth not shall be damned"—Markos (Mark) 16:15-16, KJV.

From these readings, it is clear that it is in our understanding and acceptance of repentance from sin, and baptism into *Yahushua HaMashakhYahu*, that we can be brought into the salvation of *Elohiym*. There is no other way. The *talmidim* of *Yahushua HaMashakhYahu* were, and are, to teach all nations this truth. They were, and are, to teach the *Besuras HaGeulah* and the right response to this news; which is to repent from sin and to receive baptism in the name of *Yahushua HaMashakhYahu*.

When *Yahushua HaMashakhYahu* taught *Nakdimon* (Nicodemus) in *YahuChanan (John)* 3:1-15, he made it clear then, and beyond the times of *Nakdimon*, that no one could enter the *Malchut HaElohiym* without experiencing the power and effect of living waters on him. This teaching is what he restated in *Mattityahu* and *Markos*. The born again experience that *Yahushua HaMashakhYahu* taught *Nakdimon* was to come about in baptism by complete immersion in natural living waters and the receipt of *Ruwakh HaKodesh* through this baptism.

Let us also look at three verses of scripture from *Lukas (Luke)* 24. One day after his resurrection, *Yahushua HaMashakhYahu* appeared and sat with his *Shlikhim* (the eleven "apostles") and opened their minds to understand these verses. He also commissioned them as witnesses of their fulfillment, to all nations, beginning from *Yerushalayim*. This we refer to as an indirect version of the Great Commission.

"And said unto them, thus it is written, and thus it behooved Christ (Yahushua HaMashakhYahu) to suffer and rise from the dead the third day: and that repentance and remission of sins should be preached in his name among all nations, beginning at Jerusalem (Yerushalayim). And ye are witnesses of these things"—Lukas (Luke) 24:46-48, KJV; words in parenthesis are mine.

For me, this record of *Lukas* 24:46-48 gives more explicit instructions of the Great Commission than those of *Mattityahu* and *Markos*. In *Lukas*, the Master instructed his *talmidim* to teach **repentance and remission of sin** for the salvation of the sinner. The *talmidim* were to ensure that they taught **repentance and remission of sin** to all sinners in every part of the world throughout the New Covenant Age, in order to bring them into the salvation of *Elohiym*, till *Yahushua HaMashakhYahu* returns to Earth. They were not to assume that they could preach **repentance and forgiveness** of sin, anytime their intention was to lead sinners into the salvation of *Elohiym*. The Great Commission instructions are about repentance and remission of sin; and remission of sin, is about baptism into the name of *Yahushua HaMashakhYahu*.

The timing of this teaching of *Yahushua HaMashakhYahu* was most significant. Coming after the lengthy discourses of the Last Supper, his arrest, sacrificial death, and resurrection, Yahushua's eleven *Shlikhim* learned to appreciate the Great Commission instructions in bringing the salvation of *Elohiym* to the sinner.

They therefore held them as highly sacred beliefs and committed their lives to them. These instructions of *Yahushua HaMashakhYahu* were what his eleven *Shlikhim* led their listeners to obey on the Day of the Outpouring of *Ruwakh HaKodesh* (Pentecost?) in *Yerushalayim*, which yielded startling results.

Today, anyone who claims to be a minister of the New Covenant faith, but does not understand **repentance and remission of sin,** cannot lead any person into the salvation of *Elohiym.*

No minister should switch from teaching **repentance and remission of sin** to the teaching of **repentance and forgiveness of sin** for the salvation of the sinner. The clear and strict instructions of *Yahushua HaMashakhYahu,* to teach **repentance and remission of sin** to bring about the salvation of the sinner, still stand today— under Grace.

We miss the path of *Elohiym* to our salvation in *Yahushua HaMashakhYahu,* albeit narrowly, when we are led to believe that **repentance and forgiveness of sin** would bring us into the salvation of *Elohiym.*

This feeds perfectly into the intents of the deceiver, making many a salvation seeker hold onto what looks very much like a genuine currency but which is nonetheless counterfeit.

The praying of so-called *Sinners' Prayers,* asking for forgiveness of sin as the means to enter Elohiym's salvation, is contrary to these clear instructions of *Yahushua HaMashakhYahu*—to preach **repentance and remission of sin** and bring about people becoming born again into His salvation.

We must obey the doctrines of *Yahushua HaMashakhYahu* if we are to be safe in the expression of our faith in him. Otherwise, we are in danger of erring and being denied the very salvation we seek.

I hope a lot more insight was gained regarding the meaning of remission of sin and its crucial role to our entry into the salvation of *Elohiym* in *Yahushua HaMashakhYahu,* when we dealt with it under **(1) Atonement, Forgiveness, and Remission of Sins,** a subsection of this chapter.

It is my prayer that you acquired a firm grasp of the blessing of *Elohiym* available to the salvation seeker from the interplay of repentance, baptism in the name of *Yahushua HaMashakhYahu,* and remission of sin.

It is that interplay that brings to the hearts of penitent sinners the born again experience, and not the praying of "Jesus Christ"

(*Yahushua HuMashakhYahu?*) into hearts through some *Sinners' Prayer* recitals. *HalleluYahu, HalleluYahu.*

(4) The Good News (*Besuras*) and the Response to It

Let us consider how any sinner can enter the salvation of *Elohiym* based on the message of the "Gospel" or Good News for Mankind's Redemption (*Besuras HaGeulah*), and the only appropriate response to it.

To enter the salvation of *Elohiym* in *Yahushua HaMashakhYahu*, one needs to know two things. The first is to have the right knowledge of the person and mission of the Savior to mankind. The second is to know how to respond to or what to do with this knowledge of the person, mission, and ministry of the Savior.

From the accounts in the *Holy Scriptures* about the salvation of any particular person, it was the combination of these two pieces of knowledge that brought about the person's sure entry into it, and into all the blessings that come to man on receipt of the salvation of *Elohiym*.

The teaching on the person, mission, and work of *Yahushua HaMashakhYahu*, is what is known as the *Besuras HaGeulah* or Good News of Redemption or what is commonly known as the *"Gospel"*. Many people have made mistakes in believing that the whole of the *Holy Scriptures* is the "Gospel". Since the "Gospel" is also known as the Good News of our redemption, it could not be that the entire scriptures contitutes the "Gospel", since much of the *Holy Scriptures* is not pleasant news.

It is even too broad to consider the first four books of the New Covenant teachings as the "Gospel". Of course, the books of *Mattityahu, Markos, Lukas,* and *YahuChanan* contain the accounts of the earthly ministry of *Yahushua HaMashakhYahu*. Together, they give us information about the person and mission of the Savior to earth, but cannot be said to be strictly the "Gospel".

The revelation of *Elohiym* in the *Holy Scriptures* is about who *Yahushua HaMashakhYahu* is, the essence and blessing of what he did for humanity in his death and resurrection, and how every salvation seeker can come into these blessings. This is the Good News of Redemption for mankind. This is the "Gospel". This Good News is revealed in *Ma'asim (Acts)* and the *Iggrot Kodesh (Holy Letters)*.

Various parts of the *Holy Scriptures* bring different kinds of knowledge and blessings. There are parts of the *Holy Scriptures* that teach healing, success in life, holiness, prosperity, life in eternity, etc.

But the part of the *Holy Scriptures* that teaches Elohiym's salvation, which is available only in *Yahushua HaMashakhYahu,* and how one can enter into it, is called the *Besuras HaGeulah,* Good News of Redemption or "Gospel".

The core of this Good News of Redemption which every sinner must hear is centered on *Yahushua HaMashakhYahu* being of and from *Elohiym,* who lived a perfect life on earth, was falsely accused and sacrificed, buried, and rose up to life on the third day, all according to the plan and foreknowledge of *Elohiym.*

This is the cardinal faith of all true followers of *Yahushua HaMashakhYahu.* These truths, if well-expounded and explained to any sinner seeking to enter the salvation of *Elohiym,* would bring repentance into the heart of the sinner.

The mandate to lead repentant sinners into the New Covenant family—the Body of *Yahushua HaMashakhYahu*—was given primarily to *Shimon Kefa.*

On the Day of the Outpouring of *Ruwakh HaKodesh* (Pentecost?) on him and his friends, in *Yerushalayim, Shimon Kefa* rose to the task he had been elected to, ahead of time, by *Yahushua HaMashakhYahu.* His message to salvation seekers was crisp, concise, powerful, and extremely effective in bringing his listeners to the salvation of *Elohiym.*

The thrust of it was about *Yahushua*—the *Netzer* or *Tzemach,* Hebrew words either of which means "sprout", "branch" or "offshoot" of King *Dovid*—of *Natzeret* (Nazareth), the anointed one of *Elohiym,* who was murdered by the Hebrew leaders of the day, and whom *Elohiym* raised up on the third day of his burial.

Every minister of the New Covenant teachings on salvation must keep in mind that, when the *Besuras HaGeulah* was preached for the very first time on the Day of the Outpouring of *Ruwakh HaKodesh* (Pentecost?) in *Yerushalayim,* this was the message.

Sha'ul, a latter day convert to the faith of the followers of *Yahushua HaMashakhYahu* and who was also made a *Shliakh* (sent one, emissary, "apostle") of the Savior, defending the power of the *Besuras HaGeulah* ("Gospel"), wrote, under the inspiration of *Ruwakh HaKodesh,* one of many statements that I consider to have been later on inappropriately translated into English, thus:

"For I am not ashamed of the gospel of Christ (Yahushua

83

HaMushakhYahu): for it is the power of God (Elohiym) unto salvation to every one that believeth, to the Jew (Hebrew) first, and also to the Greek"—Romans 1:16, KJV; words in parenthesis are mine.

Even though I stated this earlier on in this teaching, I must say it again that I have great difficulty accepting the words *God, Christ,* and *Jesus* used by bible translators, particularly in the quotations they attribute to characters of the *Holy Scriptures.* In this verse of *Romans* which bible translators attribute to *Sha'ul,* I can say in all certainty that he never uttered the words *Christ* and *God.*

In fact, *Sha'ul* never used any of these words in any of the writings he was inspired by *Ruwakh HaKodesh* to write, as translators of the English Bible would have all believe! *Sha'ul,* no doubt, wrote the book of *Romans* in Hebrew and so could never have used these Greek-based words.

The greatest power of the universe is the Word of *Elohiym.* So then, the Word of *Elohiym* which constitutes the *Besuras HaGeulah,* Good News of Redemption, or "Gospel", must obviously have enough power laden in it to be able to bring salvation to the sinner. This must be obvious to all since words spoken by *Elohiym* brought about the creation of all that are in the physical and unseen worlds. Elohiym's Words are His wisdom. His Word is His power.

By His Word, *Elohiym* gets things done. We must therefore understand Elohiym's power to save the sinner is in His Word, as *Sha'ul* stated in *Romans* 1:16, and that the sinner is saved only when he is led to hear this Word and properly taught to obey it.

Furthermore, *Sha'ul* tells us in *First Corinthians* 15:1-4 the following:

"Moreover, brethren, I declare unto you the gospel, which I preached unto you which also you received, and wherein ye stand; by which also you are saved, if ye keep in memory what I preached unto you, unless ye have believed in vain. For I delivered unto you first of all that which I also received, how that Christ (Yahushua HaMashakhYahu) died for our sins according to the scriptures and that he was buried, and that he rose again the third day according to the scriptures"—First Corinthians 15:1-4, KJV; words in parenthesis are mine.

From these verses we find that it is the Good News of *Yahushua HaMashakhYahu* that brings salvation and that it is, indeed, about his death, the reasons for his death, his burial, and his resurrection.

The understanding and acceptance of these truths about *Yahushua HaMashakhYahu* will always bring a certain force to the heart of every person that will help one repent of one's sins and seek Elohiym's pardon and reconciliation with Him. This is why *Sha'ul* says the *Besuras HaGeulah* is the power of *Elohiym* unto salvation.

The only way to respond to the *Besuras HaGeulah* is to seek repentance of sins and to receive baptism into the name *Yahushua HaMashakhYahu*. All accounts about the salvation of any person in *Ma'asim (Acts)* 2:41; 8:12; 8:36-38; 9:18; 10:48; 16:15; 16:33; and 18:8 reveal this response.

This has been the only way that salvation seekers have responded to the *Besuras HaGeulah* since the Day of the Outpouring of *Ruwakh HaKodesh* (Pentecost?).

Please be convinced of this truth, so that you do not do anything else like the reciting of *Sinners' Prayers* in attempt to obtain the born again experience.

In particular, let us read of a typical response to the *Besuras HaGeulah* from the following verses of *Ma'asim (Acts)*:

"Then Peter (Shimon Kefa) said unto them, repent, and be baptized every one of you in the name of Jesus Christ (Yahushua HaMashakhYahu) for the remission of sins, and ye shall receive the gift of the Holy Ghost (Ruwakh HaKodesh). For the promise is unto you, and to your children, and to all that are afar off, even as many as the Lord (Adonoi) our God (Maker) shall call"— *Ma'asim (Acts) 2: 38-39, KJV; words in parenthesis are mine.*

All through the New Covenant teachings, any persons who ever entered into the *Malchut HaElohiym* had done so through baptism into the name of *Yahushua HaMashakhYahu* as a follow-up to their repentance from sin. Elohiym's promise of *Ruwakh HaKodesh* to dwell in the hearts of men is also fulfilled in the lives of men through their repentance of sin and baptism in the name of *Yahushua HaMashakhYahu*, and in no other way. This is the only true doctrine taught in the New Covenant revelation that ushers men into *Yahushua HaMashakhYahu* and brings about the receiving of *Ruwakh HaKodesh* into the hearts of repentant men.

From the foregoing, we can see that the faith we have come to develop in the praying of so-called *Sinners' Prayers* for the born again experience is a false one. It is false because the *Holy Scriptures* do not teach it. As a result, when we express faith in it we act on a deception of the devil.

This deception keeps us in delusion of being saved, when we are actually not. We must beware of this and take some steps backward to where the Master gave us clear instructions about how we must be born of water and of *Ruwakh HaKodesh* to be able to enter Elohiym's kingdom.

It is sad that, for about two thousand years after the ascension of *Yahushua HaMashakhYahu*, the world has not been taught the right message of the *Besuras HaGeulah* and the appropriate response to it. This is sad because with the benefit of this time we should have all the mastery in the teaching of Elohiym's salvation in *Yahushua HaMashakhYahu*. But what do we live in? Are we not living in a deception of the devil?

Many overzealous and ignorant people who have not been called by *Elohiym* for any assignment are flooding the world with a wrong doctrine that is leading people into doom.

The most unfortunate thing is that neither the overzealous "man of God" who preaches this wrong doctrine, nor the hearers of it, are aware that they believe an erroneous teaching. How sad this really is!

Two Scripture Accounts of How Ignorance about Baptism into *Yahushua* Denied Some People Elohiym's Salvation

From accounts in the *Holy Scriptures*, a number of people were humble and courageous enough to receive correction when their errors concerning the salvation of *Elohiym* in *Yahushua HaMashakhYahu* were pointed out to them. People of today must have the same humility and courage to receive correction when their errors about the born again doctrine is brought to their attention. We all owe it as a duty to ourselves, and to other persons, to believe the truth of Elohiym's Word. This, we should seek to do through knowledge and understanding, humility, and courage.

There was a man named Apollos who though very knowledgeable in, and committed to the obedience of, the Old Covenant scriptures, lived in error with regards to the salvation of *Elohiym*. He, like many today, was slowly but steadily being led away from the very *rendezvous* he sought to have with *Elohiym* without knowing it, due to a wrong faith he lived by.

It was by the Grace of *Elohiym* that he was brought onto the right track by a highly discerning married couple who had the leading of *Ruwakh HaKodesh*, as well as a thorough knowledge of the New Covenant salvation doctrine and could teach it. Let us read of him from *Ma'asim (Acts)* 18:24-26:

"And a certain Jew (Hebrew) named Apollos, born at Alexandria, an eloquent man, and mighty in the scriptures, came to Ephesus. This man was instructed in the way of the Lord; and being fervent in the spirit, he spake and taught diligently the things of the Lord, knowing only the baptism of John (YahuChanan). And he began to speak boldly in the synagogue (shul): whom when Aquila and Priscilla had heard, they took him unto them, and expounded unto him the way of the Lord more perfectly"—Ma'asim (Acts) 18: 24-26, KJV; words in parenthesis are mine.

Apollos was a very educated man. As a Hebrew born in the Hebrew Diaspora, he was a native of Alexandria. Alexandria, a city in North Africa, was founded by the Greek Emperor, Alexander the Great in 331 BCE. It was a center of learning, harboring a large populace of Hebrews, Greeks and Egyptians. It had a famed library and later developed to become one of the greatest cultural and intellectual centers of the Roman Empire replacing Grecian dominion.

The Septuagint Version of the Old Covenant scriptures was written in this city in about 280-170 BCE. The fame of Alexandria as a city of intellectual and cultural significance continued into the first century. The renowned, brilliant and devout Hebrew, Philo Judaeus, lived in Alexandria in the first century and wrote his works on the **Logos** in this city at that time (cf: *Thompson Chain Reference Bible*, 1988 Edition; Condensed Cyclopedia of Topics and Texts: No. 4327—Alexandria; **p. 1724**).

The great intellectual knowledge Apollos had come to acquire, could be said to be a matter of course for a native of this important city of the then civilized world. Apollos was not only well educated, but he was also eloquent and knew the scriptures well. He not only confessed *Yahushua HaMashakhYahu* but he also proclaimed him boldly.

He had a fervent spirit, spoke and taught diligently, and had a charisma that many of today's Christian leaders would be very envious of. This man looked alright before many men, if weighed against Elohiym's Word. In fact, many professing to be Christians today might desire to be like him—even in his state of ignorance about the salvation plan of *Elohiym*.

He exuded confidence, "assurance" of salvation, and the hope of life in the presence of *Elohiym* in Eternity. Yet, he was in error concerning how to enter the salvation of *Elohiym*. He did not know how to become born again, just like many educated theologians and bible scholars today.

Apollos was in error because he believed a teaching that could not bring him into the salvation of *Elohiym* in *Yahushua HaMashakhYahu*. You could not blame him for believing an incorrect teaching concerning how he could enter the salvation of *Elohiym*, because he simply did not get the opportunity to hear the right way to respond to the teachings of *Yahushua HaMashakhYahu* on the born again doctrine. He did not meet a genuine teacher of the New Covenant faith, a true *Shliakh* of *Yahushua HaMashakhYahu*, who could show him the right way into the salvation of *Elohiym*.

Thinking that he himself was saved by the faith he professed, Apollos went on to teach others his kind of beliefs, and his understanding of the salvation of *Elohiym* for that matter. He was sincere in, and dedicated to, what he taught. In fact, he put all his human resources to this teaching, portraying an enviable zeal, fervency, passion, and diligence, as he went along. And yet he was in error? Now that is very sad.

Many people today are in exactly the same error of believing and acting on falsehood as Apollos found himself in during the early days when faith in *Yahushua HaMashakhYahu* was preached in Ephesus. They have zeal, fervency in spirit, diligence, dedication, and commitment, and yet are wrong in their preaching of the *Sinners' Prayer*, and of praying "Jesus Christ" (*Yahushua HaMashakhYahu?*) into the hearts of repentant sinners.

The crux of this error is that people do not have the patience to wait to be called to the service of *Elohiym* in His Kingdom. People just call themselves into all manner of ministries, teaching all kinds of doctrines, and yet claiming to have been called and sent by *Elohiym*, therefore, leading many away from His salvation in *Yahushua HaMashakhYahu* for mankind.

If you have the patience and humility to wait on *Elohiym* to call you into His service, you would be blessed to have the proper instructions of what to say and what to do for the people to whom you are being sent to minister the salvation of *Elohiym* in *Yahushua HaMashakhYahu*. You would then be going to these people in the spirit of a *navi* ("prophet"), or a messenger-teacher, having Elohiym's Word in your mouth.

In that case, you could say to the people to whom you are sent to help receive salvation, ***"Thus sayeth Elohiym,"*** and not be lying about it. In waiting for *Elohiym* to call and to send you, you would receive anointing, authorization, and the power of *Elohiym* to enable you carry out the assignment and achieve the desired results, which at the end will be a blessing to many.

If you sent out yourself to the mission field, however, then you went out with your own word and anointing to do a job you claim *Elohiym* had called you to do. You would definitely betray yourself to people to whom *Elohiym* did not send you. It would not be long before people get to know that you sent yourself to them.

What Apollos was not instructed on, until Aquila and Priscilla came his way, was—and is—the cardinal and fundamental doctrine believed by all genuine followers of *Yahushua HaMashakhYahu*: the baptism in the name of *Yahushua HaMashakhYahu*, which, when received in faith and understanding, brings remission of sin to the baptized penitent.

Apollos neither knew that one had to be baptized in the name of *Yahushua HaMashakhYahu* for the remission of all sins previously committed, nor that one received the gift of *Ruwakh HaKodesh* to dwell within one's heart only after baptism.

If you do not have the right kind of faith in repentance and remission of sin as the only way to receive the gift of *Ruwakh HaKodesh* to dwell within your heart, how can you have the salvation of *Elohiym*?

Apollos was ignorant of the instructions of *Yahushua HaMashakhYahu* for the repentant sinner to be baptized into his name as an initiation into him—in spirit, soul and body—and for the remission of his sins.

He did not know that baptism in the name of *Yahushua HaMashakhYahu* for the remission of sin was commanded by the Savior for all who want to be saved in his sacrifice or become born again, and thereby become his true *talmidim*.

Apollos probably did not know that *Yahushua HaMashakhYahu* was the last *Navi* of the era of the Old Covenant, whose word was to be received and obeyed to the letter for salvation.

Baptism in the name of *YahuChanan ben Zecharyahu* which Apollos knew about, accepted, and probably directed his listeners to receive, did not have the power of bringing sinners to the salvation of *Elohiym*.

This is because *YahuChanan ben Zecharyahu* did not die for the salvation of mankind. *YahuChanan* was not *HaSeh HaElohiym* (the Lamb of *Elohiym*) who took away the sin of the world.

Please do not get me wrong. *YahuChanan ben Zecharyahu*, of

course, died in the service of *Elohiym* to bring to all people knowledge about the salvation of *Elohiym* that was about to come through remission of sins.

In that sense, he died in the cause of salvation for mankind, but that death did not pay for the sins of men. It is only the sacrifice of *Yahushua HaMashakhYahu* that *Elohiym* ordained to pay for sin and to bring salvation to mankind. In that context, *YahuChanan* did not die to save anybody.

Thanks to *Elohiym* that Apollos had a humble and a teachable spirit and could receive correction. I met a general overseer of a Christian denomination who did not have the humility and courage of Apollos, and he would therefore not take any corrections.

Instead, he preferred, out of pride, to remain persistent in teaching the wrong doctrine he preached to his congregation. He remained highly stubborn and adamant in the teaching of the wrong doctrines of *Sinners' Prayer* recitals and of praying for "Jesus Christ" (*Yahushua HaMashakhYahu?*) to enter the hearts of sinners, which he believes made him born again.

Sadly, his belief and practice of these incorrect doctrines take him far away from the true salvation of *Elohiym* in *Yahushua HaMashakhYahu* because they deny him the power to become born again.

I hope that, like Apollos, you will accept correction and avert your course from the wrong and unexpected destination, where you were bound to be received by an undesirable host, to the narrow way and Elohiym's abode, *Shamayim*.

Of course, the accounts in the *Holy Scriptures* do not say in plain words that Apollos was later baptized into *Yahushua HaMashakhYahu* after his meeting with Aquila.

What was the use of this exposure of ignorance and correction of error, if it was not to lead him to the baptism in the name of *Yahushua HaMashakhYahu*, in which all repentant sinners receive remission of sin, become born again, and consequently enter into Elohiym's salvation and service?

With reference to the *Holy Scriptures*, we can be assured that Apollos was subsequently baptized into *Yahushua HaMashakhYahu*.

Why would the brethren in Ephesus recommend him by letter to those in Achaia—cf. *Ma'asim (Acts)* 18:27—if he was not properly initiated or inducted into the New Covenant family by undergoing the rite of baptism into *Yahushua HaMashakhYahu*?

How could he be such a valuable asset and pillar to the *Kehillah* (Congregation or Body of genuine Believers in *Yahushua HaMashakhYahu*) at Corinth,—cf. *First Corinthians* 1:12 and 3:4— if he was not united with *Yahushua HaMashakhYahu* in baptism into him?

Furthermore, how could he be such a useful companion and aide to *Sha'ul*—cf. *First Corinthians* 16:12 and *Titos (Titus)* 3:12—in ministering the message of the *Besuras HaGeulah*, if he himself were not genuinely led into the blessings of this Good News by being clothed with *Yahushua HaMashakhYahu* in baptism into his name?

Why is the error of Apollos revealed to us by *Elohiym* in the *Holy Scriptures* at all? Was it not for us to take the issue of baptism into *Yahushua HaMashakhYahu* far above that of *YahuChanan ben Zecharyahu*?

Was it not meant to teach every one of us to submit to baptism in the name of His only begotten Son so that we could reap all the benefits and blessings it brings? There can be no doubt in the mind of any diligent reader of the New Covenant scriptures that Apollos was subsequently baptized into *Yahushua HaMashakhYahu*, after receiving instruction from Aquila and his wife.

May *Elohiym* bless the rare Aquilas and Priscillas we have today, who, upon hearing an Apollos begin to preach, would immediately identify any falsehoods in doctrine. It takes much preparation by *Ruwakh HaKodesh* for anybody to identify the error of Apollos and to prescribe its antidote. However, we cannot but persevere in this challenging and daunting task.

We have to pray that the many "Apolloses" found everywhere today would have the humility and courage to accept their mistakes about the salvation of *Elohiym* in *Yahushua HaMashakhYahu*, when such mistakes are pointed out to them.

Though this may seem very difficult to do, they should try to accept and acknowledge their error in good faith, in obedience to Elohiym's Word.

It is interesting how *Ruwakh HaKodesh* of *Elohiym* places issues of like-nature close to each other in the *Holy Scriptures*. Leaving the issues of Apollos's error in *Ma'asim (Acts)* chapter eighteen, toward the end, we go into the chapter nineteen to be confronted with another error in faith.

Again, this error is about how to enter the salvation of *Elohiym* in *Yahushua HaMashakhYahu*. This time round, it is *Sha'ul*, after being miraculously transformed from a persecutor of believers in

Yuhushua HaMashakhYahu into becoming one of them, and, indeed, one of their most dedicated leaders and a *Shliakh* of *Yahushua HaMashakhYahu*, who now had to correct this error. Read the account of this in *Ma'asim (Acts)* 19:1-7 before continuing with the reading of this book.

Sha'ul came across some men in Ephesus who claimed to be *talmidim* of *Yahushua HaMashakhYahu*, but, looking at their lives, *Sha'ul* was not convinced that they were saved people. A little investigation led *Sha'ul* to the root of the problem, which had brought about the irksome feeling he had had in his spirit.

From the investigation, *Sha'ul* found out that all these men—all twelve of them—did not have knowledge of *Ruwakh HaKodesh*. They had never heard about *Ruwakh HaKodesh;* just like almost all Christians today!

This ignorance must have shocked *Sha'ul* greatly. "How could one be a *talmid* of *Yahushua HaMashakhYahu* and not have *Ruwakh HaKodesh* residing in him?" he must have wondered.

For a *talmid* of *Yahushua HaMashakhYahu* to be completely ignorant of *Ruwakh HaKodesh*—and of his work in the believer—it must have been a wonder of wonders to *Sha'ul*. *Sha'ul* knew that every true *talmid* of *Yahushua HaMashakhYahu* must bear the mark and evidence of *Ruwakh HaKodesh*, which he did not see in these men. Again, knowing that all *talmidim* of *Yahushua HaMashakhYahu* must receive the gift of *Ruwakh HaKodesh* in their baptism into his name, *Sha'ul* asked them what baptism they received when they first believed.

By their answers to his questions, the problem became clear to *Sha'ul*. All these twelve men of Ephesus, like zealous Apollos, knew only of, and had only received, the baptism in the name of *YahuChanan ben Zecharyahu*!

Sadly, the baptism in the name of *YahuChanan ben Zecharyahu* was not to enable *Ruwakh HaKodesh* dwell in the hearts of its subscrbers. *Elohiym* did not plan for anybody baptized in the name of *YahuChanan* to receive the in-dwelling presence of *Ruwakh HaKodesh*. The baptism of *YahuChanan*, therefore, did not, and indeed, could not bring *Ruwakh HaKodesh* to dwell in the hearts of any of his (YahuChanan's) *talmidim*.

The one and only baptism that gives *Ruwakh HaKodesh* of *Elohiym* to any believer in, and subscriber to, the *Besuras HaGeulah* is the baptism in the name of *Yahushua HaMashakhYahu*. Baptism into the name of *Yahushua HaMashakhYahu* makes the baptized person obtain or secure remission of sin in fulfillment of the requirement for receiving the promised gift of *Ruwakh HaKodesh.*

This is what these twelve men in Ephesus should have been taught. Unfortunately, they did not get the opportunity. They did not have any true *talmid* of the New Covenant doctrine on the salvation of *Elohiym* in *Yahushua HaMashakhYahu* to teach them the truths of it. As a result, they were almost excluded from the "flight" to *Shamayim,* but *Sha'ul* came their way as a messenger of *Elohiym* to bring correction to their erring faith.

Sha'ul led them to do the right thing. I am sure that, even after they were taught and led to the baptism in the name of *Yahushua HaMashakhYahu* to enable them receive *Ruwakh HaKodesh* to dwell within their hearts, their minds were still not entirely free of the incorrect doctrine they had earlier held onto for so long.

This incorrect doctrine might have become a bias or stronghold in their minds that denied them the immediate, spontaneous, and joyous manifestation of *Ruwakh HaKodesh* who had come to dwell in their hearts after their baptism in the name of *Yahushua HaMashakhYahu. Sha'ul* had to lay hands on them to "activate" *Ruwakh HaKodesh* in these believers of Ephesus.

Had it been one of today's "tongues-blasting", "charisma-cherishing", "men of God" who met with these erring *"talmidim"* of Ephesus, other than *Sha'ul,* I am sure the unfolding drama would have been completely different.

It would have been a great opportunity for one such "man of God" to organize—what is commonly known in today's Christian parlance—a *"Holy Spirit Baptism Seminar", "Life in the Spirit Seminar", "Impartation Service",* or *"Anointing Service"* in attempt to pray-down a repeat occurrence of the events in the upper room in *Yerushalayim,* on the Day of the Outpouring of *Ruwakh HaKodesh* (Pentecost?).

This "man of God" would have been zealously teaching at this seminar or service, his faith of receiving the "Holy Spirit" (*Ruwakh HaKodesh* of *Elohiym?*) in a so-called "Holy Spirit baptism", until he hears one of his students begin to utter the babbling sounds of **shandararara, shandaramama ma, shandara, shandarama, ma, ma, mama, shandarama . . .** or some strange such tongues.

Such a "man of God", in great excitement, would have encouraged the other eleven *"talmidim"* to emulate the feat accomplished by the first.

And before long, the entire church-room would have been

filled with the deafening and unstoppable melodious sounds of *shandarama, shandarama, mu mama ma, shandarama, shandarama*... from the lips of twelve men in frenzy.

Then a highly elated "man of God" would pronounce and declare his students "baptized in the Holy Spirit" and blessed with the in-dwelling presence in their hearts, "the full measure" of the "Holy Spirit" (*Ruwakh HaKodesh* of *Elohiym*?)!

The need for a proper teaching or a re-teaching, so to say, of what has been given out to many people about how to enter the salvation of *Elohiym* is more urgent today than in the past, since time is running out.

This error in doctrine, which has come about by praying for "Jesus Christ" (*Yahushua HaMashakhYahu*?) to enter peoples' hearts for salvation or enable them become born again, has gained so much root in the practices of people claiming to be followers of the Savior that it is not easy to destroy it.

Nevertheless, every true *talmid* of *Yahushua HaMashakhYahu* must do his part, in measure of the Grace of *Elohiym* given him in this regard, to expose and to correct this error.

It is imperative that we all seek to do this, in order to avert many salvation seekers from a wrong course, which leads to a wrong, undesirable and unexpected destination.

Three Classic Salvation Accounts

Shall we look at the work of three notable *talmidim* of *Yahushua HaMashakhYahu* who, on different occasions, were given specific errands to run? These were very important assignments, intended to bring the salvation of *Elohiym* in *Yahushua HaMashakhYahu* to people and, therefore, needed messengers who knew exactly what to do.

All the three people were spoken to directly, without a human agent, when they were being sent out on the assignment. An angel of *Elohiym* spoke to one of them, while *Yahushua HaMashakhYahu* himself spoke to the rest in visions. The *talmidim* in question are *Philippos* (Philip) who, at some time, when numbers of believers in *Yahushua HaMashakhYahu* was increasing in *Yerushalayim*, was elected to serve them at tables; *Chananyahu* (Ananias), a resident of Damascus; and *Shimon Kefa*, the man *Yahushua HaMashakhYahu* made his *Shliakh* and leader of his flock of sheep.

These three *talmidim* had many qualities in common. They

were all dependable *talmidim* of the New Covenant doctrine on the salvation in *Yahushua HaMashakhYahu*. They knew how to minister the New Covenant salvation of *Elohiym* to anybody in need of it. They knew where to start and where to end any assignment that led sinners to the salvation of *Elohiym* in *Yahushua HaMashakhYahu*. They were not just knowledgeable of the meaning and value of the work of salvation done by *Yahushua HaMashakhYahu* and how to genuinely direct sinners into it, but they were also available and ready to go.

For anybody today who seeks to obtain the qualities of these wonderful *talmidim* of the New Covenant faith, many important divine visitations to be assigned special duties await him. The faith, beliefs, and characters of these great *talmidim* of the New Covenant faith are what I would relish to live by.

For any people who seek correction from the error of *Sinners' Prayer* recitals and for "Jesus Christ" (*Yahushua HaMashakhYahu?*) to enter their hearts in their bid to become born again, a study and understanding of the work that these three *talmidim* did in their various assignments is recommended. That is why I cite them as case studies in presenting Elohiym's salvation to the sinner in this teaching.

Let us look at the particular assignment *Philippos* was given and how he executed it. *Philippos* was taking it cool at home, or some place, when an angel of *Elohiym* disrupted his privacy. The angel had a short instruction for him. What the angel said to *Philippos* was, **"Arise, and go toward the south unto the way that goeth down from Jerusalem (Yerushalayim) unto Gaza, which is desert"**—*Ma'asim (Acts) 8: 26, KJV; word in parenthesis is mine.*

Philippos immediately took off to do as he had been told. He did not ask any questions. He went off without any delay because he knew that the angel was a messenger from *Elohiym*. We can read about what transpired between the angel of *Elohiym*, *Philippos*, *Ruwakh HaKodesh* of *Elohiym*, and the candidate elected by *Elohiym* for His salvation in *Ma'asim (Acts)* 8:26-40. Please read these verses and strive to understand them before continuing with the reading of this book.

When *Philippos* caught up with the chariot and heard what the Ethiopian eunuch was reading, he knew what to do in execution of his assignment. Dwelling upon the scriptures the Ethiopian was reading, *Philippos* perfectly expounded the doctrine of the New Covenant salvation to him. This is what the account in *Acts* on this issue meant when it said, *"Philip (Philippos) . . . preached unto him Christ (Yahushua HaMashakhYahu)"—Ma'asim (Acts) 8:35, KJV; words in parenthesis are mine.*

What was, or is, there to preach about *Yahushua HaMashakhYahu* besides his life, sacrifice, death, burial, and resurrection? What else could *Philippos* have preached to the Ethiopian if not the meaning of the suffering and death of *Yahushua HaMashakhYahu* for mankind? What else could *Philippos* have taught his friend, if not how *Elohiym* had worked a plan and a means for any sinner to enter His salvation through the sacrificial death of *Yahushua HaMashakhYahu?*

All these issues had direct bearing on what the Ethiopian was reading from *Yeshayahu (Isaiah)* about *HaMashakhYahu* and his suffering, which he had difficulty understanding. *Philippos* taught that baptism into the name of *Yahushua HaMashakhYahu* would bring about the salvation of *Elohiym* by remission of sins, and that the receipt of *Ruwakh HaKodesh* of *Elohiym* to reside in the heart of any believer would also come about in this baptism. This was to be an everlasting ordinance of *Elohiym* until the end of time—that all men be baptized in the name of *Yahushua HaMashakhYahu*, so as to get remission of sins and obtain the gift of *Ruwakh HaKodesh* to dwell within their hearts—cf. *Ma'asim (Acts)* 2:38-39.

Philippos thoroughly and expertly taught the doctrine of the New Covenant salvation of *Elohiym* in *Yahushua HaMashakhYahu* to the Ethiopian. The Ethiopian understood and strongly desired the blessings due him from the doctrine. While these words and desires for their fulfillment were burning in the heart of the Ethiopian, *Philippos* might have wondered how his mission to the eunuch would be beneficial without water for baptism, which seemed absent in the arid desert where they were traveling. They, however, continued their chariot ride, with the hope that *Elohiym*, who sent *Yahushua HaMashakhYahu* to die in the horrible manner he did for the salvation of men, would make available water for baptism into the name of *Yahushua HaMashakhYahu*.

With time, they came to a body of natural living waters. The eunuch, on seeing the body of water, excitedly asked his teacher what could prevent him from being baptized into *Yahushua HaMashakhYahu* to receive this great salvation of *Elohiym* he had been taught. The sight of the body of water, and the question of the eunuch, must have come as a great relief to *Philippos*. He quickly went down into the water to plunge his ready-to-receive student of the New Covenant salvation into it. Thus, the Ethiopian was baptized into *Yahushua HaMashakhYahu* for the remission of his sins and for the receipt of *Ruwakh HaKodesh* to dwell in his heart.

Oh, would that men would catch the importance of the role of water to the born again experience! I am very sure that as *Philippos* was teaching the eunuch about the role of water in bringing about the born again experience, the Ethiopian was carried in the spirit to some re-enacted drama between *Yahushua HaMashakhYahu* and *Nakdimon* on the subject of water, *Ruwakh HaKodesh* of *Elohiym*, and entering into the *Malchut HaElohiym*.

The fact that *Philippos* was whisked away by *Ruwakh HaKodesh* of *Elohiym*, vanishing from the sight of the Ethiopian immediately after this act of baptism, was Elohiym's confirmation that his assignment was over, and that it had been well executed. The fact that the miraculous departure of *Philippos* from the scene did not leave the Ethiopian in confusion, bewilderment, or fear, but left him rejoicing, was a testimony that *Ruwakh HaKodesh* of *Elohiym* had found residence in the eunuch's heart. This was all that *Elohiym* wanted done in the errand of *Philippos* to the Ethiopian.

In this single baptism in natural living waters, in the name of *Yahushua HaMashakhYahu*, the eunuch received the full compliment or package of Elohiym's salvation. He missed nothing. Nothing was deducted from Elohiym's package of salvation, which was supposed to be added to him later on.

He, like the over three thousand Hebrew believers on the Day of the Outpouring of *Ruwakh HaKodesh* (Pentecost?) in *Yerushalayim*, received remission of sin and the gift of *Ruwakh HaKodesh* in that baptism in living waters. Neither the eunuch nor any one of the three thousand Hebrews saved on the Day of the Outpouring of the *Ruwakh HaKodesh* (Pentecost?) had any so-called "baptism of the *Holy Spirit*" later on, after their baptisms in natural living waters. All that they could receive from *Elohiym* in the new birth, they did receive by their expression of faith in that one baptism.

As for this eunuch, he continued his journey after this baptism in natural living waters, fully saved and full of *Ruwakh HaKodesh*, to a destination where there was nobody to lead him to another kind of baptism—a so-called "Holy Spirit baptism"—or to teach him how to receive a gift of speaking in tongues. This miracle of salvation, replete with the filling of *Ruwakh HaKodesh* in one-off execution by *Elohiym*, was made available and received by the eunuch after a few minutes of chariot ride!

I would also wish to draw the attention of all to the fact that this first African Gentile convert to the faith in *Yahushua HaMashakhYahu* became the first to propagate this faith in Ethiopia. In being used by *Elohiym* to establish any *Kehillah* of *Yahushua HaMashakhYahu*, in Ethiopia, I am sure this eunuch taught his followers how to become *talmidim* of *Yahushua HaMashakhYahu* through the doctrine of repentance and baptism in the name of *Yahushua HaMashakhYahu*. This same doctrine is the one he himself had expressed faith in, to enter the salvation of *Elohiym* in the desert of Gaza, as he was taught by one of Elohiym's most reliable messengers, *Philippos*. This eunuch, when he arrived in Ethiopia, would have performed this divinely-given function of establishing a *Kehillah* of *Yahushua HaMashakhYahu* without knowledge of a practice of raising-up of hands towards *Shamayim* while reciting a so-called *Sinners' Prayer* for salvation or to become born again.

How do all these compare with the lengthy teaching, often spanning into weeks, by some "men of God" today in leading salvation seekers to go through baptism, and later on another so-called "Holy Spirit baptism" for them to receive the infilling of a "Holy Spirit" (*Ruwakh HaKodesh?*)? This second so-called "baptism in the Holy Spirit", they claim, would always result in the speaking in some strange tongues by salvation seekers as evidence of a higher spiritual experience than that pertaining to baptism in natural living waters.

Why would people teach this falsehood of speaking in tongues as being initial evidence of a so-called "Holy Spirit baptism"? Do we not receive the revelation from *First Corinthians* 12:30: *"...do all speak with tongues?"*

Nobody from the accounts in *Ma'asim (Acts)*, after receiving baptism in the name of *Yahushua HaMashakhYahu* for the remission of sins and the receipt of *Ruwakh HaKodesh*, went through a second so-called "Holy Spirit baptism" for him to speak in some strange tongues.

Many "men of God" teach that some *"measure"* of "Holy Spirit" (*Ruwakh HaKodesh* of *Elohiym?*) is received in the reciting of *Sinners' Prayers* by salvation seekers when they invite "Jesus Christ" (*Yahushua HaMashakhYahu?*) to come into their hearts. They further teach that, to get the entire human vessel filled—to the brim or to the full *"measure"*—with the "Holy Spirit" (*Ruwakh HaKodesh?*) and rendered worthy of use by *Elohiym*, one must be "baptized in the Holy Ghost"! From the accounts of the *Holy*

Scriptures, however, it is obvious what is taught by denominations as a "baptism in the Holy Spirit or Ghost," manifested by speaking of strange tongues, is alien to Elohiym's revelation to mankind and therefore a doctrine of men.

Not even the Philippian jailor—cf. *Ma'asim (Acts)* 16:25-40— who might seem to have been hurriedly baptized into *Yahushua HaMashakhYahu* at midnight, had anything else to receive the next day or days following that midnight administration of baptism in natural living waters. He got all the blessings of Elohiym's salvation that midnight. Nobody later organized a so-called *"Holy Spirit Baptism Seminar"* to teach him how to speak in strange tongues and to demonstrate this as proof that he had been filled with *Ruwakh HaKodesh.*

I thank *Elohiym* here that no other *Philippos* was sent to meet with the Ethiopian eunuch in the desert of Gaza but this one. I am sure a different *Philippos* would have "reasoned", due to scarcity of bodies of natural living waters in the desert where they were traveling, that it would be acceptable by *Elohiym* for him to fetch some of the water the eunuch and his company were no doubt carrying for the journey and attempt to administer baptism to the Ethiopian. Such a *Philippos* would have poured or sprinkled some of this water on parts of the eunuch's body for a so-called ministration of baptism into *Yahushua HaMashakhYahu*!

Yet another *Philippos* would have said to the Ethiopian, "I was supposed to baptize you into "Jesus Christ" by immersing you in water. But, as you can see, we do not have a drop of water in this parched desert where we find ourselves. Besides, you are going on a long journey, and I do not want to waste your time sending you backwards to where we can find water for your baptism.

"Anyway, do not worry about this, so long as you believe and accept my word. My word, which is God's word for you, has washed you of sin. You simply pray this prayer after me. **Dear Jesus, I come to you just as I am. I am a sinner, but today I repent of my sins. Forgive me, wash me with your blood which you shed for me on Calvary, and come into my heart. Live your life in me. I will not turn from you anymore. Fill me with your Spirit. Thank you for saving me and making me your child. Amen.**

"Also, confess that God raised Jesus from the dead. For if you shall confess with your mouth and believe in your heart that God raised Jesus from the dead, you will become born again.

"My dear eunuch, you are unfortunate to be going to a place

where there is no Bible-believing and Holy Spirit-led church. I would have advised you to attend the services of one, so that they could baptize you to fulfill all righteousness. You will have to look for me in *Yerushalayim* when next year you come for the feast of the Hebrews, so I can baptize you to fulfill all righteousness. Until then, God be with you as you go. Amen".

That is how ridiculously many people coming after *Philippos* have sought to lead sinners into the salvation of *Elohiym* in *Yahushua HaMashakhYahu*, in a dying world in urgent need of it. For a long time many "men of God" ignorant of how to minister the salvation of *Elohiym*, have forced some falsehoods down our throats.

And we have gullibly accepted and become comfortable with their falsehoods! Now is the time to face this incorrect doctrine head-on and dismantle it. By *Elohiym* working in and through faith-filled men, this will be done. *HalleluYahu!*

Let us now consider the next *talmid* of *Yahushua HaMashakhYahu* called *Chananyahu* (Ananias), who, at the time of his assignment, resided in Damascus. The account about him, and the errand he ran for the Master, is found in *Ma'asim (Acts)* 9:10-18. Please read these verses and make sure you have a good understanding of this account before continuing with the reading of this book.

Read about the same event, recounted by the recipient of Chananyahu's ministry, *Sha'ul*, in *Ma'asim (Acts)* 22:12-16 and 26:14-19, to get the complete picture of events that unfolded in the work done by *Chananyahu* on this particular assignment.

The mission of *Chananyahu* was the same as that of *Philippos*. He was sent to minister salvation to one of Elohiym's elect, a very dreaded character, named *Sha'ul*. After an initial resistance, *Chananyahu* took off on his errand with zeal and commitment. From the unfolded drama of the vision, in which *Chananyahu* heard *Yahushua HaMashakhYahu* talk to him, he knew his mission was to bring the salvation of *Elohiym* to a person whom He had elected to receive it. The choice of him, by *Yahushua HaMashakhYahu* himself, was a confirmation that he could stand up to the task. Obviously, *Yahushua HaMashakhYahu* had already prepared him for this singular task.

In the vision, *Chananyahu* had been clearly instructed to go and do one thing for *Sha'ul*. He was to minister restoration of sight to poor old *Sha'ul*, who had been blind for three days. For this need,

Chananyahu knew exactly what to do. He did not have to ask questions about how to bring this about. He was a *talmid* who already knew this, having been properly taught how.

To bring about a restoration of sight, *Chananyahu* knew he had to lay his hands on blind *Sha'ul*. This was exactly what he did when he went to meet with *Sha'ul*. *Chananyahu* immediately laid his hands on *Sha'ul* and announced the purpose of his visit. There and then, Sha'ul's eyes opened and his sight was regained. *Chananyahu* was obviously living in the light of his rights, privileges, authority, and the powers given him—and all born again *talmidim* of *Yahushua HaMashakhYahu*—concerning the laying-on of hands of the believer on the sick for healing, as found in *Markos (Mark)* 16:15-18.

From the discourse he had with *Yahushua HaMashakhYahu* in the vision, *Chananyahu* knew his visit to *Sha'ul* was to go beyond the laying-on of hands for the restoration of sight. Note that *Yahushua HaMashakhYahu* told *Chananyahu* in the vision that *Sha'ul* was to become **"a vessel unto me, to bear my name to the Gentiles, and kings, and the children of Israel (Yisroel)"—** *Ma'asim (Acts) 9:15*. *Chananyahu*, being a seasoned and mature *talmid*, understood that to be a chosen vessel meant to be filled with *Ruwakh HaKodesh* of *Elohiym*.

Even though *Yahushua HaMashakhYahu* did not mention this aspect of the mission of *Chananyahu* specifically in the vision, *Chananyahu* knew that the main purpose of the Master sending him to *Sha'ul* was for him (*Sha'ul*) to be initiated into the salvation of *Elohiym*, so that he could become the Master's chosen vessel filled with *Ruwakh HaKodesh*. Thus, when *Chananyahu* got to *Sha'ul*, he immediately mentioned the two reasons for his visit in the following quotation:

"And Ananias (Chananyahu) went his way, and entered into the house; and putting his hands on him said, Brother Saul (Sha'ul), the Lord, even Jesus (Yahushua HaMashakhYahu), that appeared unto thee in the way as thou camest, hath sent me, that thou mightest receive thy sight, and be filled with the Holy Spirit (Ruwakh HaKodesh)"—*Ma'asim (Acts) 9: 17, KJV; the words in parenthesis are mine.*

Once the restoration of sight was accomplished, *Chananyahu* had to minister for the second blessing to be received. He then led *Sha'ul* to receive the baptism into the name of *Yahushua HaMashakhYahu*, for the remission of his sins and so he could be filled with *Ruwakh HaKodesh*. *Sha'ul* had already been prepared earlier on for this act of baptism into the name of *Yahushua HaMashakhYahu*, not only because of his encounter with *Yahushua HaMashakhYahu* on the highway to Damascus but also from what he knew about the faith and practices of the people he once persecuted.

Sha'ul was later to testify before King Agrippa that what Ministry *Yahushua HaMashakhYahu* carried in the country of the Hebrews before his sacrificial death *"was not done in a corner."* This means there was nobody living in *Yisroel* at the time of *Yahushua HaMashakhYahu* who could deny knowledge of the doctrines, teachings, and healing ministry of the Savior.

Sha'ul, a contemporary of *Yahushua HaMashakhYahu* whose age was close to his, already knew that *the people of "HaDerekh" (The Way)*—cf. *Ma'asim (Acts) 9:2, 24:14*—as the *talmidim* of *Yahushua HaMashakhYahu* were called back then and must continue to be called today, accessed the person, teachings, and ordinances of their Master through baptism into his name. *Chananyahu*, therefore, cut out lengthy talk to ask the question and to say after the restoration of sight: *"And now why tarriest thou? Arise and be baptized and wash away thy sins, calling on the name of the Lord"*—*Ma'asim (Acts) 22: 16, KJV.*

In fact, the teaching *Chananyahu* was to do in the light of the *Besuras HaGeulah* concerning *Yahushua HaMashakhYahu* was already known by *Sha'ul*. *Sha'ul* knew that *Yahushua HaMashakhYahu* was a messenger of *Elohiym* sent on a mission to *Yisroel*. He saw the entire ministry of the Savior and approved of his suffering, hanging, and death. *Sha'ul* knew the truth of the resurrection of *Yahushua HaMashakhYahu*; he just chose to join with other *Perushim* (Pharisees) to deny it. He lived his life in the knowledge of all these things, yet he chose to denounce and deny them, opting instead to persecute those who held these truths and lived by them.

The intervention of *Yahushua HaMashakhYahu* in Sha'ul's life, on his way into Damascus, brought an end to his denials of these truths, enabling him receive them with faith and to repent of his stance against *Elohiym*, His purposes, and His people.

Sha'ul had already mentally accepted the truth about the Good News of Redemption in *Yahushua HaMashakhYahu* before *Chananyahu* went to minister the salvation of *Elohiym* to him. This he had earlier done on his way to Damascus, when the lightning of

Elohiym from *Shamayim* struck him. *Sha'ul* then posed the question: *"Lord (Adoni, meaning "My Lord") what wilt thou have me do?"—Ma'asim (Acts) 9:6, KJV; words in parenthesis is mine.*

All that was now needed for *Sha'ul* to do was to profess these truths about the *Besuras HaGeulah* by accepting baptism in the name of *Yahushua HaMashakhYahu* for the remission of his sins for him to enter into the salvation of *Elohiym*.

When *Chananyahu* was a beginner *talmid* of *Yahushua HaMashakhYahu*, he had been taught the elementary doctrines of the Master. These, according to the book of *Ivriim (Hebrews)*, include the laying on of hands, baptism, etc.—cf. *Ivriim (Hebrews)* 6:1-2. So *Chananyahu*, in his early years of study as a *talmid* of *Yahushua HaMashakhYahu*, had been properly taught these doctrinal truths and was in the position to deliver in this regard. This was exactly what he delivered to *Sha'ul* in that particular assignment.

We have to understand that *Sha'ul* could not receive *Ruwakh HaKodesh* of *Elohiym* into his heart when the light from *Shamayim* struck him on the highway to Damascus. *Sha'ul* could neither become born again by his repentance of sin and show of remorse in persecuting Elohiym's people—no matter how sincerely he expressed it—nor by his sincere confession of *Yahushua HaMashakhYahu* as *Adoni* (my Lord) in his encounter with the Savior. He could also not become born again and be filled with *Ruwakh HaKodesh* when *Chananyahu* laid his hands on him.

The laying of hands by *Chananyahu* on *Sha'ul* was to pass a "shockwave" of the power of *Ruwakh HaKodesh* through him, to flush out, as it were, the blindness, and any sicknesses that might have been in his body. It was the work of *Chananyahu* in leading *Sha'ul* to baptism in the name of *Yahushua HaMashakhYahu* that brought *Sha'ul* the born again experience and the filling of *Ruwakh HaKodesh* within him. *Sha'ul* only became a vessel worthy of use by *Yahushua HaMashakhYahu* after the filling by *Ruwakh HaKodesh* within him in his baptism into the name of *Yahushua HaMashakhYahu*.

Could it also be that *Sha'ul* was ignorant of how to access the blessings of the sacrifice of *Yahushua HaMashakhYahu* as being through repentance and baptism into the name of the Savior? Was *Sha'ul* seeking to become born again through an intense three-day fast and prayer after his encounter with *Yahushua HaMashakhYahu* on the road to Damascus? If so, was *Sha'ul* one of those early subscribers to the erroneous and wrong faith and practice of *Sinners' Prayer* recitals for salvation?

I do not want to suppose that *Sha'ul* was, in three days, seeking to get *Elohiym* to write his name in *HaSefer HaChayyim* (the Book of Life) through repentance, confession of sins, and a pledge to *Elohiym* never to go back to his bad and sinful ways. I do not think *Sha'ul* was expecting that his acts in these days of spiritual examination, in themselves, would have rendered him born again. In fact, it would seem absurd for one to think so.

However, if *Sha'ul* indeed expected to be saved in these days of fasting, prayer, and change of heart, simply by his engagements in them, then he was blessed to have *Chananyahu* sent by *Yahushua HaMashakhYahu* to go and lead him to do the right thing instead. *Yahushua HaMashakhYahu* sent his able *talmid*, *Chananyahu*, to teach *Sha'ul* the right thing to do to become born again. *Chananyahu* taught *Sha'ul* that the blessings of the salvation of *Elohiym* come to every repentant and brokenhearted sinner only in baptism into the name *Yahushua HaMashakhYahu*. In furtherance to this, *Chananyahu* asked *Sha'ul* the famous question: ***"And now why tarriest thou? Arise, and be baptized, and wash away thy sins, calling on the name of the Lord.—Ma'asim (Acts) 22:16, KJV.***

The ministration of humble and more knowledgeable *talmid* of *Yahushua HaMashakhYahu*, *Chananyahu*, in leading needy *Sha'ul* to the salvation of *Elohiym* in *Yahushua HaMashakhYahu*, is, sadly, very different from that of the many seemingly more mature title-bearing pastors, bishops, archbishops and general overseers of Christian denominations today. Many are leading people to pray for "Jesus Christ" (*Yahushua HaMashakhYahu*?) to enter their hearts in order for them to gain Elohiym's salvation!

This is a clear departure from what the early *talmidim* of *Yahushua HaMashakhYahu*, who were called before us taught. And I really wonder how many of our "men of God" today are truly called, taught, and sent by *Yahushua HaMashakhYahu* to bring about the sinner's salvation.

Finally, let us look at a particular work that *Shimon Kefa*, a *Shliakh* of *Yahushua HaMashakhYahu*, executed for him. An account of this is found in *Ma'asim (Acts)* 10. Please read the entire chapter and try to get the substance of it, before you continue reading this book.

While praying in his housetop room in *Yafo* (Joppa), *Shimon*

Kefa gets a divine visitation in a trance. As a result of his lifestyle and prejudices as a Hebrew, he was very slow in understanding the meaning of the vision he had. To make things difficult for his comprehension, *Shimon Kefa* was commanded to go down from his housetop prayer room to hospitably receive three men who had come on a mission to him under Elohiym's instruction.

The events in the town of Caesarea, the third day after the vision, in the house of Cornelius, a special Gentile worshipper of the Most High One of *Yisroel,* would open Shimon Kefa's understanding to the meaning of the vision he had had in his prayer room in *Yafo.* This understanding of the vision was to leave a lasting impact on his discriminatory attitude toward people of non-Hebrew descent.

Before *Shimon Kefa* received this vision, *Elohiym* had earlier sent an angel to Cornelius, the Gentile whose holy lifestyle had come before Him as a memorial, and who He wanted to bring into His special salvation in *Yahushua HaMashakhYahu. Elohiym* told Cornelius through the angel to send for *Shimon Kefa,* who, when he comes, *"shall tell thee what thou oughtest to do,"—Ma'asim (Acts) 10:6.* These words were also echoed by the messengers Cornelius sent to *Shimon Kefa* when they met him: *". . . and to hear words of thee,"—Ma'asim (Acts) 10: 22.* Then again, when *Shimon Kefa* made entry into the presence of Cornelius and all that were gathered in his house, Cornelius said, among other things, the following:

"Send therefore to Joppa (Yafo), and call hither Simon (Shimon), whose surname is Peter (Kefa); he is lodged in the house of one Simon (Shimon) a tanner, by the sea side: who when he cometh, shall speak unto thee. Immediately therefore I sent for thee; and thou hast well done that thou art come. Now therefore are we all here present before God (Elohiym), to hear all the things that are commanded thee of God (Elohiym)"—Ma'asim (Acts) 10:32-33, KJV; the words in parenthesis are mine.

The stage was now set for *Shimon Kefa* to say what *Elohiym* had commanded him to say, which would thereafter be crucial in directing the spiritual life of Cornelius and his entire household.

Shimon Kefa neither had a lengthy speech to make, nor were his listeners ready for one. He went straight to the point. He preached *Yahushua HaMashakhYahu,* the Savior, to his devout and holy listeners. He preached the suffering, death, and resurrection of

Yahushua HaMashakhYahu and the blessings these bring to mankind. This is the Good News of Redemption for the entire world and for all times.

He did not have to speak for long. *Elohiym* bore testimony to what *Shimon Kefa* spoke as being the words He had given him to speak, as was seen in the descent of *Ruwakh HaKodesh* upon Cornelius and his household, while he yet spoke.

By this falling of *Ruwakh HaKodesh, Elohiym* was commending *Shimon Kefa* for the message he had given. This is the only message with the power to bring about a sorrowing of heart of any person that hears it and lead him to repentance of sin.

When, later on, *Shimon Kefa* had to give an account to the other *Shlikhim* about why he had to go to the Gentile Cornelius, this was what he said as part of the report: *"And he showed us how he had seen an angel in his house which stood and said to him, Send men to Joppa (Yafo), and call for Simon (Shimon), whose surname is Peter (Kefa); who shall tell thee words, whereby thou and all thy house shall be saved."—Ma'asim (Acts) 11:13-14, KJV; words in parenthesis are mine.*

The words *Shimon Kefa* was to speak to Cornelius are the very words of salvation as recorded in *Ma'asim (Acts)* 10:36-43. This is the good news of, and for, our redemption. Whenever you have to lead people into the salvation of *Elohiym* in *Yahushua HaMashakhYahu*, do not just preach any message because it can be found in the *Holy Scriptures*; preach the *Besuras HaGeulah* (the true Good News) in *Yahushua HaMashakhYahu* as *Shimon Kefa* did. The message of the hanging of *Yahushua HaMashakhYahu* will always evoke so much remorse in man, as to lead him to repentance from his sins.

Even though *Ruwakh HaKodesh* was outpoured upon the listeners of his message, *Shimon Kefa* knew his assignment wasn't over. No doubt, he had been taught everything about the salvation of *Elohiym* in *Yahushua HaMashakhYahu* and how to lead men into it. Otherwise, how was he fit to be a leader, chosen and ordained by *Yahushua HaMashakhYahu* himself, or how would he have been successful on his very first assignment in this regard on the Day of the Outpouring of *Ruwakh HaKodesh* (Pentecost?) in *Yerushalayim*?

The outpouring of *Ruwakh HaKodesh* upon Cornelius and his household notwithstanding, *Shimon Kefa* knew that they had to go through the ordinance, instructed by *Yahushua HaMashakhYahu*, to initiate them into membership of the New Covenant family. He thus commanded them to be baptized in the name of *Yahushua HaMashakhYahu.*

The manner and timing that *Ruwakh HaKodesh* was poured out upon these Gentiles, I am sure, was as astonishing to *Shimon Kefa* as it must have been for his Hebrew brethren who accompanied him from *Yafo.* Not only was the outpouring of *Ruwakh HaKodesh* on Cornelius and company unexpected, since it was considered unthinkable for them as Gentiles, but so also was the timing of the event.

There is no doubt then that this outpouring of *Ruwakh HaKodesh* was part of the teaching process of *Elohiym* for *Shimon Kefa,* which He started in *Yafo. Shimon Kefa* was taught in a manner that would break down all his Hebrew prejudices against people of non-Hebrew descent. These prejudices clouded Shimon Kefa's understanding of Elohiym's plans for Gentiles' salvation, even after the same lesson had been taught him three times in a single episode through the vision he had in *Yafo.* Shimon Kefa's prejudices taught him it was wrong for Hebrews to keep company with people of non-Hebrew origin.

He did not hide these prejudices from Cornelius in his introductory words in the latter's house. *Shimon Kefa* thought it was impossible for non-Hebrews to be considered acceptable to *Elohiym.* In this state of mind, he could not bring any spiritual blessings to Cornelius and his household.

Talking about signs, this was one of the clearest that ever came to any genuine minister of the message of the *Besuras HaGeulah.* This outpouring of *Ruwakh HaKodesh* upon Cornelius was meant to be a sign from *Elohiym* to *Shimon Kefa* that He had accepted these Gentiles for His salvation. It was as if *Elohiym* was issuing a command to *Shimon Kefa* to **"arise, and baptize these non-Hebrews into the name of my Son, into Life, for I have approved of them for my salvation."**

This outpouring of *Ruwakh HaKodesh* was not to mean that these non-Hebrews had become born again. That would have contradicted Elohiym's Word in *YahuChanan (John)* 3:5, *Markos (Mark)* 16:16, and *Ma'asim (Acts)* 2:38-39. After all, the account says *Ruwakh HaKodesh* fell on these non-Hebrews but not that they were filled with him in their hearts.

Not only did this outpouring of *Ruwakh HaKodesh* awaken *Shimon Kefa* to the spiritual realities of the situation he found himself in, but he also realized he could never withstand *Elohiym.*

Shimon Kefa then concluded that *Elohiym* must have His way. He was left with no option but to lead these non-Hebrew believers through the ordinance commanded by *Yahushua HaMashakhYahu* for the initiation of all salvation seekers into the new birth.

This he did, daring any of the brethren who went along with him from *Yafo* to resist the move of *Elohiym*. After all, if *Elohiym* Himself considered Gentile Cornelius and his family eligible for His salvation, who was he *Shimon Kefa* to resist the plan of *Elohiym* by refusing to baptize them into *Yahushua HaMashakhYahu*?

This was the only experience *Shimon Kefa* had in his entire ministering life where people were blessed with an outpouring of *Ruwakh HaKodesh* upon them **before** their initiation into the new birth by way of baptism into *Yahushua HaMashakhYahu*. This was also the only experience of a minister of *Elohiym* of the New Covenant salvation doctrine ever documented. For this to have happened at the hand of *Shimon Kefa*, a leader ordained by *Yahushua HaMashakhYahu*, at the time it did, was certainly of great significance to the *Malchut HaElohiym*.

The conversion of the Gentile world would have been slow in coming, considering all the prejudices the Hebrew *Shlikhim* of *Yahushua HaMashakhYahu* had against Gentiles. *Elohiym* just had to let things happen the way they did in the home of Cornelius to kick-start and to speedup the salvation process of the Gentile world.

Even after the outpouring of *Ruwakh HaKodesh* upon Cornelius and his family, and their subsequent guided entry into life through baptism, the acceptance of Gentiles by Hebrews as being qualified for Elohiym's salvation was still slow in coming. When by reason of persecution in *Yerushalayim* the *talmidim* were forced to scatter abroad, they still preached *Yahushua HaMashakhYahu* to only Hebrews in all the towns they fled to—cf. *Ma'asim (Acts)* 11:19— not considering non-Hebrews being worthy to receive the salvation of *Elohiym*.

At the end of this teaching process of *Elohiym*, I am sure *Shimon Kefa* had come to accept the active participation of the Master in any worthy ministration of the New Covenant salvation by any of his *Shlikhim* or *talmidim*. Any ministration of the New Covenant salvation, going strictly by the doctrines of *Yahushua HaMashakhYahu*, will have the Master show himself in some way in that ministration.

He will be present as to urge one on, as well as lead, direct, encourage and commend as one does the genuine work one is called into his service to do. *Yahushua HaMashakhYahu* will be present in that ministration and will announce his presence through signs and wonders.

Every minister of the New Covenant salvation must always allow room, in their ministrations of the word of salvation, for the Master to do as he pleases. When the Master plays his role, acting like he did in the home of Cornelius, it should not confuse the able minister of the New Covenant faith in carrying out to the end his part of the work as instructed by the Master. Every minister of the New Covenant faith must constantly bear in mind that the Master himself is a co-laborer with him in all genuine ministrations of the doctrines and instructions of the New Covenant.

All ministers should be comforted and strengthened by the Word of *Elohiym* in *Mattityahu (Matthew) 28:19-20, Markos (Mark) 16:20, First Corinthians 3:9,* and *Second Corinthians 6:1,* where we have been assured of the presence of the Master in our ministrations of the word of faith. In the same way, ministers of the New Covenant must understand that it is the prerogative of the Master to play his part in their ministries at any point in time, and in any manner he chooses. The work of ministers must be to carry out the instructions of the Master to the letter, allowing him to do as he wills in support and confirmation of their activities, as and when he pleases.

I am particularly pleased with *Shimon Kefa,* because he led these non-Hebrew believers to their baptism into the name of *Yahushua HaMashakhYahu* in fulfillment of his obligation to, and role in, the Great Commission of the Master. I know of many people, who, upon seeing the outpouring of *Ruwakh HaKodesh* upon those Gentiles, would just stop there and end the ministration of salvation to their listeners, thinking that salvation or the born again experience had come.

Not so for *Shimon Kefa*—he knew his role in this ministration of salvation was only to end in the ministering of baptism in the name of *Yahushua HaMashakhYahu,* which he did. He also knew for sure that in the matter of *Elohiym* giving *Ruwakh HaKodesh* to dwell within the heart of any person, the Master could only give *Ruwakh HaKodesh* after the able minister of the New Covenant had finished his role of properly administering baptism.

If any of today's ministers of the New Covenant salvation doctrine want to see people receive an outpouring of *Ruwakh*

HaKodesh before baptism, in a manner as was evident in this particular ministration of salvation by *Shimon Kefa* to Cornelius, they must re-create the same situation as it took place then. At that time, *Shimon Kefa* and the other *Shlikhim* believed that it was wrong and unacceptable to *Elohiym* to go to Gentiles with the message of the *Besuras HaGeulah*. How could it have been possible for them to go to these people with the blessing of *Elohiym* for their salvation in this state of mind and attitude, with an unholy prejudice against these people?

Today, no minister should expect to have *Ruwakh HaKodesh* of *Elohiym* fall on any people, as in the vivid manner as happened in the home of Cornelius, before the ministration of baptism into *Yahushua HaMashakhYahu*. We should understand that it is, **in, at, through,** or **after**—not before—the ministration of baptism in the name of *Yahushua HaMashakhYahu* that *Ruwakh HaKodesh* is received to dwell within the hearts of any penitent sinners.

For sure, *Shimon Kefa* saw this outpouring of *Ruwakh HaKodesh* upon these Gentiles as an Old Covenant phenomenon. *Shimon Kefa*, at that time, might have been led by *Ruwakh HaKodesh* to the scriptures in *Bamidbar (Numbers)* 11:25-26. There, is the account of *Ruwakh HaKodesh* of *Elohiym* coming upon seventy elders of the house of *Yisroel* simultaneously! Immediately afterwards, they all "prophesied"—meaning they spoke or sang praises to *Elohiym* in tongues, known or unknown—in a manner very much akin to the experience of Cornelius and his household.

Even as those elders of *Yisroel* had *Ruwakh HaKodesh* of *Elohiym* that was in *Moshe* come upon them, their yearning desire was to receive *Ruwakh HaKodesh* in the manner of the New Covenant dispensation. After all, did these elders, who could "prophesy" by *Ruwakh HaKodesh* of *Elohiym*, not see through faith that the New Covenant would be characterized by better promises than the Old—cf. *Ivriim (Hebrews)* 8:6—and would come with, and through, a better priesthood—cf. *Ivriim (Hebrews)* 7:20-28—as well as a better resurrection—cf. *Ivriim (Hebrews)* 11:35? Did they not see ahead of them, a better way to enter the salvation, kingdom and family of *Elohiym*, by being born again through repentance and remission of sin, than what existed in the Old Covenant—cf. *Ivriim (Hebrews)* 1: 1-4 and *Kefa Alef (First Peter)* 1: 10-13?

Did these elders not know that in the New Covenant dispensation *Ruwakh HaKodesh* would come to dwell within the hearts of the elect of *Elohiym* and not stay upon them, hovering over their heads? Did these elders not also know that without the New Covenant believers they could not be made perfect—cf. *Ivriim (Hebrews)* 11:40—and so their yearning would have been to enter the salvation of *Elohiym* like the New Covenant folks would?

Shimon Kefa knew all about that incident of *Bamidbar (Numbers)*, and it was also a known fact to him that those elders were looking forward to receiving *Ruwakh HaKodesh* in the more excellent manner of the Grace Dispensation and according to the better promises and clearer instructions of *Elohiym*. These promises, *Elohiym* said, would only come about by repentance from sin and baptism into the name of His son *Yahushua HaMashakhYahu*.

Shimon Kefa therefore commanded his listeners to be baptized in the name of *Yahushua HaMashakhYahu*, so that they could receive remission of sins and the gift of Elohiym's *Ruwakh HaKodesh* to dwell within their hearts. This was to be the norm in the era of Grace for the receiving of the salvation of *Elohiym* in *Yahushua HaMashakhYahu*, and *Ruwakh HaKodesh* as a gift of *Elohiym* to dwell within the hearts of men.

Shimon Kefa held as highly sacred the parting words of the Master in the Great Commission statement, by which he was instructed to ensure that everybody who received the message of the *Besuras HaGeulah* was baptized in his name—*Yahushua HaMashakhYahu*—for salvation (*Markos* 16:15-16). *Ruwakh HaKodesh* of *Elohiym*, who resided in Shimon Kefa's heart, constantly brought him into remembrance of the instructions of the Master to baptize all in his name for salvation.

How could *Shimon Kefa* ever forget these instructions of the Master to baptize in his name for salvation? Woe unto him if he ever forgot this or did anything different. How could it ever get into his heart to direct salvation seekers to pray some *Sinners' Prayers* for their salvation? Sadly, the devil has been able to deceive many people coming after *Shimon Kefa* to lead people to say prayers after them for salvation!

Many people casually familiar with the accounts of *Ma'asim (Acts)* 10:44-47 believe erroneously that the outpouring of *Ruwakh HaKodesh* upon Cornelius and his family meant they had become born again! But it would be wrong to believe so, since that would mean man can become born of *Ruwakh HaKodesh* before they were born of water, that is to say, before they were baptized in natural

111

living waters into the name *Yahushua HaMashakhYahu*. The Word of *Elohiym* says that man is born again of water and of *Ruwakh HaKodesh*. Man is not born again **of *Ruwakh HaKodesh* and, then, of water.**

Elohiym is the only true wise Being. *Elohiym* is that one source of all wisdom. Every word from His mouth is pure wisdom. His thoughts manifest wisdom. If, *Elohiym* wanted to get man born again **of *Ruwakh HaKodesh* and, then of water**, in which case baptism into *Yahushua HaMashakhYahu* would follow salvation, He would have said so. *Elohiym* conveys His will, purpose, power and wisdom in what He says.

When one day at a prayer meeting in Antioch *Ruwakh HaKodesh* of *Elohiym*, who is the *Ruwakh* (Spirit) of wisdom and understanding, counsel and might, knowledge and the fear of *Elohiym*, manifested, he spoke as to reveal His will. In that prayer meeting, *Elohiym* spoke to His people to ***"separate me Barnabas (Bar-Nabba) and Saul (Sha'ul) for the work that whereunto I have called them"—Ma'asim (Acts) 13:2, KJV; words in parenthesis are mine***. Why did the *Ruwakh* of Wisdom not say for the people of *Elohiym* to separate ***Sha'ul* and *Bar-Nabba*** instead?

The *Ruwakh* of Wisdom speaks to reveal the mind of *Elohiym*. By saying ***"Bar-Nabba and Sha'ul,"*** the *Ruwakh* of Wisdom was revealing the leadership in the mission these two servants of the Savior were to be assigned. *Bar-Nabba*, by that utterance of *Ruwakh HaKodesh*, was ordained and anointed by *Elohiym* as the leader of that missionary journey.

All the subsequent details of that mission are proof of this fact. It was later on in *Ma'asim (Acts)* 15:36-40, when *Sha'ul* started to act like the one in charge and dissented sharply with *Bar-Nabba* over one *YahuChanan*, also known as *Markos* (John-Mark), that a leadership crisis ensued, leading to the breakup of that partnership that was established by *Ruwakh HaKodesh*.

Elohiym is the Great One of order: His Creation manfests this fact. Every word from His mouth will always attest to this. No word of His will ever bring confusion or disorder, but confusion and disorder are what ensue when some of Elohiym's listeners take it that man is ***"born of water and of Ruwakh HaKodesh"***, while others believe that man is born of *Ruwakh HaKodesh* and of water.

Elohiym is angered and disappointed by this avoidable confusion among people who claim to obey His instructions. In fact, when *Elohiym* says ***"of water and of Ruwakh HaKodesh"***, He means just that. *Elohiym* is offended when men think He ought to say that man is born **of *Ruwakh HaKodesh* and of water** to bring about the born again experience.

In seeking to obey and to follow *Elohiym*, we ought to understand that the order and sequence of His instructions to us are very important. We should never reverse the order of instructions that He gives to us. I am happy that, up until now, I have not found any group of "celebrants" of the *Last Supper* reversing the order or manner of that memorial event, even though many other things are done wrongly today in its celebration by many so-called believers of *Yahushua HaMashakhYahu*.

It would seem stupid of any people to go drinking the wine before eating the bread in the celebration of the *Last Supper*. That reversal would be unbecoming of people who claim to be followers or copyists of the Master.

Let me tell you a secret; why one must first be born of water and then of *Ruwakh HaKodesh*. The secret is that water does not inhabit *Ruwakh HaKodesh*; rather, *Ruwakh HaKodesh* inhabits waters—cf. *Bereshis (Genesis)* 1:2. Water must first be there and available before *Ruwakh HaKodesh* of *Elohiym* can come to brood over it. The Old Man must, therefore, be born of water first before he can be inhabited by *Ruwakh HaKodesh*.

Being born of water is becoming water. Natural man must first become water before *Ruwakh HaKodesh* of *Elohiym* can come into him. Nobody can be born again **of *Ruwakh HaKodesh* and of water**. If you believe you can and claim that in your spiritual experience you were first born of *Ruwakh HaKodesh* of *Elohiym* and then of water, that experience will be tested by fire and I am sure it will not stand up to the test.

I am the more convinced, by my understanding of Elohiym's Word, that even by the outpouring of *Ruwakh HaKodesh* on Cornelius and his household, they were not yet born again. They were like the many people referred to in the *Holy Scriptures* upon whom *Ruwakh HaKodesh* of *Elohiym* descended, after which they spoke in tongues and prophesied, but were not yet born again.

I do hope you understand and accept that many people under the Old Covenant, upon whom *Ruwakh HaKodesh* of *Elohiym* descended at sundry times and for varying reasons, did not get born again. Everybody in the accounts of the Old Covenant scriptures blessed with the coming of *Ruwakh HaKodesh* upon them for diverse reasons, and at sundry times and seasons, were not born again. All of them, from righteous *Chanokh* (Enoch) through *Noach, Moshe, Bezalel* (Bezaleel), *Shmuel* (Samuel), *Sha'ul, Dovid, Yeshayahu*

(Isaiah), *Yechezkel* (Ezekiel), Daniel, etc., down to the last Old Covenant folk upon whom *Elohiym* put His *Ruwakh HaKodesh*, were not born again.

We also have to understand that not even one of the experiences of dead people, who were raised back to life by the power of *Ruwakh HaKodesh* of *Elohiym* in any of the incidents preceding the resurrection of *Yahushua HaMashakhYahu*, could be considered as born again experiences.

Readily coming to mind are such incidents as involving the dead son of the widow of *Tzarphat* (Zeraphath) recorded in *Melekhim Alef (First Kings)* 17:17-20; the dead son of a woman of Shunem recorded in *Melekhim Bais (Second Kings)* 4:18-37; and a dead warrior's body coming into contact with the bones of *Elishah* the *navi* in a cave recorded in *Melekhim Bais (Second Kings)* 13:20-21. None of these coming to life from the dead events were born again experiences.

Not even those accomplished at the hand of *Yahushua HaMashakhYahu*, as he confronted the forces of darkness during his pre-*Gulgotha* ministry, brought the born again experience to any of the people who benefited from those raising-back-to-life feats.

Therefore, neither the raising to life from the dead by *Yahushua HaMashakhYahu* of the son of the widow of *Naim* (Nain) as found in *Lukas (Luke)* 7:11-15; nor the return to life of the dead daughter of *Ja'ir* (Jairus) found in *Lukas (Luke)* 8:41-42 and 49-56; nor the all-too-famous coming back to life of dead *El'azar* (Lazarus) of *Beit-Anyah* (Bethany) as recorded in *YahuChanan (John)* 11:1-14, could be considered as born again experiences.

The born again experience, a glorious mystery of *Elohiym*, was only to come to His blessed elect in the death and resurrection of *Yahushua HaMashakhYahu*. This mystery was to be manifested in, and by, the power of natural living waters and *Ruwakh HaKodesh* of *Elohiym* to repentant believers of *Yahushua HaMashakhYahu*, and of his work of salvation to mankind. Only the repentant sinner under the bequeathed Will of *Yahushua HaMashakhYahu* within the New Covenant revelation can be born again according to the dictates of that will.

I am not surprised that *Ruwakh HaKodesh* of *Elohiym* became visible, or manifested in the speaking in tongues, by Cornelius and his company as they listened to the word of *Shimon Kefa*. You see, *Ruwakh HaKodesh* of *Elohiym* was already all over Cornelius and his sin-abhoring household before *Shimon Kefa* went to him.

You cannot live in holiness and righteousness as Cornelius did, and not have *Ruwakh HaKodesh* upon you, about you, and around you. You cannot live in a state where you get the testimony by angels that your righteous deeds are a memorial before *Elohiym*, and not have *Ruwakh HaKodesh* over your head and about you.

You cannot live in the presence of the holy angels of *Elohiym*, and not have *Ruwakh HaKodesh* about you. Therefore, even before *Shimon Kefa* went to the home of Cornelius, *Ruwakh HaKodesh* of *Elohiym* was all about him and his home.

Shimon Kefa could never see or know this because he was much too prejudiced against non-Hebrews to ever think they could be blessed with the presence of *Ruwakh HaKodesh* of *Elohiym* around them. *Elohiym*, by bringing about that manifestation of the presence of His *Ruwakh Kodesh* in a manner resembling, but not of the same essence as, that of the expectant *talmidim* already baptized in *Yahushua's* name in the upper room, was simply opening the eyes of *Shimon Kefa* and his friends from *Yafo* to the spiritual state of Cornelius before their visit to him, which was now manifesting audibly as they listened to the words of *Shimon Kefa*.

I hope you remember the words of *Yahushua HaMashakhYahu* to his *talmidim* in *YahuChanan (John)* 14:16-17, where he said he would send them *Ruwakh HaKodesh* who was already **dwelling with** them at the time. *Yahushua HaMashakhYahu* went on further to say that he was going to send to them *Ruwakh HaKodesh* of *Elohiym* to **reside in** them, forever, at the opportune time. Shall we read these verses of *YahuChanan (John)*?

"And I will pray the Father (HaAv) and he shall give you another Comforter (Melitz Yosher), that he may abide with you forever. Even the Spirit of truth (Ruwakh HaEmes); whom the world (Olam Hazeh) cannot receive, because it seeth him not, neither knoweth him; but ye know him; for he dwelleth with you, and shall be in you"—YahuChanan (John) 14:16-17, KJV; the words in parenthesis are mine.

Remember that as *Yahushua HaMashakhYahu* spoke to his *talmidim* in these words they were not yet born again. At that instant, all these *talmidim* were of the same spiritual standing as any good Hebrew who was living in obedience to the *Torah* and the holy word of the *Neviim* ("prophets") of *Elohiym*. This is because, up to this time, the New Covenant of *Yahushua HaMashakhYahu* in which sinners are born again was not yet in force.

And yet *Ruwakh HaKodesh* of *Elohiym* was **dwelling with** them. The *talmidim* got to be born again on the Day of the Outpouring of *Ruwakh HaKodesh* (Pentecost?) in *Yerushalayim*, when they received *Ruwakh HaKodesh* to **dwell within** their hearts in completion of their new birth which started in the baptism they received in the name of *Yahushua HaMashakhYahu* during the early days of his ministry—cf. *YahuChanan (John)* 3:22, 26; 4:1-2; and 7:39.

Let us look closely at the account in *Ma'asim (Acts)* about the coming of *Ruwakh HaKodesh* (on Day of "Pentecost"?). Three things stand out very clearly. Two of these announce the descent of *Ruwakh HaKodesh*. The third reveals the destination and final dwelling place of *Ruwakh HaKodesh*—in the hearts of the men gathered.

Ma'asim (Acts) 2:2 talks about the sound as of a rushing mighty wind from *Shamayim* filling the entire house where the *talmidim* were gathered. *Ma'asim (Acts)* 2:3, talks about the parting as tongues of fire upon the heads of all the *talmidim* of *Yahushua HaMashakhYahu* who were in the upper room. These two verses together announce the advent of *Ruwakh HaKodesh* in fulfillment of the promise of *Yahushua HaMashakhYahu*.

Ruwakh HaKodesh had to announce his coming in that way for all those gathered, many of whom were like *Toma* (Thomas)— sense-ruled and not faith-minded—to know that the promise of *HaAv* (the Father) had come. The sound of a mighty rushing wind and the tongues of fire that parted on the heads of all the *talmidim* gathered in the room were simply to inform them that *Ruwakh HaKodesh* had come. After this announcement came the actual descent of *Ruwakh HaKodesh* into their hearts to fill or dwell within them.

This filling of hearts by *Ruwakh HaKodesh* was the main reason for his coming. Without this filling up of the hearts of the *talmidim*, they were as hollow as empty barrels, and not the precious vessels that were worthy of use by the Master in his work.

If those gathered were faith-minded people, they would have known that *Ruwakh HaKodesh* was already with them, saturating the entire atmosphere of the upper room, in and out, and resting upon their heads, before this dramatic display. The mighty wind and the fire came to manifest what was already in existence, and to let them know that the promise of *HaAv* to send *Ruwakh HaKodesh* to dwell within their hearts forever had finally been fulfilled to them.

So we can understand that *Ruwakh HaKodesh* could be around Cornelius and his family and yet not dwell within their hearts, in the manner that born again people are blessed with.

All born again people receive the dwelling presence of *Ruwakh HaKodesh* within their hearts along with their faith in repentance of sin and baptism in the name of *Yahushua HaMashakhYahu*.

Baptism in the name of *Yahushua HaMashakhYahu* is the only ordinance of *Elohiym* which, when received properly in faith after genuine repentance from sin, brings the descent of *Ruwakh HaKodesh* to dwell within the hearts of men in completion of their new birth.

The baptism in the name of *Yahushua HaMashakhYahu*, which was ministered to Cornelius and company, brought about the descent of *Ruwakh HaKodesh* from hovering over their heads into their hearts, to dwell within them forever.

We should, as is said elsewhere in this book, let the spirit of the entire New Covenant scriptures carry us along as we read it. When that happens, we can see the character, the heartbeat or pulse, the feelings, and indeed the very power of this covenant. We would then understand the wisdom that brought it into being, appreciate the orderliness of it, and therefore receive its blessing.

If the spirit of the New Covenant scriptures takes us along as we read it, we would understand, for example, what *Yahushua HaMashakhYahu* meant when he said in *YahuChanan* 20:22, *OJB*, **"Receive Ruwakh HaKodesh,"** as he breathed on his *Shlikhim*. Did they receive *Ruwakh HaKodesh* to dwell within their hearts by that act, or was there the need for the occurrence of the events of *Ma'asim (Acts)* 2:2-4? Think about this.

If we let the spirit of the New Covenant scriptures carry us along as we read this great document meant to lead us to our salvation, we will know when and by what manner and means *Ruwakh HaKodesh* is received. This allows us to avoid the errors that have come into our faith today about the born again doctrine, and a so-called "Holy Spirit baptism" wrongly believed by many Christians to be a secondary spiritual experience to being born again.

I am convinced that it was the act of baptism rendered to Cornelius and company that brought *Ruwakh HaKodesh* to dwell within them, rendering them born again. Nobody can ever become born again except of water and of *Ruwakh HaKodesh.* That is my humble attempt to echo the words of *Yahushua HaMashakhYahu* to *Nakdimon,* **"Omein, omein, I say to you: unless someone is born of mayim (water) and Ruwakh HaKodesh he is not able to enter the Malchut HaElohiym (Kingdom of Elohiym)."—OJB.** This is the truth of Elohiym's Word, which His integrity cannot violate or change.

This assignment of *Shimon Kefa,* like his very first one on the Day of the Outpouring of *Ruwakh HaKodesh* (Pentecost?), in *Yerushalayim,* ended in the ministration of baptism in the name of *Yahushua HaMashakhYahu* to his followers. *Philippos* and *Chananyahu* also ended their ministrations of the salvation of *Elohiym* to their candidates in baptism into the name of *Yahushua HaMashakhYahu.*

In fact, all true *Shlikhim* or *talmidim* of *Elohiym* sent to bring His salvation to any people would do this by ministering baptism in the name of *Yahushua HaMashakhYahu* to their candidates in the same hour of executing their assignments.

No called-and-sent minister of the *Besuras HaGeulah* should delay baptism to repentant salvation seekers for an hour. All ministers should see the urgency to baptize their repentant followers and should not delay for any reason for a day, let alone one month, in baptizing them. This is because every minister of the New Covenant faith must remain focused on the instructions of the Master in the Great Commission statement, understanding that baptism in the name of *Yahushua HaMashakhYahu* now saves in today's Dispensation of Grace.

For today's ministers to delay baptism for four Sundays, and up to fourteen Sundays in some cases, is puzzling. Can we see any minister in the accounts of the *Holy Scriptures* delaying baptism that long? What are ministers of today teaching the salvation seeker about baptism, in the period of four Sunday lessons, which the *Shlikhim* of *Yahushua HaMashakhYahu* did not teach for even an hour?

The Master said we should baptize the repentant sinner and then, teach him *"all things"—cf. Mattityahu (Matthew) 28:19-20.* Are today's ministers seeking to overturn the instruction of the Master by trying to teach the sinner *"all things"* before baptizing him?

In all the three errands of *Philippos, Chananyahu,* and *Shimon Kefa,* we see people called of *Elohiym* given assignments and words to speak in the execution of their various tasks. They had the same call, the same mission, the same anointer—the same level of anointing?—and the same message from the same Master which all brought the same results. Is that not wonderful?

How contrasting are these accounts of how *Philippos, Chananyahu,* and *Shimon Kefa,* led people into the salvation of *Elohiym* in *Yahushua HaMashakhYahu* with what many pastors, bishops, general overseers, television evangelists, etc., present to salvation seekers in our world today for salvation or the born again experience.

Where from these *Sinners' Prayers*? What good comes from these practices of praying "Jesus Christ" (*Yahushua HaMashakhYahu*?) into hearts? Who started this corruption of Elohiym's pure holy doctrine on His salvation for the sinner?

My prayer is that you receive correction from this false doctrine that teaches that people can become born again by saying a so-called *Sinners' Prayer* by inviting "Jesus Christ" into their hearts, before the trumpet of the archangel of *Elohiym* is sounded for His holy people to be gathered Home. Please do not delay in doing this.

This is the sum of all that we have been saying in this chapter. We are saved by the power of the Good News of Redemption in *Yahushua HaMashakhYahu* and our genuine response to it. Acceptance of baptism in the name of *Yahushua HaMashakhYahu* upon hearing this Good News of Redemption about his suffering, death, burial, and resurrection to life according to the power of *Elohiym,* will bring to the repentant sinner the born again experience, the means for entering into the *Malchut HaElohiym,* and thus the salvation of *Elohiym.*

The Great Commission bears witness to these facts and reveals, in particular, the indispensable role of natural living waters to the salvation of the sinner. Anybody, who receives the Good News message in humility, shows remorse for his sins, repents of them, and is baptized in the name of *Yahushua HaMashakhYahu* by any of his true messengers in natural living waters, gains entry into the salvation of *Elohiym* and the Body of *Yahushua HaMashakhYahu.*

Baptism has, since the Old Covenant days, been the wisdom and power of *Elohiym* that separates the saved from the unsaved. Today, repentant sinners baptized in the name of *Yahushua HaMashakhYahu,* with understanding, become born again—that is, gain the new birth and thus enter the family of *Elohiym.*

The *Holy Scriptures* reveals that remission of sin, and not forgiveness of sin, is the power of *Elohiym* and His wisdom, which brings sinful man into His salvation in *Yahushua HaMashakhYahu*. And that remission of sin is only accessible through repentance from sin and baptism into the name of *Yahushua HaMashakhYahu*. These facts of *Elohiym* should constitute our faith in Him so as to bring us His salvation.

The practice of praying so-called *Sinners' Prayers*, in our attempt to enter the salvation of *Elohiym* in *Yahushua HaMashakhYahu*, is alien to the revelation of *Elohiym* in the *Holy Scriptures* for our salvation. The *Sinners' Prayer* doctrine is a detraction of the devil meant to confuse our understanding of the plan of *Elohiym* for our salvation, and therefore deny us its blessing.

The *Sinners' Prayer* has no power to save. It only brings simple-minded people into a delusion of being saved when they still remain in their weaknesses to sin. We must wake-up to the realities of Elohiym's plan and instructions for our salvation and move away from this detraction of the devil in praying *Sinners' Prayers* for salvation. This move, we must make now.

Chapter Three

Truths of Baptism Laid Bare

Before going into the next chapter of this book to embark on what I consider the most unpleasant part of this teaching assignment—why *Sinners' Prayer* recitals do not save—let me bring out, for the benefit of readers, some hidden truths on baptism from the *Holy Scriptures*. I suppose it would be easier for me, in the next chapter, to lay bare why the recitations of so-called *Sinners' Prayers* do not lead salvation seekers into the born again experience, and for readers to appreciate why this is so, if we first look at these revelations on baptism in this chapter.

I shall start to unfold these rare truths of *Elohiym* about baptism by teaching a few things about the malefactor, who was hanged beside *Yahushua HaMashakhYahu* and was promised paradise by him on that day the Savior was sacrificed.

Though many people know about this criminal blessed to enter paradise with *Yahushua HaMashakhYahu*, they are ignorant about the facts of his ancestry and history, in relation to his baptismal status before his death. A revelation about this malefactor in this regard will open up many hidden issues on baptism, and, hopefully, bring further understanding to readers about the great importance and indispensability of baptism for the salvation of any sinner, and for one's eligibility to enter *Shamayim*.

I would go on to look at the people who were in the upper room in *Yerushalayim* on whom *Ruwakh HaKodesh* was outpoured for the first time: "Pentecost"? Many people are ignorant that these upper room residents were baptized in the name of *Yahushua HaMashakhYahu* ahead of this day of outpouring and, therefore, were eligible to receive *Ruwakh HaKodesh* in their hearts.

Many people today think that these upper room residents received *Ruwakh HaKodesh* without baptism in natural living waters. As a result, many seek to obtain *Ruwakh HaKodesh* into their hearts without exercising true faith in the ordinance of baptism into the name of *Yahushua HaMashakhYahu*.

A teaching on the baptismal status of these upper room residents prior to the accounts of *Ma'asim (Acts)* 2:2-4 should bring to readers a clearer understanding of the teaching of *Yahushua HaMashakhYahu* to *Nakdimon* about the indispensability of water to being born again and of his Great Commission instructions of *Mattityahu (Matthew)* 28:18-20 and *Markos (Mark)* 16:15-16.

We shall consider in this chapter, in some detail, the question of who is eligible for baptism. Does *Elohiym* have a minimum age for baptism, or is a soul—whether aged a day or a hundred years— simply just a soul who needs salvation, and so should be eligible for baptism?

Though the question of where to administer baptism—which is, in natural living waters—might seem to have been answered already in this teaching, I would still like to go a little deeper into the issue. Must baptism be administered only in bodies of natural living waters or in man-made pools or tanks as well?

How must we administer baptism: Are we permitted to sprinkle, pour, or spray water with pumping machines on parts of peoples' bodies in our attempt to administer baptism into the name of *Yahushua HaMashakhYahu?* We shall look at all these issues in this chapter that showcases a lot of great revelations about baptism.

The Repentant Robber at *Gulgotha* and His Baptismal Status Before His Death and Other Related Issues.

Let us start the teachings of this chapter by looking at some issues related to the malefactor who was hanged along with *Yahushua HaMashakhYahu* who went to the defense of the Savior. We should refresh our memories by going to read the accounts of him in *Lukas (Luke)* 23:39-43:

"And one of the malefactors which were hanged railed on him saying, If thou be the Christ (HaMashakhYahu), save thyself and us. But the other answering rebuked him, saying, Dost not thou fear God (Elohiym), seeing thou art in the same condemnation? And we indeed justly, for we receive the due reward of our deeds: but this man has done nothing amiss. And he said unto Jesus (Yahushua HaMashakhYahu), Lord, (Adoni), remember me when thou comest into thy kingdom. And Jesus (Yahushua HaMashakhYahu) said unto him, Verily I say unto thee, To day shalt thou be with me in paradise."—Lukas (Luke) 23: 39-43, KJV; the words in parenthesis are mine.

Many people who read these verses conclude that, since this malefactor entered paradise—Avraham's Bosom (cf. *Luke* 16:23, KJV) or *Gan Eden* (cf. *Lukas* 23:43, OJB)—with *Yahushua*

HaMashakhYahu, apparently without baptism into his name, anybody today can enter the *Malchut HaElohiym* without baptism. I do not know when, or by whom, such a teaching came to mankind. The teacher of such an idea is ignorant of the teachings of the New Covenant faith. This malefactor is able to give clear and tangible proof of his baptism to anybody who confronts him anywhere beyond Earth on the issue. I shall soon tell you how.

Well, this malefactor, a robber, hanged beside *Yahushua HaMashakhYahu* did enter paradise with him without personally undergoing baptism into Yahushua's name—and so did many before him. *Avraham, Dovid, Shlomo* (Solomon), *Yechezkel* (Ezekiel), *El'azar* (Lazarus), and all the other Old Covenant holy men entered paradise without baptism into *Yahushua HaMashakhYahu,* as they all lived before the advent of the New Covenant.

He, like these men, met the conditions on baptism which were in place or needed to enter paradise at the time in the Law Dispensation. He was neither given any special concession to enter paradise, nor did he enter without baptism.

The curtain on the Law Dispensation was about to be brought down. In fact, this robber had only a few minutes or hours to act on the provisions of the Old Covenant, so as to redeem his image and qualify to enter paradise to be in the bosom of *Avraham.*

He was a Hebrew who run afoul of the *Law* and had to die for his bad ways. That was why he was hanged. He admitted himself that his punishment was deserved, and accepted it. By what he said, he had regretted his bad ways and repented of them as he hung beside *Yahushua HaMashakhYahu.*

Looking at the suffering *Yahushua HaMashakhYahu* hanged beside him, this thief saw how deserving his own punishment was for him as a wrong-doer. But for *Yahushua HaMashakhYahu,* who knew no wrong-doing, why should he suffer in the same manner as he, a robber? This would have led him deeper into repentance and a desire for Elohiym's mercy for the sinful life he lived on earth, which was soon to end for him.

His genuine repentance, recognition of *Yahushua HaMashakhYahu* as coming from *Elohiym,* and he humbly paying homage to him, earned him the right to be in paradise. He met the requirement at the last minute of what is seen in *YahuChanan (John)* 1:11-13 to be a child of *Elohiym* and to be in paradise, Avraham's bosom, after physical death. Let us capture these verses of *YahuChanan (John)* here:

"He came unto his own, and his own received him not. But as many as received him, to them gave he power to become the children of God (Elohiym), even them that believe on his name: which were born, not of blood, nor of the will of the flesh, nor of the will of man, but of God (Elohiym)"—YahuChanan (John) 1: 11-13, KJV; the words in parenthesis are mine.

Maybe these verses bring confusion to the minds of some people into believing that *Yahushua HaMashakhYahu* ministered salvation to non-Hebrews or Gentiles. This, however, is a complete misunder-standing of these verses. Many people who read these verses incorrectly interpret them to mean that *Yahushua HaMashakhYahu* came for Hebrews, but the Hebrews did not receive him, so to the many Gentiles who received him, he gave them power to become children of *Elohiym*.

Fact is that, *Yahushua HaMashakhYahu* did not, at any time during his earthly ministry, turn from Hebrews to Gentiles. He remained focused and committed to the few (**as many**) Hebrews who received him, to give them the power to spiritually become Elohiym's children. As *Yahushua HaMashakhYahu* said himself, and demonstrated in his actions, he came to bring the *Seh Oveid HaBais Yisroel* (lost sheep of the House of Yisroel) back to the fold—cf. *Mattityahu (Matthew)* 10:5-6, 15:24, and *Lukas (Luke)* 19: 9-10.

We should understand that *Yahushua HaMashakhYahu* lived his entire life in the Old Covenant. Oh yes, if you did not know this, let me say it again that *Yahushua HaMashakhYahu* lived all his years on earth in the Old Covenant as the last *navi* ("prophet") of that covenant. He lived in obedience to the rules, regulations, ordinances and privileges of the *Torah*.

He himself said he came to fulfill the *Torah*. How was he to fulfill it if he came at a time the Old Covenant had ended? He lived his entire earthly sojourn in the *Torah*, demonstrating to all that one could obey it entirely.

While *Yahushua HaMashakhYahu* lived in the *Torah*, he worked to write a new covenant for those who would believe in his work of salvation and have the wisdom of *Elohiym* to act so as to receive it. This work he did within his teaching and healing ministry. The climax of that written document is taught in the meaning of his sacrificial death, his resurrection, and the benefits arising thereof to sinful man.

By demonstrating the power of every part of that written

document in the way he lived, many people today seem to think that *Yahushua HaMashakhYahu* lived during the time the New Covenant was in effect or operation. Not so. He was simply living beyond his time and beyond his contemporaries, demonstrating to all what life under the New Covenant would be.

That is why many Hebrews of his days did not understand his teaching. It was when *Yahushua HaMashakhYahu* concluded the writing of the New Covenant document that he brought the Old Covenant, as it was then, to an end—cf. *Romans* 10:4. The life of *Yahushua HaMashakhYahu* was a foreshadowing of the good things and power of *Elohiym* that man would receive in his sacrifice, a demonstration of the *Elohiym* kind of life every believer in him was to receive and live.

You see, the New Covenant is the bequeathed Will of *Yahushua HaMashakhYahu* and could only come into effect after it was promulgated in *Shamayim* by *Elohiym*, after the death of *Yahushua HaMashakhYahu*. *Yahushua HaMashakhYahu* had to present to *HaAv*, in *Shamayim*, his blood of sacrifice before he could table a motion for the adoption of that written document of the New Covenant. When *Elohiym* accepted the motion of His only begotten Son, He added His Life (*Ruwakh HaKodesh*) to that document.

Then was *Ruwakh HaKodesh* of *Elohiym* made available to descend to Earth and dwell within the hearts of all people baptized in the name of *Yahushua HaMashakhYahu*, even taking into retrospective effect those baptized in his name before his death and resurrection. Therefore, even if one agrees with publishers of *The Bible* in their sectioning of a part of it as the "New Testament", such a section could only legally start with *Ma'asim (Acts)* 2:2 and not with *Mattityahu (Matthew)* 1:1, which is arbitrarily considered by many to be the beginning of the New Covenant document.

Clearly, therefore, the dispensation in which this robber was hanged was almost at the tail end of the Old Covenant dispensation. In that dispensation, anyone of *Yisroel* who lived in repentance of his sins, obeyed the *Torah*, and gave recognition and honor to the *neviim* ("prophets"), past or present—as messengers, bearers of good tidings, and information ministers, if you like—sent from *Elohiym*, earned life in the bosom of *Avraham* in paradise after physical death.

All these conditions and requirements this repentant robber satisfied, by his utterances, as he hung beside *Yahushua HaMashakhYahu*. It seems to me this robber was the last Hebrew man of the *Law Age* to enter life as a direct beneficiary of the earthly ministry of *Yahushua HaMashakhYahu*. I shall presently explain why I say this robber was the last direct beneficiary of the Savior's ministry on earth to the righteous people of the Old Covenant.

For the next fifty-three days after *Yahushua HaMashakhYahu* gave up the ghost at *Gulgotha*, any Hebrew who found his way into Avraham's bosom got there because he believed the testimony of *Yahushua HaMashakhYahu* based on revealed signs of him at the time and or in the historic past of *Yisroel*. Such a person believed *Yahushua HaMashakhYahu* to be indeed a messenger of *Elohiym* because of the signs that his death brought about, or that were foretold of by the prophets.

What I mean to say is that, within the days marking the death of *Yahushua HaMashakhYahu* and the coming of *Ruwakh HaKodesh*, Hebrews who came to believe in him, because they then saw signs about him in the *Neviim* manifested, got to Avraham's bosom, if they passed on within the period. Any Hebrew in these particular days who came to reality with the strange events surrounding the death of *Yahushua HaMashakhYahu* could reap some rewarding benefits that entitled him to enter paradise.

This was an open window of opportunity—not a door in a real sense, but an opening cut through the door—for the last crop of Old Covenant folks to finish their courses of life on earth in such a way so as to be qualified to enter paradise. This period marked the transition between the Old and New Covenants.

Yahushua HaMashakhYahu, HaSeh HaElohiym, had been led to the slaughter outside the walls of *Yerushalayim*. He neither defended himself, nor had anybody to defend him! An unusual darkness covered the earth for three hours before he yielded up his spirit at *Gulgotha*. The *Parochet* (curtain) of the *Beis HaMikdash* (Place of Sanctuary or *Yerushalayim* Temple) was torn into two—cf. *Mattityahu (Matthew)* 27:27-33, 45, and 50-51.

Then the earth quaked, cracked open, and caused some long dead holy people of *Yerushalayim* resting in their graves to wake-up and to make an obviously scary march into the Holy City to say hello to their living kinsmen—cf. *Mattityahu (Matthew)* 27:51-54. There was also the fact of the Savior's empty tomb. Oh, how the very wicked and most cruel soldiers would have beaten on their chests in deep repentance.

This period of fifty-three days was one characterized by silence. There was nobody to speak for *Elohiym*. *Yahushua HaMashakhYahu,*—the orator and crowd-pulling Savior—was, no longer present to teach on the hills, seashores, in the *Beis HaMikdash*, or in any *shul* (synagogue). His *talmidim* were nowhere to be found to say anything in his name. Every serious-minded Hebrew stayed to himself; reflecting, meditating and contemplating on the events, strange as they were, that characterized the death on earth of *Elohiym's* only begotten Son.

In their reflections on these strange events of Yahushua's death, some Hebrews living at the time could come to the conclusion that he who was killed outside the walls of the Holy City was indeed a true messenger of *Elohiym* sent to bless *Yisroel*. Once such a member of the house of *Yisroel* came to this conclusion and lived in repentance of sin for his role, and that of his fathers—the leaders of *Yisroel*—in the death of the Savior, he was on the way to reconciliation with *Elohiym* so as to qualify him to enter Avraham's bosom; that is, if such a person died before the Savior's bequeathed testament or will came into full force to affect his friends living at the time, and also those who would befriend him later on beyond these days.

Anyone of the house of *Yisroel* who did not receive *Yahushua HaMashakhYahu* during the time of his physical presence in ministry on earth had these days to believe in him as Elohiym's messenger, accept him, and obey him posthumously so as to qualify to enter paradise, if they died within this period. These were the last Hebrews of the Old Covenant dispensation, those who I consider not to have been direct or first-hand beneficiaries of the ministry of *Yahushua HaMashakhYahu* while he was physically present on earth to discharge it.

The window of opportunity, as earlier on mentioned, was one designed by *Elohiym* for those very drunk with the old wine to wake-up from their drunkenness and accept the reality of a change. The old wine had simply become vinegar and was, therefore, undrinkable. They had this short period to understand and accept this fact and to act in faith on the mission of *Yahushua HaMashakhYahu*, so as to qualify to enter Avraham's bosom if they died within this same period.

Beyond this time or opportunity, they were to be treated as dumb, stone-dead, cursed dogs, (Gentiles), who would need to be "physically" scrubbed-clean of their filthy sins in baptism in natural living waters, in the name of *Yahushua HaMashakhYahu*, together with all non-Hebrews, in order to qualify to enter paradise after death.

Nobody today can enter life in the similitude of the robber at

Gulgotha. This is because the dispensation in which this robber lived has long since rolled away. A new dispensation is now in place in today's times and it has its own ordinances, faiths, doctrines, and instructions as to how one can enter the *Malchut HaElohiym*, both on Earth and in the New *Yerushalayim* being prepared and to be delivered from *Shamayim* by *Elohiym* as the dwelling for all holy men, from righteous Seth, to *Noach*, *Avraham*, and to them that live throughout the Dispensation of Grace.

In today's Dispensation of Grace, repentance from sin, baptism in the name of *Yahushua HaMashakhYahu* for the remission of sins, and the receipt of the presence of *Ruwakh HaKodesh* to dwell within the hearts of faith-led people, bring them into the salvation of *Elohiym*. There is no other way.

Baptism in the name of *Yahushua HaMashakhYahu* is the one true ordinance that initiates penitent sinners into the salvation of *Elohiym*. It is sad that, even though many people have heard of Yahushua's born again teaching to *Nakdimon*, they are not taught to understand that it is in baptism that it is made real, and that it is only in baptism that one enters Elohiym's Kingdom.

I have met many people of today who want to enter paradise without baptism, presuming that the robber at *Gulgotha* did enter without it. They argue that if they do not have water to be baptized in, because they find themselves in some arid place where they come to hear the *Besuras HaGeulah*, can they not be saved?

What if, upon hearing the message of the *Besuras HaGeulah* and before they could respond to it in repentance and baptism, they die in, say, a motor accident, would they not enter the *Malchut HaElohiym*? I am persuaded that they will not, because they did not get to obey the instructions of *Elohiym* for salvation to the letter.

I hope that people will see these as funny hypothetical situations and not believe that they could become real in their lives. Dear reader, think about this: can *Elohiym*, who provided all the waters in the world and controls time for His pleasure, and who, for your salvation, sent *Yahushua HaMashakhYahu* to you, jeopardize your becoming born again by not sending you the needed natural living waters and time to bring this about? If this is your understanding of the Most High One, then I wonder if you truly have faith in Him.

Any sinner who hears the *Besuras HaGeulah*, and comes to the point of repentance from his sins, becomes a very valuable person before *Elohiym*. *Elohiym* will make sure such a person is given all the security and time to enable him rush into life—into *Yahushua HaMashakhYahu* in baptism. *Elohiym* is not going to leave such a person unprotected for the devil to kill him in any motor accident while on his way to obey Him for the baptism into *Yahushua HaMashakhYahu*.

All day long, *Elohiym* waited for the sinner to come to reason with himself and to repent of his sins so He could show him love. And now that the sinner has repented of his sins, *Elohiym* leaves him to the devil? No way. *Elohiym* sent His son, *Yahushua HaMashakhYahu*, to ensure our deliverance from the destruction of the devil.

The one who was killed in such a manner did not come to the point of repentance from sin. If he did, he would not be left exposed, without angelic protection, for the wicked one to touch him. In fact, any person who repents of his sins on hearing the message of the *Besuras HaGeulah* would be given the best angelic escorts to lead him to a place for baptism.

I am highly persuaded that the person who is killed in an accident after hearing the *Besuras HaGeulah*, but could not respond to it in baptism into *Yahushua HaMashakhYahu*, did not come to the point of repentance. Do not let the devil toy with your salvation by allowing him to hold your mind captive to such hypothetical and absurd situations alluded to earlier. Get real and get wise. Believe the Word of *Elohiym* and experience the joy and realities of being born again, of natural living waters and of *Ruwakh HaKodesh* of *Elohiym*.

To be born again of water and of *Ruwakh HaKodesh* is Elohiym's only formula for you to obtain the new birth, and He has committed all His power, love, resources and time towards you to bring it about. Run and accept life in His way. The instruction of your spiritual leader to seek to be born again through prayer—and of *Ruwakh HaKodesh*—will not earn you the salvation of *Elohiym* in *Yahushua HaMashakhYahu* that you seek. Do beware of this.

Please stop and think about why water is the most bountiful and most common commodity on Planet Earth. Waters cover about three quarters of the earth's surface and not in shallow depths. The earth's atmosphere is heavily laden with waters. The underground reserves of waters are huge. Waters are everywhere. There is no human community that is not crisscrossed by long and big rivers made by *Elohiym* for the convenience and comfort of His Creation.

Every year, *Elohiym* sends great replenishing in the form of rain, snow, and ice. *Elohiym* is forever committed to your needs of copious amounts of water and holds stocks of it in seas, rivers, lakes, ponds, and aquifers across the world for you. Water is crucial for biological life, but more importantly, water is crucial for spiritual life, and this is why it is readily available for our baptism into *Yahushua HaMashakhYahu.*

Elohiym says that water and His *Ruwakh Kodesh* will work together to bring you the new birth. *Yahushua HaMashakhYahu* says that, verily, verily, without water, you cannot enter life. In the midst of all the waters we can find everywhere in the world, you want to tell *Elohiym* that you did not get any for your baptism??

So, in your desperation, you decided that it was alright to pray the *Sinners' Prayer* to obtain the born again experience! You decided to copy the formula of the robber at *Gulgotha* to enter paradise. As he asked *Yahushua HaMashakhYahu* to remember him when he enters his kingdom, you too say a similar prayer to God (*Elohiym?*) to bring you the born again experience and His salvation??

I fear for you and your kind of faith, because *Elohiym* will one day ask you what use you put to all the waters He provided for humanity. When He sent His only begotten Son to let you know that without water you cannot enter the *Malchut HaElohiym*, you still did not have any faith in Him to go out to search for that body of living waters so crucial for your born again experience.

If you were with me in Ghana, Africa, and *Elohiym* had said to you to go get baptized in the name of *Yahushua HaMashakhYahu* in the *Yarden* of the Middle East in order to be born again, I would urge you to go sell enough of your possessions to make that trip. My advice would be based on two reasons.

The first would be based on my knowledge of how *Elohiym* demands complete and absolute obedience to His instructions. Being perfect in all He does, *Elohiym* demands perfection from all He deals with. I, therefore, would have advised you not to end up in the Volta, the Nile, or any well-known river of your home country since your born again experience was not ordained by *Elohiym* to come about anywhere but in the *Yarden*.

I would have reminded you of how *Na'aman* (Naaman) almost went back to his better fancied *Avana* (Abana) and *Parpar* (Pharpar) rivers of his native *Aram* (Syria), instead of going for his miracle destination, the *Yarden*, and nearly missed his healing from leprosy—cf. *Melekhim Bais (Second Kings)* 5:8-14.

Secondly, I would urge you to undertake the long, arduous and expensive trip to the *Yarden*, knowing the blessings of being born again. To be born again is to have *Elohiym* make you His child. To be born again is to gain entry into Elohiym's Kingdom.

To be born again is to have your name written in blood, in *HaSefer HaChayyim* (the Book of Life). To be born again is to have *Sha'arei HaShamayim* (the Gates of Heaven) open to you unconditionally, any time you ever arrive there to visit or to stay through eternity.

So do not be ridiculous; *Elohiym* is not sending you to far away *Yarden* to be born again. Go out there and seek out that nearby body of living waters and get baptized in it in the name of *Yahushua HaMashakhYahu*, so you can be born again and eligible to spend eternity with *Elohiym* in *Shayamin*.

Follow the example of *Yahushua HaMashakhYahu*. He walked without the ease, convenience, or comfort of a camel, donkey or chariot ride, from far up-country *Galil* (Galilee) to the parts of *Yarden* near Bethabara (Beit-Bar?—meaning, House of Cleansing?) to get baptized by *YahuChanan (John)*—cf. *Mattityahu (Matthew)* 3:13 and *YahuChanan (John)* 1:28-29. That was how important baptism was to him even though he had no sins to wash away or any need to be made a child of *Elohiym* since he was, up to that time, the only Son begotten of *Elohiym*. He only did so to set an example to his followers. So follow his example—keep walking until you get to that body of water needed for your baptism.

Maybe, you should also follow the example of the Ethiopian eunuch who kept on riding in his chariot with his eyes widely opened, looking out for that natural body of water of crucial value for his baptism. In Philippi, as an example to you, dear reader, a jailor literally ran out of his home to get his baptism at midnight, no doubt in the river on whose bank the city was built—cf. *Ma'asim (Acts)* 16:12-13 and 25-33.

Why not emulate the determination of many people who, when under demonic oppression, would travel long distances from their homes in search of deliverance from "men of God". Get out there and take a walk to your baptism and into life. Do not stay in that arid place complaining of lack of water and, in a sense, blaming *Elohiym* for that lack.

Why would you wish to enter life in the manner of the robber at *Gulgotha*, ignorant of what his ancestor did for him, spiritually, centuries before his birth, in the act of crossing the *Yarden* into Canaan under the leadership of *Yehoshua*? Why damn and throw away all the evidence in the accounts of the *Holy Scriptures* of how believers of the message of the *Besuras HaGeulah* in the early days of the Grace Dispensation did enter their salvation? Why do you not find, in those accounts of the early followers of *Yahushua HaMashakhYahu*, a deeper desire to enter life in the same manner that they did, rather than in a manner after the similitude of the robber at *Gulgotha*?

My dear reader, please accept the only true way that *Shimon Kefa* led over three thousand people into the salvation of *Elohiym* on the Day of the Outpouring of *Ruwakh HaKodesh* (Pentecost?) in *Yerushalayim*, to ensure that yours is also genuine and sure. I entreat you by the mercies of *Elohiym* to do this with a sense of urgency so that your name can be written in *HaSefer HaChayyim*.

I shall give you a great revelation pointing to the indispensability of baptism for the sinner's entry into the *Malchut HaElohiym*. Not many people know about it, even though it is conspicuously placed in the *Holy Scriptures*.

Only the few people who spend valuable time meditating on the significance of baptism can be blessed to have this understanding from the *Holy Scriptures*. Many theologians and other professors of Christianity miss this revelation simply because they do not apply their hearts and minds to fathom out the great value of baptism.

Elohiym would not easily or readily give the kind of wisdom He gave to King *Shlomo* (Solomon) to one of the king's errands-men for one simple reason—the errands-man of the king would not be a person who was likely to apply his heart to puzzling issues of conflict resolution and the judgment of evil deeds done in secret.

That is the worry of any king in his judgment seat. It is the worry of kings to obtain wisdom in discerning which of the parties before their thrones are guilty. It is therefore more natural for *Elohiym* to grant revelation knowledge to those who desire it and seek for it from Him with all diligence, rather than to those who do not.

For a long time, I meditated on the issue of the robber at *Gulgotha* entering paradise seemingly without baptism. Then, one day, *Elohiym* gave me a revelation while I meditated on this issue. This revelation is what I call a "breakthrough" revelation on the indispensability of baptism to becoming born again.

Of course, if you believe that baptism is a post-salvation rite, which does not really add to or subtract from the salvation you claim to have received in the reciting of a so-called *Sinners' Prayer*, you will not be blessed to receive from *Elohiym* this revelation about the baptismal status of this robber at *Gulgotha*. Why? Because you've found what you seek!!

What you do not seek is unimportant to you, so why would *Elohiym* lead you to His secrets in that direction? Now get ready for Elohiym's revelation about the baptismal status of this robber long before he was hanged at *Gulgotha* beside *Yahushua HaMashakhYahu*.

Elohiym has given me the revelation that everybody I will meet in *Shamayim* can give me legal proof to his baptism. According to this revelation to me, everybody who finds his way into *Shamayim* will get there through baptism. Oh yes, everybody. Every holy worshipper of *Elohiym*, before, in and after Noach's flood till now, and unto the end of time, enters *Shamayim* through baptism.

This includes the repentant robber at *Gulgotha*. He has proof of his baptism to show you if you ever get to meet him in *Shamayim* or try to challenge *Elohiym* about it. So why do many people suppose that the robber at *Gulgotha* entered paradise without baptism?

Lack of knowledge is the answer. I mean lack of revelation knowledge: the kind of deep insight from the mind and wisdom of *Elohiym* given by *Ruwakh HaKodesh* to people who seek the deep, rich secrets of the Most High One. I could take you to a place in the *Yarden* River, opposite the plains of *Yericho* (Jericho), where this robber at *Gulgotha* was baptized while in the loins of his ancestor in the days of *Yehoshua*.

Noach and his family will enter *Shamayim* with proof of the baptism they received in the flood—cf. *Kefa Alef (First Peter)* 3:20-21. When *Noach* and his family were baptized in the flood, his three sons had in them the seed of all mankind in their loins. Their descendants who lived holy lives in the sight of *Elohiym* will find their way into *Shamayim* because their ancestors, Noach's sons, were baptized on their behalf while they were held captive in the loins of these ancestors.

Such holy descendants of *Noach* and his sons came down to include *Avraham*, *Yitzchak* (Isaac), and *Ya'akov* (Jacob). All these had their ancestor Shem, Noach's eldest son, baptized for them while they were in his loins.

Yosef, the son of *Ya'akov*, and his brothers who went to live in *Mitzrayim* could all trace their baptism to Shem's. They will therefore have in *Shamayim* the legal proof of their baptism received in Noach's flood.

When the premier generations of the nation of *Yisroel* who lived in *Mitzrayim* died, their descendants were ready to be moved by *Elohiym* to their Land of Promise given to their great ancestor, *Avraham*. As they journeyed with *Moshe* toward this Promised Land, they were baptized in the Red Sea—cf. *First Corinthians* 10:1-2—as their first spiritual experience of that journey. Every male member of the house of *Yisroel* who was of age militarily, and biologically matured to reproduce, was baptized unto *Moshe* in the Red Sea, and so all the seed of coming generations of *Yisroel* held in their loins were also baptized.

These men misbehaved in the wilderness, however, and made their baptism unto *Moshe* of no effect. All the biologically mature and militarily capable men who left *Mitzrayim* under *Moshe*, died because of their disobedience to *Elohiym*. The children born unto these men while in the wilderness, together with those who left *Mitzrayim* when they were not of age militarily, later came face to face with the River *Yarden* on their journey to the Promised Land. *Elohiym* planned it that way so that they had to cross the *Yarden* into Canaan.

At the *Yarden*, all the now militarily mature men aged twenty and above, who were for that matter also of reproductive age, were led to cross the *Yarden* under *Yehoshua* in exactly the same fashion that their disobedient ancestors crossed the Red Sea. They were all therefore baptized unto *Yehoshua* in the crossing of *Yarden* with all yet-to-be born children of *Yisroel* in their loins.

Ever since that historic crossing of *Yarden*, every child born to *Yisroel* can legitimately trace his ancestry to one of those mature men that crossed the *Yarden* under *Yehoshua*, and can show proof of his baptism in theirs.

Every child of *Yisroel* at the point of being conceived received in his "spiritual DNA" vibrant "baptismal genes" from his great, great, ancestor, who was part of the convoy that made the historic crossing of the *Yarden* into Canaan under the leadership of *Yehoshua*. These "baptismal genes" were passed on to him in a relay-race fashion by that ancestor, through the men of his lineage.

The evidence of these "baptismal genes" in the "spiritual DNA" of every child of *Yisroel* was proof that he was a child of *Avraham* and legally put him on the way to paradise or Avraham's bosom—a stopover to *Shamayim*—after death. At the gates of paradise, every member of the house of *Yisroel* was "scanned" for this special "baptismal gene" in his "spiritual DNA." Anyone without it was refused entry.

You could lose the "baptismal gene" in your "spiritual DNA" and be negative when you are "scanned" for it. You would then be considered a Gentile and not eligible to enter paradise, Avraham's bosom, when you arrived at the gate.

How could one lose these "baptismal genes" in one's "spiritual DNA"? One could lose them through sin. When one sinned at will and became incapable of receiving chastisement, admonition, and correction, one progressively darkened one's "baptismal genes" until they became invisible in that person's "spiritual DNA."

These genes became blurred in the initial stages of the sinful life. They continued to grow darker and darker every day in sin and, with the passage of time, these genes became dark and undetectable by the "scanning machine." In that state, the "scanning machine" would come out with no evidence of the sinner's status as a member of the house of *Yisroel* fit for entry into paradise, Avraham's bosom. Then that person would be turned away from entering the gate.

The good thing for every sinful member of the house of *Yisroel* was that, anytime he went back to his senses and stopped sinning he had the "baptismal genes" in his "spiritual DNA" brought back to life with renewed shine, as to be detectable by the "scanning machine." If the member of the house of *Yisroel* who enjoyed sinning, now came to the point of repentance, obeyed the *Torah* about how to secure atonement of and cleansing from sin, and lived in the obedience and honor of the *neviim*, paying them their due respect as teachers or messengers sent to him from *Elohiym*, he had his "baptismal genes" brought back to such dazzling brightness as to be able to pass the sensitivity tests of the "scanning machine." This condition of his "baptismal genes" cleared him for entry into paradise.

The repentant robber at *Gulgotha*, at the last minute, did all that was required of him to meet the compliance sensitivity test of the "scanning machine" for his "baptismal genes" at the gates of paradise. He probably did not know this himself. However, *Yahushua HaMashakhYahu* knew that this criminal, by his state of heart while at *Gulgotha*, could pass this "Baptismal Gene Sensitivity Test", and that he had these genes in his "Spiritual DNA" so highly sensitized to the "scanning machine" that it qualified him for entry into paradise.

Do not try to challenge *Elohiym* as to why the robber at *Gulgotha* entered paradise, seemingly without baptism, if you are denied entry into *Shamayim* because you did not wise up to the revelations of the *Holy Scriptures* and, consequently, did not rush for baptism into *Yahushua HaMashakhYahu*.

You may be thinking that the robber at *Gulgotha* was blessed more than you are because he did not have to physically go through the act of baptism, or because his ancestor was baptized on his behalf. Well, in that latter sense, you might be right.

Do you not understand, however, that the New Covenant holy ones are rather the envy of the Old Covenant folks? In fact, all the Old Covenant folks are waiting for you to quickly get born again of water and of *Ruwakh HaKodesh* so that, in that birth, they can be made perfect. You delay their attainment of perfection by your ignorance of how one is born again into the *Malchut HaElohiym*—of water and of *Ruwakh HaKodesh* in baptism.

Of all men of the house of *Yisroel*, Elohiym's chosen people, there is none born into this world without being baptized ahead of his birth; that is, before the New Covenant dispensation. *Yahushua HaMashakhYahu* is the only exception. Why was that so? It is simply because he did not come through the male line of *Yisroel*. He had no biological father as a man of *Yisroel*. He could therefore not be found in the loins of any of the men that crossed *Yarden* under *Yehoshua*, at the time they did.

Yahushua HaMashakhYahu had only an affiliation with the tribe of *Yahudah* (Judah) for Dovid's sake, which was why he was called the son of *Dovid*. *Yahushua HaMashakhYahu* identified with *Yahudah* in just the same way that he did with all sinners in his vicarious death. He could not be part of the corruption and immoral sexual stains of the bloodline of *Yahudah* that ran from the days of Tamar (I), *Rahav* (Rahab), Ruth, the wife of *Uriyah* (Uriah), and Tamar (II), to the uncontrollable sexuality of *Shlomo*, by descending from it.

To meet the righteous requirements of *Elohiym* for his entry into paradise with this robber, and re-entry into *Shamayim*, *Yahushua HaMashakhYahu* himself had need to be baptized by *YahuChanan ben Zecharyahu*. *YahuChanan ben Zecharyahu* was also baptized long before his birth, so he could be qualified to baptize the Savior!

You can now understand the ***"Fulfillment of all righteousness"*** statement of *Yahushua HaMashakhYahu* that has been grossly misunderstood and developed into something else. Every person who leaves Earth, homebound, must show the evidence of his baptism while on earth at the gates of paradise—and of *Shamayim*—before being cleared to enter.

That is Elohiym's law: and thus, even *Yahushua HaMashakhYahu* was not made immune to that law. Because *Yahushua HaMashakhYahu* knew of this fact, he could cry out to *Nakdimon*, **"Omein, omein, I say to you: unless someone is born of mayim (water) and of Ruwakh HaKodesh, he is not able to enter the Malchut HaElohiym (Kingdom of Elohiym)"—YahuChanan 3:5, the Orthodox Jewish Bible, OJB; words in parenthesis are mine.**

Let me say that after *Yahushua HaMashakhYahu* resurrected and ascended to *Shamayim*, and had his New Covenant ratified by *HaAv*, all the "baptismal genes" in the "spiritual DNA" of all living children of *Yisroel* were wiped out. Every living child of *Yisroel*, together with all Gentiles after Yahushua's New Covenant came into being and effect, had to acquire a special "baptismal gene," possessed by *Yahushua HaMashakhYahu* only, into his or her "spiritual DNA" to qualify to enter *Shamayim*, Elohiym's Abode. These special "baptismal genes" come into the "spiritual DNA" of every repentant sinner who understands and receives the baptism in the name of *Yahushua HaMashakhYahu*. This is the mystery of the born again experience.

Baptism is the invention of *Elohiym* to bring salvation to mankind. This is Elohiym's plan; it has not and will not change. Baptism since the days of *Noach* has served the same purpose: it brings people into the salvation of *Elohiym*.

Noach's baptism was in 2348 BCE, according to historians. It had the potency of bringing salvation to him and his family at the time. That baptism also gave spiritual power to all righteous people of his lineage to live holy lives. This continued for about 427 years, up to the year 1921 BCE. Such righteous descendants of *Noach* came down to include *Avraham*, who was born out of the loins of Shem, Noach's eldest son.

In 1921 BCE, when the time of Elohiym's plan to establish the nation of *Yisroel* became due, He called *Avraham* and told him to leave his father's house of idol worshippers to a land he was to give him and his descendants for an inheritance. *Elohiym* then led *Avraham* to cross the Euphrates River—cf. *Yehoshua (Joshua)* 24:2-3, the OJB; the New Living Translation; and the Living Bible,—an act (of baptism by *Elohiym*?) that made Him sever his links with the land of his ancestors, and from his people, forever.

The crossing of the Euphrates was Elohiym's manner of purifying *Avraham* and his seed—then in his loins—which made them holy, separated from the rest of the world, and His own, forever. Many years after *Avraham* crossed the Euphrates, the time became due for him to bring forth the seed in his loins that had been made pure and holy by *Elohiym* in the rite of crossing the Euphrates.

Later, this holy seed of *Avraham*, begotten through *Ya'akov*, went to live in *Mitzrayim* according to the plan of *Elohiym*. While in *Mitzrayim*, this seed enjoyed the potency and blessing of the baptism in the Euphrates of their great grandfather, *Avraham*. When the potency of that baptism seemed to be waning, they were ready to be moved by *Elohiym* to their Promised Land.

In the year 1491 BCE, exactly 430 years after the *Call of Avraham*, *Elohiym* led *Yisroel* to cross the Red Sea on pilgrimage to Canaan. By that crossing, *Elohiym* gave a big boost to the potency of the baptism of the Euphrates. Sadly, however, the children of *Yisroel* did not understand the spiritual significance of the crossing of the Red Sea, so they misbehaved against *Elohiym* in the wilderness.

Forty years later in 1451 BCE, this baptism of the Red Sea was revitalized in the crossing of the *Yarden* for more deserving children of *Yisroel* than those who crossed the Red Sea. The potency of that baptism in the *Yarden* sustained *Yisroel* until about 26 to 30 CE, in this case, for over 1400 years.

Everyone of the house of *Yisroel* who was spiritually alive in the expectation of the Savior knew that the Age of *HaMashakhYahu* would be characterized by mass baptisms. Many knew that baptism was to be a characteristic of the Age of *HaMashakhYahu*. When many saw *YahuChanan ben Zecharyahu* ministering baptism freely in the *Yarden*, they thought he was their expected Savior from *Elohiym*.

It was as if the Old Covenant symbolism of baptism, seen in the permanently buried twelve-stone altar (the Twelve Tribes of *Yisroel*?) in the waters of the *Yarden*—cf. *Yehoshua (Joshua)* 4:9— had then sprouted into reality in a vibrant spiritual life as *HaMashakhYahu* was about to surface. The spiritual leaders of *Yisroel*, therefore, sent to *YahuChanan ben Zecharyahu*, *Levi'im* (Levites), to inquire if he were *HaMashakhYahu* from *Elohiym*. He told them he was *Kol Korey Bamidbar* (The Voice of One Crying in the Wilderness)—cf. *Yeshayahu (Isaiah)* 40:3. Surprised at or disappointed with his answer, they asked him why he baptized if he was not *HaMashakhYahu*—cf. *YahuChanan (John)* 1:19-27.

Yahushua HaMashakhYahu came with the final and everlasting boost of this invention of *Elohiym* to bring eternal salvation to all. Baptism in the name of *Yahushua HaMashakhYahu* is the ordinance of *Elohiym*, which, when received in faith, understanding and in accordance with the instructions of the Master, will bring any sinner into Elohiym's salvation.

When *Yahushua HaMashakhYahu* talked with *Nakdimon*, he expressed surprise about his ignorance of the importance and indispensability of baptism as the entry requirement into the *Malchut HaElohiym*. *Yahushua HaMashakhYahu* was, in a sense, not only reproving *Nakdimon* for not knowing what lay ahead of *Yisroel* in this regard, but he was also unhappy with *Nakdimon* for not applying his heart to the meaning of the many shadows of baptism in the Old Covenant document of the *Holy Scriptures*.

Nakdimon ought to have understood these shadows, which at sundry times brought salvation to *Yisroel*, as being forerunners to the baptism to be received in the name of *Yahushua HaMashakhYahu* with understanding in his sacrificial death and in his resurrection. *Nakdimon*, being a spiritual leader of *Yisroel*, ought to have known that to be born of water and of *Ruwakh HaKodesh* through baptism in the name of *Yahushua HaMashakhYahu*, properly understood in the context of the prototype baptisms of *Noach*, *Moshe* and *Yehoshua*, was the only way into the *Malchut HaElohiym*.

Yahushua HaMashakhYahu was disappointed with *Nakdimon* in that, despite the ongoing baptism of *YahuChanan ben Zecharyahu*, this spiritual leader of *Yisroel* did not see in it the reechoing of events of the past (shadows), which brought salvation to *Yisroel*, and the imminent one by *HaMashakhYahu* as the fulfillment of these shadows. Do we have any people like *Nakdimon* today? I shudder to think we have an awful lot of them.

Where do all these teachings on "baptismal genes" in "spiritual DNA" from ancestors and our entry into *Shamayim* come from? Let us go to the book of *Ivriim (Hebrews)* for the answer. Please read in *Ivriim (Hebrews)* the account about *Avraham* giving tithes to *Melekh-Tzedek* (Melchizedek).

Tithes? Yes, tithes. Go to *Ivriim (Hebrews)* 7:9-10. *Avraham* gave tithes to *Melekh-Tzedek* (My King of Righteousness) on behalf of his great, grandson, Levi, while Levi was in his loins.

Loins, loins, loins! It must be clear now. How did we miss this for so long? Every person who came out of *Avraham* after he gave tithes to *Melekh-Tzedek* was a tithe-giver legally, all his lifetime.

By this same principle must the issue of the baptism of any son of *Yisroel* for his entry into paradise be understood! If you were a son of *Yisroel*, because your ancestor was baptized—with you in his loins—you were bound to the blessings of *Elohiym* arising from that act of your ancestor on your behalf, while the relevance of that baptism remained.

The repentant robber at *Gulgotha* entered paradise while the relevance of the baptism that his ancestors received in the crossing of the *Yarden* under *Yehoshua* lasted. The potency of that baptism lasted until the Day of the Outpouring of *Ruwakh HaKodesh* (Pentecost?) in *Yerushalayim*. Then, the baptism in the name of *Yahushua HaMashakhYahu* came into effect and replaced this particular one, which had then waxed powerless, and had became irrelevant and defunct under a new dispensation.

I hope you do not forget that all mankind sinned in the First Adam. Because every human being was held in the loins of the First Adam when he sinned in the *Gan Eden*, all men sinned then, even before being born into the world. Today, all unsaved mankind sin not by choice, but by cause. The First Adam made all his descendants sinners when he sinned while they were in his loins!

Yahushua HaMashakhYahu, the Second Adam, came to rescue man in this—cf. *Romans* 5:12 and 17-19. Everybody today who wants to get to *Shamayim* must of need obey the command of *Yahushua HaMashakhYahu* to be baptized into him for the remission of sin, and thereby be born of water and of *Ruwakh HaKodesh*. Baptism is the only way to be begotten by, made the seed of, and transformed into the image of the Second Adam, *Yahushua HaMashakhYahu*. *HalleluYahu!*

Well, this big shout of *HalleluYahu* did not end the matter entirely. I still had questions about how the righteous of the pre-flood generations would be cleared to enter *Shamayim* in baptism, because they too, like our friend the repentant robber at *Gulgotha*, do not seem to have received any before death. For this, *Elohiym* proceeded to teach me gradually. The revelation about their baptismal status that enables them to enter *Shamayim* came to me after days of living in *Bereshis (Genesis)* chapters one and two, and meditating also on the earthly ministry of *Yahushua HaMashakhYahu*.

I shall soon tell you more about what I learned in *Bereshis* chapter one. For now, let me tell you just this: take it or leave it, the First Adam was baptized. If you can take it further up the ladder of faith, the First Adam was baptized since the Earth that brought him forth was called out of waters.

Please understand that the First Adam is a product of the earth, which was itself brought forth by and of waters. The First Adam was in the loins of "Father Earth" when the Earth was begotten by and of waters. As the First Adam was baptized while in the loins of Father Earth, so were all his descendants in his loins with him!

You see how far the shadows of baptism can be from ours in *Yahushua HaMashakhYahu*, which is the reality! Remember *Yahushua HaMashakhYahu* came to earth not for his own benefit but for that of the entire humanity—those who lived from Creation, including those who will be living at the end-time.

Yahushua HaMashakhYahu came to do the will of *HaAv* so that by that obedience, *Elohiym* would ratify the deeds of all the righteous people who ever lived on earth before the advent of his coming. He also established the legal document, *The Kingdom Constitution*, if you will, by which any mortal after his advent to earth would be enabled to enter the *Malchut HaElohiym*.

Elohiym, in the baptism of *Yahushua HaMashakhYahu* by *YahuChanan ben Zecharyahu* ratified all the shadows of baptism we can find in mankind's history from the time of Creation. Elohiym's wisdom and grace are so deep. They are beyond measure. The fulfillment of the righteous requirement of *Elohiym*, for *Yahushua HaMashakhYahu* to take baptism at the hand of *YahuChanan ben Zecharyahu*, marked the beginning of a process to bring all the pre-flood and post-flood righteous into the salvation of *Elohiym*.

Yahushua's baptism at the hand of *YahuChanan* qualified all the righteous people from Creation until his advent to enter *Shamayim* with proof or evidence of their baptism. That baptism of *Yahushua HaMashakhYahu* by *YahuChanan ben Zecharyahu* gave legal validity to all manner of shadow baptisms, inclusive of that received by all of the post-Creation righteous as they were baptized while in the loins of our first ancestor, the First Adam. This legal validity qualifies them to enter *Shamayim* with a tangible proof of their baptism.

To ratify means to give legal recognition, backing, or approval to something that has happened in the past, is happening in the present, or will happen in the future, a combination of these or all of these. *Elohiym*, by ratifying all shadows of baptism from Creation to the time of Yahushua's baptism, gave legal recognition to all these shadow baptisms as the means and proof for entry into the *Malchut HaElohiym*.

By that same ratification, He gave legal backing to all baptisms into the name of *Yahushua HaMashakhYahu* following his resurrection to be adequate, valid, and sufficient proof of qualification for the entry of any person into the *Malchut HaElohiym*. The Master would not have *Nakdimon* be ignorant of this, and so he cried out loudly to him; *"Omein, omein, I say to you: unless someone is born of mayim (water) and of Ruwakh HaKodesh, he is not able to enter the Malchut HaElohiym (Kingdom of Elohiym)"—YahuChanan 3:5, OJB; words in parenthesis are mine.*

You can say that *Elohiym* did credit card business with all the post-Creation righteous of humanity before the coming of *Yahushua HaMashakhYahu*. In anticipation of the scope and efficacy of the redeeming work of *Yahushua HaMashakhYahu*, *Elohiym* credited righteousness to those worthy humans who lived in manners that pleased Him. *Elohiym* did credit business with such people, with the plan and scheme in place, with the knowledge that their Savior and Redeemer, *Yahushua HaMashakhYahu*, would come to pay-up their debts of sin on their behalf. Oh, what love *Elohiym* has shown to humanity in His gift of *Yahushua HaMashakhYahu* to the world.

Yahushua HaMashakhYahu comes onto the spiritual scene of Planet Earth as its Savior sent by *HaAv*. Then he starts paying for the sins of men, left, right, and centre. He pays for the sins of all past humanity committed before his coming. He pays for the sins of those living at the time of his sacrifice. Then, He pays in advance for all manner of debts due *Elohiym* for the sins of those to be born into humanity after his departure from earth!

This deposit payment for those following him into the Earth after his sacrifice must have been huge and inexhaustible. Every human being coming to the earth after Yahushua's physical exit can freely draw from this bank at anytime, with no hindrance, and have his debts of sin paid, so he can live happily and free of sin on earth thereafter. What a grace of *Elohiym* this is!

That is to tell you how powerful the sacrifice of *Yahushua HaMashakhYahu* was in its ordained plan of *Elohiym* to take away the sins of the world. The sacrifice of *Yahushua HaMashakhYahu* had efficacy to cover and take away the sins of mankind, from the times of the First Adam to the End-time. It was a great sacrifice with retroactive power and of retrospective effect, which had been excellently designed by a mind that could only belong to *Elohiym*.

The righteous of the pre-flood generations were later to have the second stage of their redemption unfold in the ministry of *Yahushua HaMashakhYahu*, as he went to preach to their spirits in prison—cf. *Ephesians* 4:8-11, *Kefa Alef (First Peter)* 3:19-20 and 4:6. Do remember that *Yahushua HaMashakhYahu* said he had other sheep in another sheepfold that needed to be brought together with those of *Yisroel*—cf. *YahuChanan (John)* 10:16. This was long after *Yahushua HaMashakhYahu* had received his baptism at the hands of *YahuChanan ben Zecharyahu* in fulfillment of the righteous requirement of *HaAv*.

Mark the words of *Yahushua HaMashakhYahu* in this verse very well. *Yahushua HaMashakhYahu* said he already had some sheep elsewhere that needed to hear his voice as *Ro'eh HaTov* (the Good Shepherd), to be brought into the sheepfold of *Yisroel*. *Yahushua HaMashakhYahu* was not talking then about Gentiles who were to be saved later in his sacrifice. At the time *Yahushua HaMashakhYahu* was speaking, he did not have any Gentile sheep as yet.

Yahushua HaMashakhYahu was talking about the dead pre-flood righteous—cf. *YahuChanan (John)* 5:25—whose deeds were worthy of the ratification of *HaAv* to enable them enter *Shamayim*, when its gates are flung open for all righteous people to enter for the Great Feast—cf. *Mattityahu (Matthew)* 22:2-14, *Lukas (Luke)*. *Yahushua HaMashakhYahu* undertook the ministry of preaching the *Besuras HaGeulah* to these pre-flood righteous people, between the hours immediately following his resurrection and just when it became public knowledge through the activities of *Miryam* of *Magdala* (Mary Magdalene), and *Shimon Kefa* and *YahuChanan*, two of the inner core *Shlikhim* of *Yahushua HaMashakhYahu*.

At the end of that ministry, he burst forth toward *Shamayim* with a cloud of the righteous men of the pre-flood generation (*Ephesians* 4:8) to send them to their prepared stopover place of rest (Second Heaven?—*HaSheni HaShamayim?*) to continue their wait there for the final events of Kingdom Calendar—the resurrection of the dead, the Judgment of the Lamb, and the Great Feast of the King of all kings.

Maybe, and I mean maybe, there are three distinct places of rest for the spirits of the departed righteous since Creation, where they await the End-time Resurrection. There is, as we are told in the

Holy Scriptures, Avraham's bosom, a transit quarters for the spirits of *Avraham* and all his righteous children, awaiting the resurrection. Then there is a Third Heaven (*HaShlishi HaShamayim*), visited by *Sha'ul*—cf. *Second Corinthians* 12:2. This is a place distinct from Avraham's bosom. It has its own inhabitants whose life and worship of *Elohiym, Sha'ul* was blessed to observe on a visit there. *HaShlishi HaShamayim* (Third Heaven) might possibly be a place of waiting for the spirits of *Noach,* his sons, and their righteous descendants of the post-flood generations just before the *Call of Avraham.*

Having been told of a Third Heaven, there must be a Second and a First where *Sha'ul* was never taken to by *Elohiym* on a visit. First Heaven might be the same as the Highest Heaven (*Shomei HaShamayim*) the place of Abode of *Elohiym,* while Second Heaven (*HaSheni HaShamayim*) could be the stopover location of the pre-flood righteous of Seth and the righteous among the generations after him, but not including *Noach.*

It might seem we have three departed grandfathers to whom all righteous people who depart this earth gather: Seth, *Noach,* and *Avraham.* Each might seem to have their own city of abode in the Heavens. Anyway, all this is pure conjecture. I am not presenting a doctrine in this.

Let me give you some revelation on baptism by sharing with you more on what I learned from my studies of *Bereshis* chapter one. From the time of Creation, *Elohiym* has manifested His wisdom and power in waters. All the birds of the air, the beasts of the fields, and the fishes of the seas were brought forth by waters and are, therefore, of waters. The earth is the child of waters, begotten of and by waters. As mentioned earlier on, the First Adam was begotten indirectly of waters since the dust he was formed of was begotten of waters.

Please read *Bereshis* chapter one once again: note well the verses 9-10, 20-22, and 24-25. It is awesome when we understand what story of creation we are told in this chapter. Waters brought forth all things, inclusive of light, the firmament, sun, moon, stars, and planets. For those who can stretch their faith and understanding of Elohiym's revelation on His work of Creation, they are able to accept this fact.

In the book *Hisgalus (Revelation),* we are told that all the dead in the seas would be begotten in a resurrection for judgment. This is in *Hisgalus (Revelation)* 20:13. We do not see the dead bodies of men in the sea now, do we? No, we do not.

The dead bodies of men in the sea have been dissolved and recycled into the molecules of seawater; thus, in effect returning to the waters they came from! The molecules of seawater are Elohiym's storage tanks of the dead in the sea, and await His command to resurrect from there.

You know how sugar granules are dissolved and lost in water and yet exist in the water? That is how the dead in the sea have become over the years after reaching there. The seawater will bring them forth on *Yom HaAcharon* (the Last Day) for judgment.

Between Creation and *Yom HaAcharon*, *Elohiym* maintains a consistency in bringing forth the new life in waters. The New Creation, therefore, is one made in, by, and of, waters. The New Creation is not a product of dry land or of a dry, airy church-room; it is one born of waters, and in waters, as was in the beginning and shall be in the end.

Causing waters to bring forth has always been Elohiym's way of bringing forth new life into the world; bringing forth the sinner into a New Creation as a product of waters in baptism is His special invention and miracle.

When sinful man submerges, momentarily, in baptismal waters, he is completely dissolved in the nanoseconds of reaching the water. This is the wisdom of *Elohiym* and therefore a mystery. Elohiym's plan to recreate mortal man demands that man should enter the waters of baptism for Him to dissolve his elements into the waters from which he is raised to a newness that boggles the mind.

Sinful man enters the waters of baptism as earth material, dust in fact, with almost zero water content as it were. Man's Adamic nature is the dust. This is lost in the waters as he is reconstituted into the Second Adam—*Yahushua HaMashakhYahu*.

The Second Adam—*Yahushua HaMashakhYahu*—is only water and blood, cf. *YahuChanan Alef (First John)* 5:6, with no dust or earth in him, so the recreated man coming out of the waters of baptism, begotten into the image of this Second Adam, is also water and blood. Otherwise, how is he compatible to be grafted into the True Vine, who is the Second Adam, as a branch? Read more on this thought in *YahuChanan (John)* 15:5, *Romans* 11:17-24, *First Corinthians* 6:15, and *Ephesians* 5:30.

Let me see how I might help you understand that when sinful man is recreated into the image of the Second Adam, he becomes water and blood. You see, to be born of *Elohiym* means you are a son of *Elohiym*. To be born of *Bapuohyele* means you are a son of *Bapuohyele*. To be born of *"water"* means you are a son of *"water"*. The son of *"water"* has in him everything that is *"water"*, so when you are born of *"water"* it means you are *"water"*.

To be recreated into the image of the man from *Shamayim*, who is begotten of things in *Shamayim*, is to become as "Shamayimly" as he is—and no more earthly! It would seem a miracle to be born of the heavenly (*Shamayim*)—water and blood—and still remain earthly—dust—in constitution. I hope, somehow, this helps us to see the value and power of our New Creation reality.

In its listing of the word **hudatos (entry number 5204)** of the Greek Dictionary of the New Testament, **The New Strong's Exhaustive Concordance of the Bible** makes an interesting comment on the Greek text of *YahuChanan (John)* 3:5. In this verse, we find the Greek words **ek hudatos,** meaning **out of water**, describing baptism. Dr. James Strong teaches the proposition **ek** gives the understanding that, **"the New Birth is, in one sense, the setting aside of all that the believer was according to the flesh, for it is evident that it must be an entirely new beginning."** Personally, I am yet to read a more profound statement of fact on baptism, and I could not agree more with this great man of letters.

Baptism in the name of *Yahushua HaMashakhYahu* is Elohiym's way and means of preparing earth-based man to be able to live a life in fellowship with Him. Earth-based natural man must be recreated to be able to succeed in any walk with *Elohiym*. In Elohiym's wisdom, He chose this recreation in the rite of baptism in water, in the name of His son *Yahushua HaMashakhYahu*.

All what *Elohiym* does in baptism is to deal with the Adamic nature of man, which is man's earth (dust) component. Our earth nature is the hindrance to us in our bid to obey *Elohiym*. This earth nature wars against us all the time. All our natural appetites and desires are earth based and stem from the fact that we are of the earth. Being earth in constitution, we naturally have a high affinity to the earth, which is our father.

Think about this: every food, drink, and medicine that we take into our bodies is from the earth. Our bodies are flesh, fattened by what we take as the products of the earth. Our flesh is earth based, and, therefore, earth sustained. Everything our bodies need is from the earth.

From foods to raw clay-product medicines, all of man's needs are from the earth. Our clothes, shoes, cars, airplanes, toys, weapons, and ammunitions are all from the earth. We love them because they are our kinsmen derived from our roots. Natural man cannot hate these, because that would be as though he hated himself.

Our high affinity to the things of the earth, and our love for them, take us away from any love we may have for *Elohiym* and for fellow man to a love for ourselves and our egos. We war against each other in competition for the things of the earth because our self-based ego dictates to us to do so. We kill each other for the things of the earth, perishable things bound to return to dust!

It amazes me looking at the piles of bricks and marble we use to build habitations for our frail and small bodies. I have often wondered what we would build for our homes if we were giants like some of Elohiym's beastly creatures. We don't even think that there is a place beyond earth that we will go to, and thus will have to leave all these things for.

We build these homes strong, to last forever if it were possible, simply because we are so much in love with earth that we do not wish to leave it. It never occurs to us to erect some makeshift homes or foxholes for our temporary sojourn on earth.

There was this compatriot of mine who was interviewed on television. He had been involved in a plane crash and lost one of his legs. He said that, at the time of the crash, he had as many as four hundred pairs of shoes! For one person living in the "Third World" country of Ghana to have that many shoes, this was shocking to me.

What if he lived in Japan or some such "First World" country and was a successful businessman or professional? How large would his shoe collection have been then? He had to lose a limb to stop his madness. That is a pity.

Did you hear as I did of the past president of an African country whose suits collection needed an entire warehouse for his wardrobe? Well, that is the fact of it; he made problems for his countrymen and for himself trying to gratify natural man. You could not blame him, though: he misunderstood warehouse to mean wear-house. After His Excellency was driven out of the Presidential Lodge, he had a big problem finding a suitable storage place for his suits.

Back home in Ghana, Africa, south of the Sahara, I was told of this pastor who had sixteen automobiles. He himself gave a testimony to this effect and sought to impress his listeners regarding how, in that, he was blessed by *Elohiym* in his ministry as a flock leader. I wished to know this pastor and to pry into the spiritual condition of the flock he led; or should I say, misled?

Talking about retired African presidents, I heard of one who, upon leaving office as a septuagenarian, continued to show a high fleshly human nature. I had thought that at that age, he would have slowed down trying to live in gratification of the flesh and be more preoccupied with plans about the journey back Home to *Shamayim*.

Not so for this septuagenarian. He fought tooth and nail to surround himself with toys and gadgets he claimed his nation owed him, so he could presumably continue to enjoy the pleasures he had been indulging in since his youth. I was so sad to hear this about a retired septuagenarian.

He seemed compelled by the desires of the flesh, to seek the state to supply to him with high-speed automobiles that had the potential to kill him instantly. His story told me a lot about our human nature relentlessly warring against us, all the way to our graves.

If crazy things like these lifestyles are seen in Africa, the poorest continent of the world, can you imagine what kind of life would be lived in France, Canada, USA, Germany, UK, etc., by such people who want to pay fabulous respects to their earth natures? *Elohiym* is sad when He looks down on earth.

Our high affinity to the things of the earth puts too much stress on the resources *Elohiym* made for all humanity to last from Creation to End-time. If *Elohiym* permits all of His Creation to go for warehouses as wardrobes, I don't think there will be any resources left for future generations. Our earth nature takes us far away from *Elohiym*.

So *Elohiym* must act fast. The solution is sure: kill the earth nature of man. Let him die, and be sure he is buried and laid to rest forever in deep water. He must not be permitted to rise again. In place of natural man, raise a new creature—one devoid of earth, one who is of water and of *Ruwakh HaKodesh*. And so *Elohiym* brings in baptism.

Baptism kills natural man and raises in his place a new man whose earth nature is killed. Did you know this? If you did not, then you probably did not get what you claim to have received in baptism. Maybe, your faith was in something else—like baptism being just a formality to fulfill some kinds of righteousness, as is popularly taught by many Christian denominations.

Baptism gives the repentant sinner the image of *Yahushua HaMashakhYahu*. Baptism brings to mankind a spiritual connection or link to Elohiym's power, grafting man to the True Vine, *Yahushua HaMashakhYahu*. Baptism is the means to the acquisition of the divine nature of *Elohiym* into one's being. In baptism, one receives *Ruwakh HaKodesh* of *Elohiym* as a gift who comes to reside in one's heart to ensure that the dead human nature does not resurrect. For those who walk or live in the power of *Ruwakh HaKodesh*, they cannot gratify the desires of the flesh—cf. *Romans* 8:8-10 and *Galatians* 5:16.

Elohiym does not just command you not to love the things of the earth without helping you to be able to do this. *Elohiym* deals with our earth-based natures that propel us toward the things of the earth. He kills that earth-based nature in us so we can obey His commands. This He does in the waters of baptism, according to His power and His wisdom—cf. *Yechezkel (Ezekiel) 36*:25-27.

Every unsaved person lives in two very powerful worlds in which, by his own strength, he is unable to resist their controls. The first is that which controls his appetites and character. This is the world of carnality: the lust of the flesh, lust of the eye, and the pride of what one possesses and who one is in the world. This world resides within every unsaved person. It is invisible but has a strong influence and control on the lifestyle of the sinner. This is our Adamic nature, the earth or dust component of the unsaved man.

The second world is made-up of the visible things of the earth. This is the material world of natural and man-made things that attracts and stirs up the appetites of the Adamic nature.

This material world is strengthened and advertised through our cultures, secular education, industry, trade, economics, governance, social life, etc.

Living within the powers of these two worlds evolves that proud, arrogant, intolerant, selfish, greedy hedonist who is insatiable in the desires of his human nature.

This lifestyle is what keeps the unsaved person from loving *Elohiym* and fellow man. Unsaved man only loves himself and does not have the power to do otherwise, even if he so wished.

To deliver sinful man from this life of enslavement to self is to make him born again or to recreate him into a new creature via a new birth. This is done in the waters of baptism through the wisdom and power of *Elohiym* acting with the faith of the repentant sinner; one who is fed up with a life of enslavement to self.

There is no other environment or medium or some vacuum where the new birth comes about; it is only in, by and of natural living waters. This is the design and will of *Elohiym*—that sinful man become born again of waters and of *Ruwakh HaKodesh*.

Elohiym does great things in baptism. We do not understand much of what He does in baptism. As a result, many of us do not benefit from this great ordinance of *HaAdon* (the Master).

Baptism makes us conform to the image of *Elohiym*. Baptism makes us Elohiym's children. It is in baptism that we become genuine and true followers of *Yahushua HaMashakhYahu*.

New life, the *Chayyei Olam* of *Elohiym* given as gift to mankind to enable him live like Him while on earth, is received in baptism. We leap from humanity to divinity in the baptism we receive in the name of *Yahushua HaMashakhYahu* in natural living waters.

Let me tell you something: *Elohiym* does very great things in natural living waters. He impregnates in waters. Everything *Elohiym* brings forth, he brings forth in waters.

Water is Elohiym's conception chamber; it is His labor ward; it is His delivery table. Water brings life. Water is life in itself. Water is Elohiym's creating power.

You can only understand what Living Waters are, and who Living Water is, if you can catch a glimpse of Elohiym's wisdom and power displayed in, by and of waters.

The mystery of what happens in the waters of baptism cannot be fully understood. We do not even need to understand all of this mystery of baptism to benefit from the blessing of recreation that it affords us. Ours is simply to obey the instruction of *HaAdon* to be baptized in his name.

If we do so in simple faith, we allow him to do as he pleases to give us his *Chayyei Olam* (Everlasting Life). That is why we have to believe *HaAdon* when he says we cannot be born again outside of natural living waters.

Let me show you what it means to believe. To believe in *Yahushua HaMashakhYahu* is to act on his Word. Everybody who is recorded to have believed *Yahushua HaMashakhYahu* for salvation acted on his Word of instruction to repent of sin and be baptized in his name.

To believe in *Yahushua HaMashakhYahu* is not just to hear about him and keep that knowledge about him in your head or to your bosom as the truth, because that is not enough. That will not help you, just as it does not help *shedim* (demons) all of whom also keep this same knowledge in their minds.

Let me caution you, dear reader, that many of the words *Elohiym* uses are not so easy to understand with human minds. Either you have to be taught by Him in the *Holy Scriptures* through your familiarity with them, or you have to acquire His mind and wisdom through *Ruwakh HaKodesh* to understand them.

Some of Elohiym's powerful words include *emunah* (meaning "faith", or verbalized by Bible translators as "have faith" or "believe") and *tikvah* ("hope", or as verbalized "have hope"), and *ahavah* (love). These words are not easily understood and acted on, as is the case with simple verbs like eat, sing, run or sit.

If you want to understand what *Elohiym* means when He commands us to "love", go find wisdom in *First Corinthians* 13:1-13 to enable you do so. There you will find out what *Elohiym* means by His command to us to love.

That understanding will kill lust, take away selfishness, and render greed tasteless in any man. When *Elohiym* commands us to love, He means we should give out good things to other people whether they are good to us or not. This is because, in the mind of *Elohiym*, true love always gives, while selfishness which is the opposite of love, keeps or takes.

When *Elohiym* tells us to have "hope", He means we should live in expectation of a happy and blessed future. If you live in the expectation of that future, you will live in a way that meets or falls in line with the instructions or commands of *Elohiym*. You will live in acts of good deeds and a worthy character.

You cannot say you are living a life of hope in *Elohiym*, when you just sit down expecting the future you desire to come by itself. If some things do come in the future while you sat down and simply waited for them, they will not come as you expect. You have to act in such a way as to bring about the manifestation of the things you hope for.

You must live in the appropriate way to get that expectation. Remember the Word of *Elohiym* in *YahuChanan Alef (First John)* 3:3: **"And every man that hath this HOPE IN HIM PURIFIETH HIMSELF, even as he is pure."**

Hope, we must know, aside being a noun, is also a verb, an action-packed word. Therefore, when living in hope, act appropriately to obtain your desired goal.

So what does *Elohiym* mean when He commands us to believe or have *emunah* in His Word? He simply means we should act on His Word. We must act appropriately on His Word if we claim to believe it. Just how we must act, we have to be told by *Elohiym* Himself in His *Holy Scriptures*.

A large group of Hebrews "believed" Elohiym's Word for salvation on the Day of the Outpouring of *Ruwakh HaKodesh* (Pentecost?) in *Yerushalayim*. They all acted appropriately and therefore received the salvation of *Elohiym*.

They acted appropriately in repentance and baptism, in the name of *Yahushua HaMashakhYahu*,—cf. *Ma'asim (Acts)* 2:14-41— and so could not be denied Elohiym's salvation.

In the city of *Shomron* (Samaria), a large number of *Shomronim* (Samaritans) "believed" the Word of *Elohiym* for salvation. To act their "belief" or showing that they had *emunah* or faith in *Elohiym* and His Word that they heard, they repented of their sins and received baptism in the name of *Yahushua HaMashakhYahu*.

They acted appropriately on their belief and were, thus, ushered into the born again experience. This is in *Ma'asim (Acts)* 8:5-25 for our study.

In the desert region of Gaza on his way from *Yerushalayim* to Ethiopia, our now-familiar friend, the eunuch, Minister of Treasury to the Queen of ancient Ethiopia, "believed" the Word of *Elohiym* for salvation. Then, he acted his "belief" by repenting of his sins and by receiving baptism into *Yahushua HaMashakhYahu*.

His actions were most appropriate and therefore earned him the salvation of *Elohiym* in the born again experience, which allowed him to be filled with *Ruwakh HaKodesh*. We have already examined this "belief" of the Ethiopian eunuch in *Ma'asim (Acts)* 8:26-40; please read of this account in these verses again.

Anytime we come across a detailed account about the *emunah* or "beliefs" of any seekers of the salvation of *Elohiym*, as in *Ma'asim (Acts)* 2:14-41, 8:5-25, 8:26-40, 9:1-18, 10:1-48, etc., we see repentance and baptism into *Yahushua HaMashakhYahu* coming into play, as the only appropriate way to act, showing evidence of how these salvation seekers acted on their "beliefs" to receive the salvation of *Elohiym*.

Where the word "believe" is found without baptism being explicitly mentioned in relation to the salvation of any people, we should understand that the actions of these salvation seekers were in the only appropriate way of repentance and baptism into *Yahushua HaMashakhYahu*.

This we should understand to be the case where mention is made in *Ma'asim (Acts)* in reference to peoples' salvation—cf. *Ma'asim (Acts)* 13:12, 48; 14:1; 17:4, 12, 34—and in other places of scripture where baptism in the name of *Yahushua HaMashakhYahu* is silent.

Baptism, as a show of evidence of the "belief" of any salvation seeker in these verses of scripture, should not be thought to have been unsubscribed to, or that these salvation seekers received the salvation of *Elohiym* without showing faith in baptism into *Yahushua HaMashakhYahu*. No salvation can come to any "believer" without him acting in repentance and baptism as confirmation and proof or evidence of his "belief".

Sha'ul and *Sila* (Silas) told a jailor in the city of Philippi, to **"believe in the name of Yahushua HaMashakhYahu"** for salvation—cf. *Ma'asim (Acts)* 16:30-33.

I am sure if they did not proceed fast enough after saying that to explain themselves, the jailor would have started to ask a string of questions.

He would ask to know, for example, exactly what about *Yahushua HaMashakhYahu* he was to "believe", and what was he to do with any such information he received about him.

Sha'ul and *Sila* proceeded quickly to tell him what they meant by saying he should "believe" in *Yahushua HaMashakhYahu* for salvation.

The jailor understood them clearly and, at an odd midnight hour, received baptism in response to the command of *Sha'ul* and *Sila* to "believe" or have *emunah* in *Yahushua HaMashakhYahu*.

To "believe" in *Yahushua HaMashakhYahu* for salvation is to have enough faith in him so as to act on his foremost and easy-to-obey instruction to repent and to be baptized in his name, for the remission of sin and for the receipt of the gift of *Ruwakh HaKodesh* to dwell firmly within one's heart.

We should take every word of *Yahushua HaMashakhYahu* as sacred wisdom. When he said *YahuChanan ben Zecharyahu* should baptize him, we should seek his wisdom to understand what he meant by insisting on that baptism **"to fulfill all righteousness"**.

If we see his wisdom beyond our understanding and accept

every instruction of his to us as the means for us to be blessed, we would not have many people like *Nakdimon* today.

Yahushua HaMashakhYahu has said that without baptism no one can enter the *Malchut HaElohiym*. It is so for the pre-flood righteous, and the post-flood righteous led by *Noach*, and for *Moshe*, *Yehoshua*, *Dovid*, etc., to the last Old Covenant holy man.

The New Covenant is also replete with evidence of how the holy men of *Elohiym* entered His salvation and the *Malchut HaElohiym* through repentance of their sins and baptism into the name of *Yahushua HaMashakhYahu*.

My dear, it has to be so also for you today and for your descendants tomorrow that you all enter the *Malchut HaElohiym* through repentance and baptism into the name of *Yahushua HaMashakhYahu*. Otherwise, *HaAdon* did not mean what he said in *YahuChanan (John)* 3:5. Please believe and act on his Word to be blessed to be in *Shamayim* with those who obey him without doubt.

Did you ever consider why *Elohiym* always passes people He sets on pilgrimage through natural living waters? It is as if when such people pass through the waters, it is their manner of saying farewell to a past life or lifestyle, faith, status, and former place of abode.

Think about it deeply; after the crossing, they neither continue in the same faith, nor in that previous way of life, nor do they return to their former place of abode.

When *Elohiym* set our ancestor the First Adam on pilgrimage to earth, He did so by passing him through waters. When He set *Noach* on errand to repossess the earth and regain the dominion that was lost by the First Adam to the devil, He passed him through waters.

Avraham was called out of his father's house and made to cross or pass through the river Euphrates on pilgrimage to the Land of Promise—cf. *Yehoshua (Joshua)* 24:2-3.

Avraham's grandson, Ya'akov, also passed over this river with his wives and children as they returned to the homeland of *Avraham* from *Padan Aram* (Padanaram), the hometown of *Lavan* (Laban)—cf. *Bereshis (Genesis)* 31:21.

On pilgrimage from *Mitzrayim* to Canaan the children of *Yisroel* under *Moshe* were made to pass across the Red Sea. Later on in this pilgrimage, a younger generation *Yisroel* passed over the *Yarden* under *Yehoshua*.

Before *Eliyahu* could end his pilgrimage to *Shamayim* (Heaven), he passed over the *Yarden*—cf. *Melekhim Bais (Second Kings)* 2:8-9.

Elishah, the successor of *Eliyahu,* also passed over the waters of *Yarden,* at the start of his prophetic pilgrimage—cf. *Melekhim Bais (Second Kings)* 2:8, 9, 14. This he did twice in one day. No wonder he had a double portion of the power that rested on his master, *Eliyahu.*

Every great friend or servant of *Elohiym* had contact with natural living waters at one time or the other. The greatest ministers of *Elohiym* are ministers of waters.

Just think of all of Elohiym's great servants: *Noach, Avraham, Yitzchak, Ya'akov, Moshe, Yehoshua, Eliyahu,* and also, *Elishah, YahuChanan ben Zecharyahu, Shimon Kefa, Philippos, Chananyahu, Sha'ul,* and Apollos. They all worked or ministered with, and or in waters. As for *Eliyahu,* when he wanted fire on a mountain top, he asked for water. Can you imagine that? He ministered with waters to produce fire!

I can understand very clearly why baptism in living waters in the name of *Yahushua HaMashakhYahu* produces the fire of *Ruwakh HaKodesh* to dwell within the one baptized.

If you want fire in your life, allow yourself to be passed over or through waters, either by *Elohiym* Himself or by any of His accredited and anointed servants.

What a mystery of *Elohiym!* Every passing over waters brings salvation, a permanent deliverance from some place and influence. When an angel of *Elohiym* passed over your home, it meant you and your first born were safe.

If *Elohiym* passes you over or through waters, then it means eternal salvation from the dominion of the devil for you and your family or house. What a display of wisdom by *Elohiym* in His "pass overs". How I wished my generation understood the ways of *Elohiym* in these regards.

Yahushua HaMashakhYahu started his journey to *Gulgotha* in the baptism he received from *YahuChanan ben Zecharyahu* in the waters of the *Yarden.*

That baptism revealed to mankind the purpose of *Yahushua HaMashakhYahu* coming to earth as *HaSeh HaElohiym* (the Lamb of *Elohiym*) to take the sin of the world away—cf. *YahuChanan (John)* 1:33.

After that baptism, there was no turning back from the purpose of *Elohiym* for Yahushua's life. The hand had been laid upon the plough—*Gulgotha,* all the way and no turning back.

Today, any sinner who wants to embark on pilgrimage to

Shamayim must be passed through living waters. You cannot genuinely start the journey toward *Shamayim*, without being passed through living waters in the baptism into *Yahushua HaMashakhYahu*.

Do we not understand these spiritual issues? We must, dear reader, so that we deliver ourselves from the error of praying so-called *Sinners' Prayers* in our pursuit of the born again experience.

Baptismal Status of the Men in the Upper Room before the Coming of *Ruwakh HaKodesh* and Related Issues

Shall we look at the people who were in the upper room in *Yerushalayim*, upon whom *Ruwakh HaKodesh* fell the forty-nineth day (or was it on the fiftieth day?) after the resurrection of *Yahushua HaMashakhYahu*. No doubt, those in the upper room were all staunch followers of *Yahushua HaMashakhYahu*.

They had gathered there to pray on many issues, to have fellowship with each other—that is, to be together in unity of mind and purpose—and to share in every way conceivable, while awaiting the coming of *Ruwakh HaKodesh* in obedience to the instructions of *Yahushua HaMashakhYahu*.

All of Elohiym's actions are done according to seasons and times. For *Elohiym*, there is a time for everything under the sun. *Yahushua HaMashakhYahu* tells us that it is when he has physically departed from the Earth to *Shamayim* that he would send *Ruwakh HaKodesh* of *Elohiym* to his *talmidim*.

This means that while *Yahushua HaMashakhYahu* was on Earth with his *talmidim*, they could not receive *Ruwakh HaKodesh* to dwell within their hearts. He could, however, prepare them to receive *Ruwakh HaKodesh* in due time.

One way, and in fact the most important of all, by which *Yahushua HaMashakhYahu* prepared his *talmidim* to receive *Ruwakh HaKodesh* was through baptism into his name. Many people professing to have knowledge of the *Holy Scriptures* do not know that *Yahushua HaMashakhYahu* baptized his followers.

They do not know that, as a prelude to and prerequisite for the receipt of *Ruwakh HaKodesh*, *Yahushua HaMashakhYahu* baptized his followers in his name. Where do we find this? We find this in *YahuChanan (John)* 3:22, 26, and 4:1-2.

There is so much evidence that *Yahushua HaMashakhYahu* baptized. I can count over five hundred people that were baptized by him, or in his name, by the end of his earthly ministry. These were those prepared ahead of time to be the first witnesses of the resurrection and first fruits of *Ruwakh HaKodesh*—cf. *First Corinthians* 15:5-6.

Shall we read the following from *YahuChanan (John)*: *"After these things came Jesus (Yahushua HaMashakhYahu) and his disciples (talmidim) into the land of Judæa; and there he tarried with them and BAPTIZED. And they came unto YahuChanan, and said unto him, Rabbi he that was with thee beyond Yarden, to whom thou bearest witness, behold, THE SAME BAPTIZETH, and all men come to him."—YahuChanan (John) 3:22, 26, KJV; caps and the words in parenthesis are mine.*

Let us also read from *YahuChanan (John)* 4:1-2: *"When therefore the Lord knew how the Pharisees [Perushim] had heard that Jesus [Yahushua HaMashakhYahu] made and BAPTIZED MORE DISCIPLES [TALMIDIM] than YahuChanan, (though Jesus [Yahushua HaMashakhYahu] himself baptized not, but his disciples [talmidim])..."—YahuChanan (John) 4:1-2, KJV; caps and the words in square brackets are mine.*

From all of these verses, it is very clear that *Yahushua HaMashakhYahu* baptized some of his followers personally and also caused others to be baptized in his name by some of his *talmidim*. Whether *Yahushua HaMashakhYahu* himself baptized, or his *talmidim* did the act of baptism, the fact is that all of his true *talmidim* were baptized in his name. Why did *Yahushua HaMashakhYahu* do this for his followers? This is a very important question to consider.

By now, from the many accounts in this book about how *Ruwakh HaKodesh* was received in the early days of the New Covenant dispensation, I hope you see the indispensability of baptism in the name of *Yahushua HaMashakhYahu* to the receipt of *Ruwakh HaKodesh*. If there is no baptism into the name of *Yahushua HaMashakhYahu*, there can be no receipt of *Ruwakh HaKodesh* by the salvation seeker to dwell in his heart.

From the day *Yahushua HaMashakhYahu* arrived in *Shamayim* after his resurrection and presented to *Elohiym* his blood of the New Covenant, everybody coming out of the waters of baptism in his name carries or bears in him and around him *Ruwakh HaKodesh*. This is so if, and only if, one's repentance from sin, and one's understanding of baptism in the name of *Yahushua*

HaMashakhYahu, was well informed by the *Holy Scriptures* and one was sincere about observing the rite.

For those baptized in the name of *Yahushua HaMashakhYahu* before he went to *Gulgotha*, rose, and ascended into *Shamayim*, they could not have this dwelling presence of *Ruwakh HaKodesh* within them as a gift of *Elohiym* as they came out of the waters of baptism. Why? For the simple reason that the age or season of *Ruwakh HaKodesh* had not yet come. *Yahushua HaMashakhYahu* himself said that he had to go back to *HaAv* before their **Melitz Yosher** (*Praklit*, Advocate, Comforter, Counselor, or Helper in Court), *Ruwakh HaKodesh,* would come.

This is what *Yahushua HaMashakhYahu* says in *YahuChanan (John)*: *"**Nevertheless, I tell you the truth; it is expedient for you that I go away; for if I go not away, the comforter will not come unto you; but if I depart, I will send him unto you"—YahuChanan (John) 16:7, KJV.**

Obviously then, for those who were baptized in the name of *Yahushua HaMashakhYahu* during his earthly ministry—that is to say, before he went to *Gulgotha*—they were to receive the gift of *Ruwakh HaKodesh* later, after he had ascended to *HaAv*.

All the residents of the upper room were qualified to expect and to receive *Ruwakh HaKodesh* since they had been baptized in the name of *Yahushua HaMashakhYahu*, and they had been instructed by him to await the coming and receipt of this gift.

Let us also look at another important verse, *YahuChanan (John)* 7:39, which is seldom seen or understood by many readers of the *Holy Scriptures.*

*"**(But this spake he of the Spirit, which they that believe on him should receive: for the Holy Ghost [Ruwakh HaKodesh] was not yet given; because that Jesus [Yahushua HaMashakhYahu] was not yet glorified.)"—YahuChanan (John) 7:39, KJV; the words in square brackets are mine.**

The people in the upper room were people waiting to receive *Ruwakh HaKodesh* into their hearts for the very first time. They had no previous filling within their hearts of *Ruwakh HaKodesh*, and neither did they now need a boost, nor a replenishing of him, as some Christian denominations are erroneously teaching and wanting us to believe.

We have to constantly keep in mind that, until the Day of the Outpouring of *Ruwakh HaKodesh* (Pentecost?), in *Yerushalayim*,

Ruwakh HaKodesh could not come to dwell within the heart of any man for the very simple reason that He had not been given out as yet by *Elohiym* for the receipt of men.

All the residents of the upper room were Hebrews. There were no Gentiles among them. You see, up to this time, *Shimon Kefa* and the other Hebrew *talmidim* of *Yahushua HaMashakhYahu* could not come to grips with the fact that Gentiles could ever become saved or enter the *Malchut HaElohiym*.

You could not blame them since *Yahushua HaMashakhYahu* himself did not minister salvation to any Gentile while he was physically present on earth. *Yahushua HaMashakhYahu* himself taught his *talmidim* not to minister the salvation of *Elohiym* to non-Hebrews, the Gentiles, until after his resurrection! Check out this fact from *Mattityahu (Matthew)* 10:5-6:

"These twelve Jesus (Yahushua HaMashakhYahu) sent forth, and commanded them saying, go not into the way of the Gentiles and into any city of the Samaritans (Shomronim) enter ye not, But go rather to the lost sheep of the house of Yisroel"— Mattityahu (Matthew) 10:5-6, KJV; the words in parenthesis are mine.

Did I hear somebody whisper that *Yahushua HaMashakhYahu* ministered salvation to the people of *Shomron* by using a serially divorced woman as an "evangelist"? This is a complete misunderstanding of the facts. *Yahushua HaMashakhYahu* did not preach, teach, or minister for the on-the-spot salvation of the *Shomronim*. You see, all Gentiles, including the *Shomronim*, were to enter the salvation of *Elohiym* by faith in the person, mission, sacrifice, and resurrection of *Yahushua HaMashakhYahu*.

Once *Yahushua HaMashakhYahu* was yet to die, no *Shomroni*, and for that matter Gentile, could enter the salvation of *Elohiym*. Gentiles, who believed in *Yahushua HaMashakhYahu* while he walked this earth, could only act in faith in his name to gain relief from *shed* (demon) possession, sickness, diseases, and hunger. That was the best any Gentile could get from Yahushua's earthly ministry, and not salvation, while he was yet to go to *Gulgotha*.

The interaction between *Yahushua HaMashakhYahu* and the woman of *Shomron* at Ya'akov's well and his subsequent two-day stay in *Sh'khem* (Sychar) a city of *Shomron*, as recorded in *YahuChanan,* did not at that time bring the salvation of *Elohiym* to the *Shomronim*, who *Yahushua HaMashakhYahu* himself considered as strangers (Gentiles) to *Yisroel.* Let us read the following in *Lukas (Luke)* 17:16-18:

> *"And fell down on his face at his feet, giving him thanks: and he was a Samaritan (Shomroni). And Jesus (Yahushua HaMashakhYahu) answering said, Were there not ten cleansed? But where are the nine? There are not found that returned to give glory to God (Elohiym), save this stranger"—Lukas (Luke) 17:16-18, KJV; the words in parenthesis are mine.*

The fact of the *Shomronim* being strangers to *Yisroel*, Gentiles in reality, is made plain in these words of *Yahushua HaMashakhYahu.* From the accounts of *Melekhim Bais (Second Kings)* 17:24-41 and *Ezra* 4:9-10, we are told that the *Shomronim* were colonists from *Ashur* (Assyria). They were not the children of *Avraham* or of *Ya'akov*, as they had come to believe centuries after the colonization—cf. *YahuChanan (John)* 4:12, 20.

Their copying or imitation of the spiritual faiths and practices of true children of *Yisroel* did not make these Assyrian colonists of *Shomron* any more than strangers to *Yisroel.* At the time of *Yahushua HaMashakhYahu*, they even had their own Temple built on Mt. Gerizim. They also had their own kind of the Old Covenant scriptures—*The Samaritan Pentateuch.* Yet, they were considered strangers to both the spiritual and social lives of the children of *Avraham.*

The people of *Yisroel* resented the *Shomronim* because they came as the representatives of the King of *Ashur* (Assyria) who sometime in their history carried *Yisroel* into captivity. Ever since the arrival of these colonists, they had been regarded as strangers that could not be allowed to mix socially or spiritually with Hebrews—the children of *Avraham* and of *Ya'akov.* This was the status of the *Shomronim* in the eyes of the children of *Yisroel*, even during the time of *Yahushua HaMashakhYahu.*

The two-day ministry of *Yahushua HaMashakhYahu* in *Shomrom*, during his earthly sojourn, was meant to be a groundbreaking work. *Yahushua HaMashakhYahu* was in that interaction with *Shomron*, preparing the ground for the sowing of the seed of the *Besuras HaGeulah* message in the subsequent preaching campaigns of his chosen *Shlikhim* and *talmidim*, which he structured for them to start from *Yerushalayim*, to *Yahudah* (Judæa), and through *Shomron* to the ends of the world.

You see, the ground of *Shomron* had to be well prepared if the message of the *Besuras HaGeulah* were ever to take effect and bear fruit there. Spiritually, *Shomron* was a hard, rough, stony, infertile land to the Word of *Elohiym*. This situation had developed over centuries through a religion that was an unholy fusion of the Hebrew faith and idol worship, practiced by Assyrians and a hybrid of people of *Yisroel* and Assyria. At the time of *Yahushua HaMashakhYahu*, *Shomrom* had just the semblance of the spiritual beliefs of the Hebrew religion, having evolved and developed its own faith over centuries.

The wrong religious doctrines of the people of *Shomrom* had to be dealt with if the Word of *Elohiym* was ever to bear fruit there. Their wrong faiths, arrogance, misconceptions, and delusions had to be made known to them and dealt with.

Their false claim of being descendants of *Ya'akov* had to be exposed to their face. As they lived in the delusions of safety, acceptability to *Elohiym*, and the hope of a life in the bosom of *Avraham*, Ya'akov's grandfather, what else could they ever expect from *Elohiym* in this state of contentment with themselves?

These are, to me, the issues *Yahushua HaMashakhYahu* spent two days in *Shomron* dealing with, so as to make the subsequent *Besuras HaGeulah* spreading campaigns of his *Shlikhim* (sent ones, emissaries, "apostles") beneficial to the *Shomronim* and to the *Malchut HaElohiym*.

Thank *Elohiym* that many people in *Shomron* believed in this groundbreaking work of *Yahushua HaMashakhYahu* which turned out to be of great benefit eventually, as seen in their response to the message of the *Besuras HaGeulah*.

In fact, it seems to me that it was in the pre-ascension speech of *Yahushua HaMashakhYahu*, recorded in *Ma'asim (Acts)* 1:8, that his ban on sending the salvation message of *Elohiym* to the *Shomronim* was lifted. This was to take affect from the day when *Ruwakh HaKodesh* fell on the *Shlikhim* of *Yahushua HaMashakhYahu*. Let us read of this from *Ma'asim (Acts)*:

"But you will receive ko'ach (power), when Ruwakh HaKodesh has come upon you, and you will be the Eidus (the Witnesses) of me, in Yerushalayim, and in all Yahudah, and Shomron and as far as ad ketzeh ha'aretz, (unto the uttermost parts of the earth)"—Ma'asim (Acts) 1:8, OJB.

The events, as recorded in *Ma'asim (Acts)* 8:5-25, were meant to break the news for the first time of the first crop of *Shomronim* that ever entered the salvation of *Elohiym*. This news came as a bit of a surprise to even the *Shlikhim* of *Yahushua HaMashakhYahu*.

All the residents of the upper room were full-blooded Hebrews, baptized in the name of *Yahushua HaMashakhYahu*, taught as his *talmidim* by him over a good period of time, and to whom the promise to be given *Ruwakh HaKodesh* to dwell within their hearts had directly been made. These were the ones chosen of *Elohiym* to be the very first crop of people to enter the New Covenant at a time when it was freshly signed in the *Dahm HaSeh* (Blood of the Lamb).

They were the first entrants into the Body of *Yahushua HaMashakhYahu*, the first to be grafted into the True Vine, and the very first into the salvation of *Elohiym* under the New Covenant. These were the first fruits or first eligible recipients of *Ruwakh HaKodesh* under the Grace Dispensation.

We should not forget that when *YahuChanan ben Zecharyahu* said to his fellow members of the house of *Yisroel* that one of them standing in their midst **"shall baptize you with the Holy Ghost (Ruwakh HaKodesh) and with fire (eish)"—cf. Mattityahu (Matthew) 3:11, Markos (Mark) 1:8, Lukas (Luke) 3:16, and YahuChanan (John) 1:26-27; words in parenthesis mine;** he was speaking in "prophecy" about *Yahushua HaMashakhYahu*.

Was this "prophecy" ever fulfilled by *Yahushua HaMashakhYahu* while he was "standing" in the midst of *Yisroel?* Yes, of course. When? At the only times we see *Yahushua HaMashakhYahu* ever baptize in natural living waters—not in fire—by the accounts of *YahuChanan (John)* 3:22, 26 and 4:1-2, to include all the residents of the upper room.

These baptisms, administered by *Yahushua HaMashakhYahu* in natural living waters, were the only occasions that he ever baptized, and they were to bring about the fire of *Ruwakh HaKodesh* into the lives of the baptized.

For all those baptized by *Yahushua HaMashakhYahu* in natural living waters, before he went to *Gulgotha*, this coming of fire into their hearts was delayed for obvious reasons, to fit into the times and seasons of *Elohiym*. This is all there is to understand about the occurrences of the Day of the Outpouring of *Ruwakh HaKodesh* (Pentecost?) in *Yerushalayim* in the upper room, of fiery tongues of fire on the heads of people and the glow of spiritual heat energy in their hearts.

Again, we should not forget that, back in *Bereshis*, before the times of new beginnings anywhere there were waters there was also *Ruwakh HaKodesh* of *Elohiym* brooding over those waters—cf. *Bereshis (Genesis)* 1:2.

In coming out of the waters of baptism, one is born of waters. And when born of waters, one indeed becomes water. All the upper room residents were born of waters in their baptisms many months ahead of the Day of the Outpouring of *Ruwakh HaKodesh* (Pentecost?). They were therefore water and, as such, were eligible to have *Ruwakh HaKodesh* come to brood over and dwell within them on the day when He was outpoured from *Shamayim*.

Today, anywhere there is any person born of waters who literally becomes a bag of waters, there must be *Ruwakh HaKodesh* of *Elohiym* to rush into the heart of that person to dwell within him and brood over him immediately and forever.

The baptism that these upper room residents received at the hand of the Master, ahead of the day *Ruwakh HaKodesh* was finally outpoured, was also to make them the first eligible ministers of the New Covenant to administer on behalf of *HaAdon* this great ordinance of the New Covenant faith. For any person to be eligible to baptize people, he must have himself been baptized into *Yahushua HaMashakhYahu*.

You are not worthy to baptize anybody if you have not been baptized into *Yahushua HaMashakhYahu*. This has been Elohiym's requirement since Creation, when this great invention of His first came into being.

While the ordinance of baptism existed in its shadows, *Elohiym* Himself took direct responsibility for baptizing the leaders of those dispensations. *Elohiym* directly ministered baptism to *Noach* and his sons, *Avraham*, and then to *Moshe*, so they could in effect also minister it to their followers subsequently.

For *Noach* and his sons, *Elohiym* started the process by shutting them in, in the ark. Then the downpours of rainwater came. The rains literally saturated them with water over a period of forty days and nights—cf. *Bereshis (Genesis)* 7:16-17, 24. After that, the rising vapors and sprays of seawater for a hundred and fifty days after the rains continued to saturate them, while their ark drifted about directionless on the sea. That was how they were baptized by *Elohiym* Himself.

As said earlier on, *Avraham* was baptized by *Elohiym* so he could be a dispensation leader. Now, this was how it happened. *Elohiym* escorted *Avraham* from his father's house to cross the Euphrates River, as he obeyed Him to go out in search of the land of Canaan. As he crossed the Euphrates, it was Elohiym's manner of personally baptizing him and his seed, so he could be the father and leader-founder of *Yisroel*. Of course, *Avraham* had no inkling of what *Elohiym* was doing to him as he waded through the ford of the River Euphrates. However, that was Elohiym's way of purifying him and his seed in a rite of baptism, so he could produce the holy Nation of *Yisroel* in due time.

As for *Moshe*, his baptism occurred during his infancy. That is not to say *Elohiym* approves of infant baptism by any ministers of the New Covenant faith today.

The birth of *Moshe* coincided with the edict of Pharaoh to kill all male-born babies of *Yisroel*. Fearing the consequences of being caught with a male child, his mother dumped him on the Nile waters, after hiding him for three months. This baby was later drawn from the Nile waters by the Pharaoh's daughter. He was given the name *"Moshe"*, which means ***"because I drew him out of the water"—Shemot (Exodus) 2:10, KJV.***

Moshe lived because he was saved by waters just as his ancestors *Noach* and sons. Paradoxically, the Nile waters were what would kill every male-born baby of *Yisroel* as the Pharaoh's edict was for them to be cast into these waters after birth—cf. *Shemot (Exodus)* 1:22.

You could then say that the child *Moshe* died as a result of the Pharaoh's edict. You could also say that *Moshe* was buried in the waters of the Nile where he was dumped, and then was resurrected from the same waters! See Elohiym's wisdom in baptism manifest in this? *Elohiym* said he raised the Pharaoh to fit into His scheme of things!

To qualify to lead *Yisroel* into baptism in His name in, and by, the Red Sea crossing, *Moshe* had to be baptized by *Elohiym* Himself, eighty years ahead of that event.

Yehoshua was eligible to lead *Yisroel* into baptism by the River *Yarden* crossing because he first received baptism in the Red Sea in the days of *Moshe*. This seems to be some kind of baton-changing activity in a baptism for salvation race. *Elohiym* knew of the *Yarden* crossing and the significance of it, and He prepared *Yehoshua* to qualify to deal with the needs of *Yisroel* forty years ahead of time.

YahuChanan ben Zecharyahu was only eligible to baptize *Yahushua HaMashakhYahu* because he was baptized ahead of his birth. He was baptized while in the loins of his ancestor at the historic crossing of *Yarden* into the Promised Land.

Yahushua HaMashakhYahu, on receiving baptism at the hand of

YahuChanan, could also minister this blessing of *Elohiym* to his *talmidim* during the days of his sojourn on earth. From these *talmidim,* baptism has come down to us.

The ways of *Elohiym* do not change. *Elohiym* is neither a respecter of any persons, nor of any of their wishes which do not conform to His Will. You must be baptized into salvation, into life, and into the *Malchut HaElohiym* to be eligible to minister baptism with its accompanying blessings to your followers. Your eligibility to baptize is based on Elohiym's Law.

I am of the conviction that the power to live the new life of faith in *Yahushua HaMashakhYahu* is unreceivable by many people simply because they do not understand the spiritual significance and value of baptism. Life is dull and a drudgery to many salvation seekers because the power to live the new life in *Yahushua HaMashakhYahu,* which is obtained only in baptism into his name, is denied them due to their ignorance about the value of baptism.

Baptism is an impartation of power from *Elohiym* to repentant man. Baptism turns natural man into a heavenly being. Baptism is the genesis or beginning of a new life in *Yahushua HaMashakhYahu.* If this beginning is not right due to ignorance, it becomes impossible to live this new life, and therefore the desired destination, *Shamayim,* is also ultimately denied. We should all be aware of this and study to understand baptism, so we can reap all its blessings intended for us.

There is one thing that unites humanity from Creation to End-time. All humanity is born biologically and genetically through a woman's receipt of male sperm, which are nourished in her womb to result in the production of a human being at birth. The resultant birth brings to earth an image of humanity's first father, the First Adam. The will of a man and a woman since Creation, in reproduction, has always resulted in the coming to earth of offsprings in the image of the First Adam.

Elohiym, in *Yahushua HaMashakhYahu,* has given an opportunity to mortal man to be reborn or recreated into His image. This rebirth into the image of *Elohiym* grants man the right to walk this earth as His representative, as well as the chance to live with Him in *Shamayim* at the end of Time.

Elohiym has clearly taught humanity in His Word that this rebirth into His image is made possible only by the joint action of natural living waters and His *Ruwakh Kodesh.* Unless one is born of water and of *Ruwakh HaKodesh,* one cannot obtain the image of

Elohiym that will entitle one to live with Him in His Kingdom. The born again experience is obtained in repentance and baptism and in no other way, as the teaching in this book has sought to make known to all its readers from the beginning.

All who will be found in *Shamayim* at the end of time will bear evidence of this rebirth by and of natural living waters and of *Ruwakh HaKodesh*. If you can count all the people who will be in *Shamayim* from Creation to End-time, you can unite all of them in the baptism they received according to the plan of *Elohiym* and or in obedience to His instruction.

The reason why *HaAdon* chose fishermen as his first four of twelve *talmidim* is not farfetched. Three of these men were *Shimon Kefa*, *Ya'akov* (James?), and *YahuChanan*, who turned out to be the closest to the Savior. None of his activities were hidden from them. The other was Andrew, a younger brother of *Shimon Kefa*.

Shimon Kefa and Andrew, the two sons of a man called *Shimon*, were called while casting a net into the sea—cf. *Mattityahu (Matthew)* 4:18-20. *Ya'akov* and *YahuChanan*, were also called while in the company of their father, *Zavdai* (Zebedee), when in the process of mending their nets in preparation to go fishing—cf. *Mattityahu (Matthew)* 4:21-22. *Yahushua HaMashakhYahu* told all four that he would turn them from being ordinary fishermen into fishers of men—a rare kind of promotion, if you ask me.

These men had great skills in catching fishes in waters. Now that they have been promoted to be fishers of men, where were they to exhibit their skills and talents?

In waters, of course! Not just any waters, but in the living waters of baptism! Fishes (men) for *Yahushua HaMashakhYahu* are only caught in the waters of baptism and not in some air-conditioned "church" room. Any catch of men for *Yahushua HaMashakhYahu*, and for the kingdom of *HaAv*, must be made in the waters of baptism and in no other places. *HalleluYahu!*

Elohiym's nature is brought into the "DNA" of human beings by baptism. You could say humans obtain Elohiym's seed, His nature, His looks, His mind, and His character traits when born again of water and of *Ruwakh HaKodesh*. It is when you are born again of water and of *Ruwakh HaKodesh* that you can claim to have been begotten of *Elohiym* and given the potential to be like Him in every aspect, just as *Yahushua HaMashakhYahu* mirrored *HaAv* while on earth.

Please take the issue of baptism seriously so you can obtain its blessings of granting you the divine life of *Elohiym* and the chance it accords of living forever in *Shamayim* after exiting this earth. May the peace of *Elohiym* be yours in this!

I am sure that any person who diligently and open-mindedly follows this teaching on baptism in this chapter, and in the one preceding it, will not find himself among the many simple-minded people who have grossly misunderstood Sha'ul's teaching in *First Corinthians* 1:17. This verse states:

"For Christ (Yahushua HaMashakhYahu) sent me not to baptize, but to preach the gospel: not with wisdom of words, lest the cross of Christ (Yahushua HaMashakhYahu) should be made of none effect."—First Corinthians 1: 17, KJV; the words in parenthesis are mine.

Many simple-minded people have concluded, upon reading this verse, that if *Sha'ul*, a *Shliakh* of *Yahushua HaMashakhYahu* of all people, could say he was not called by *Yahushua HaMashakhYahu* to baptize, then baptism is not necessary for salvation or the born again experience of the sinner. This is probably why such people teach with so much passion their faith in *Sinners' Prayer* recitals for the salvation of the sinner.

Is it not obvious that such people have grossly misunderstood *Sha'ul* by what he said in this verse of *First Corinthians*? How could any genuine minister of the New Covenant faith preach the *Besuras HaGeulah*, without understanding and accepting one's role in dispensing Elohiym's salvation through the ministration of baptism in natural living waters? *Sha'ul* could not, by what he said in this verse, render baptism into the name of *Yahushua HaMashakhYahu* irrelevant to the salvation of the sinner. On the contrary, he upheld and emphasized baptism for the salvation of the sinner in this teaching.

If we read *Sha'ul* in *First Corinthians* 1:12-17 very well, we would see the great importance he attached to baptism in the name of *Yahushua HaMashakhYahu*. *Sha'ul* established in this teaching that all baptisms in the names of any persons bring to those persons loyal *talmidim* and dedicated followers.

Many people are ignorant of this significance of baptism. Let me state that if any person were baptized **in the name of** *Bapuohyele*, that person became his loyal *talmid* (disciple) bound by his authority, blessed by his status, and identified by his total personality.

Faith in baptism into the name of *Yahushua HaMashakhYahu*,

therefore, brings to the repentant sinner a relationship with *Yahushua HaMashakhYahu*, in which one is blessed by His kingly authority, royal resources, spiritual power, eternal destiny, etc.

Sha'ul taught that baptism in the name of *Yahushua HaMashakhYahu*, ministered by any genuine servant of the *Malchut HaElohiym*,—whether he is named *Sha'ul*, Apollos, or *Kefa* (Cephas)—establishes the repentant sinner into *Yahushua HaMashakhYahu* to be with him, in him, of him, and for him, forever.

The Corinthian body of believers in *Yahushua HaMashakhYahu* was warned by *Sha'ul* that they should not misconstrue the fact that they were baptized by him, Apollos, or *Kefa* to mean that they were baptized into these ministers or servants of *Yahushua HaMashakhYahu* and not into *Yahushua HaMashakhYahu*.

Since no member of the Corinthian body of believers in *Yahushua HaMashakhYahu* was baptized into any name other than *Yahushua HaMashakhYahu*, they should not break their oneness in *Yahushua HaMashakhYahu* into factionalism, in which *Sha'ul*, Apollos or *Kefa* are crowned, worshiped and made into cult personalities.

Sha'ul stressed to breaking point the need for cohesion and homogeneity of the Corinthian body of believers in *Yahushua HaMashakhYahu*.

He explained to them that, if it is the baptisms rendered by the ministers of *Yahushua HaMashakhYahu* that led to the factionalism among them, then, they should understand that he, *Sha'ul*, was called to preach the full message of the *Besuras HaGeulah*, not to major on baptizing people into his personal name.

If *Kefa* and Apollos also baptized, they should be understood to have worked as ministers of *Yahushua HaMashakhYahu* and not thought to have baptized people into their own names, since none of them was sacrificed for the salvation of men.

This is all what *Sha'ul* is teaching the salvation seeker today in *First Corinthians* 1:17, and not the misguided interpretation by many "men of God", asserting that baptism in the name of *Yahushua HaMashakhYahu* is irrelevant to the born again experience.

By the way, did *Yahushua HaMashakhYahu* send *Shimon Kefa* as his messenger to baptize Cornelius and his household? The answer to this question is, yes. Did *Shimon Kefa* obey *Yahushua HaMashakhYahu*? The answer again is, yes.

Did *Shimon Kefa* personally baptize Cornelius? No, he did not. Cornelius and company were baptized under the command of

Shimon Kefa by the brethren who accompanied him from *Yafo* to Caesarea.

Would *Shimon Kefa* at a later date be wrong in saying that Cornelius and family could not claim he, *Shimon Kefa*, baptized them into his name and person—because he did not personally baptize them—if they started behaving in funny ways of not showing loyalty to *Yahushua HaMashakhYahu* but to him?

If Cornelius and his family ever behaved in any strange ways by showing loyalty to *Shimon Kefa*, and not to *Yahushua HaMashakhYahu*, could they push *Kefa* to take the same stand that *Sha'ul* took on the behavior of the Corinthian body of believers in *Yahushua HaMashakhYahu*?

Could we even say that because, while *Yahushua HaMashakhYahu* was on earth, he himself did not baptize some of his followers, even though they were baptized by his *Shlikhim* in his name—cf. *YahuChanan (John)* 4:2,—*Yahushua HaMashakhYahu* did not baptize them?

I think we should always be careful in taking single verses of scripture in isolation, not being mindful of the entire revelation of the *Holy Scriptures*.

Many of the distortions of the teachings of the faith of the Savior's *Shlikhim* of the first century stem from the carelessness of many students of *The Bible*, who have the habit of taking verses out of context and against the general grain of the entire record of the *Holy Scriptures*.

Eligibility for Baptism

As earlier on promised, this teaching on baptism cannot be brought to an end without mention of the eligibility of the baptismal candidate. The candidate for baptism must be eligible in the faith he expresses in the understanding of baptism, as a follow-up to his repentance from sin.

The teaching of who is eligible for baptism in the name of *Yahushua HaMashakhYahu* might seem unnecessary at this time and age after almost two millennia into the resurrection of *Yahushua HaMashakhYahu*. Unfortunately, it is one issue that has kept many a salvation seeker from the *Sha'arei HaShamayim* (Gates of Heaven) because we have not sought Elohiym's will about it. A great number of people who are not eligible for baptism, have been misled or forced into being "baptized" and, therefore, have not received the blessings of *Elohiym* intended for humanity in baptism.

Baptism into the name of *Yahushua HaMashakhYahu* is not for babies, infants, toddlers, or teenagers. The revelation of *Elohiym* about the ineligibility of the teenager group for baptism might come as a shock to many people. Unearthing this revelation from the *Holy Scriptures*, I have been very much shocked myself, but that is the fact of faith of all genuine believers in *Yahushua HaMashakhYahu*.

Let us first look at the ineligibility of teenagers for baptism to enable us appreciate more why babies, infants, and toddlers are not served any blessing when they are "baptized". Even as I fear to think about teenage pregnancies, because of their harmful and disastrous effects to teenage mothers and fathers, I am scared stiff even the more thinking about teenage baptism because of the problems it brings to the spiritual lives of many a salvation seeker.

Baptism is no plaything. Baptism is a very serious decision that every salvation seeker must make. It is a decision to follow *Yahushua HaMashakhYahu* as his *talmid* ("disciple"), with all the resolve and eagerness to be like him in every way. It is a decision to pledge loyalty to the name of *Yahushua HaMashakhYahu* and subscribe to his power.

You decide to be on the side of *Elohiym* and His Holy Son, to fight against the devil, when you opt for baptism. *Elohiym* and the devil are in a war that seems to be unending. You make a choice to fight on the side of *Elohiym* and His loyal angels when you decide to receive baptism in the name of *Yahushua HaMashakhYahu*.

You must understand what you are getting into in opting for baptism. You are supposed to pick up a sword in your hand to go and fight the enemies of *Elohiym*. This sword is the Word of *Elohiym*. After baptism, you go straight into warfare against the devil. You are conscripted and enlisted into the army of *Elohiym* for this war against the devil in your baptism.

You wear a helmet of salvation; put on a breastplate of righteousness; gird your loins with the belt of truth; put shoes on your feet in readiness to go out and preach the *Besuras HaGeulah* in *Yahushua HaMashakhYahu*; take a shield of faith to stop all the fierce fiery darts, bullets, and sling-stones of the enemy, when conscripted into the army of *Elohiym*—cf. *Ephesians* 6:13-17.

The soldier of Yahushua's Army must stand clean, strong, fearless and robust, in his personality and weaponry if he must face the devil and his cohorts. This does not give the picture of a child soldier! You must, as a soldier in the Army of *Yahushua HaMashakhYahu*, know that you are standing up to the *Golyats*

(Goliaths) of the devil; otherwise, you are their mincemeat. Baptism therefore is for mature, willing, and determined people.

Baptism also brings *Ruwakh HaKodesh* of *Elohiym* to take-up His residence in the body of the salvation seeker. Do you know the responsibility of hosting in your home His Excellency the President of our Republic, not for just one day or a week but forever?

Think about that very seriously. Then when you invite His Excellency the President, you may measure up to the task of hosting him in your home. Now go beyond your thought of hosting Mr. President to taking up into your body *Ruwakh HaKodesh* of *Elohiym*. That responsibility is not for children to take up, and yet that is the decision made at baptism.

If teenagers are unable, inadequate in every way, to host Mr. President, how could they wish to receive *Ruwakh HaKodesh* into their bodies to reside there as His dwelling places?—cf. *Yeshayahu (Isaiah)* 57:15. You ought to know that once *Ruwakh HaKodesh* takes up residence in your body you are responsible for all His moods.

You could make Him happy, sad, disappointed, or angry by where you take Him as you perambulate the earth, or by the kind of life you live. I would not offer baptism to teenagers. I would scare off teenagers who stand in wait for baptism, not knowing the responsibilities associated with it.

Let us now go into the *Holy Scriptures* to find out who was eligible for baptism. I find in the *Holy Scriptures* only one instance of baptism preceding the Old Covenant dispensation. I see many within the Old Covenant dispensation; and a lot more in the New Covenant dispensation. In whatever times or during whatever dispensation these baptisms were conducted, it is obvious that all the baptismal candidates were mature adults.

The first record of baptism in the *Holy Scriptures* is that which involved *Noach* and his family—cf. *Kefa Alef (First Peter)* 3:20-21. *Noach* was five hundred years old when he begot his three sons who were with him in the ark—cf. *Bereshis (Genesis)* 5:32. He entered the ark with them at the age of six hundred—cf. *Bereshis (Genesis)* 7:11—and was deemed baptized in the ark at that age, while his sons were one hundred for the oldest, and close to that age for the younger and youngest of the three.

The second record of baptism involved the children of *Yisroel* who left *Mitzrayim* under *Moshe* and were baptized unto *Moshe* in the Red Sea—cf. *First Corinthians* 10:1-2. It has already been taught elsewhere in this book that only those who could be held spiritually accountable were considered baptized as they crossed the Red Sea. The baptism of the Red Sea was a selective one. It covered males only, but excluded all boys below the age of twenty—cf. *Bamidbar (Numbers)* 1:2-3, 26:2, & 32:11-12.

Elohiym in His wisdom and will made a selection for baptism to involve only men who were aged twenty and above. In this account of baptism in the Old Covenant scriptures, eligibility for it was strictly based on your sex as a male in the house of *Yisroel* and as one aged twenty and or above. Teenagers, toddlers, infants and babies were all excluded.

Though teenagers, toddlers, infants and babies were part of the convoy that crossed the sea, like the other living non-human beings in the convoy, they were not involved in the baptism. Please do not be offended or repulsed by my language. The fact is that all females, underaged males, and all animal beings in that convoy, inclusive of a mixed multitude of people who were not of the blood of *Avraham,* were not baptized unto *Moshe* in the sea.

In the third account of baptism, which was for the *Yehoshua*-Caleb army of the children of *Yisroel* who made the historic crossing of the *Yarden* into Canaan, all the people who were baptized were of the same eligibility status as those baptized under *Moshe* in the Red Sea. That baptism was for adult males only. Their minimum age was twenty.

However, the modal age of these men would have been between forty and fifty-nine, indicative of those men who were born just before the departure from *Mitzrayim* and those who had not turned twenty at the time of the Red Sea crossing. All teenagers, toddlers, infants and babies were also excluded from that baptism.

In *Yisroel,* when a child was born, his parents started to read aloud to him the *Torah* right from the first day of his birth. They did this, teaching him the *Law,* until he turned twenty. Before twenty, if he was not obedient to his parents, they handed him over to the elders who usually sat in council at the city gate. The elders would sentence such a child to death by stoning. Such a disobedient child would then be quickly stoned to death—cf. *Devarim (Deuteronomy)* 21:18-21.

If the child was a good one, however, and grew up obediently under the tutelage of his parents, he became spiritually accountable to himself at the age twenty, when he was considered to have known, trusted, and matured in every aspect of the *Torah* enough to be able to live it by himself.

The age twenty was also the age of military service and biological maturity, and so it was a permissible age for marriage and reproduction. At twenty, you could fight Elohiym's wars and also release a holy seed from your loins for His kingdom.

Note that, *Elohiym* did not grant the sons of *Noach*—Shem, *Cham* (Ham), and *Yephet* (Japheth),—the chance to release any seeds in their loins until they and their seeds were made pure in their baptism in the ark.

Before twenty, you were tied to the shoelaces of your father, while rendering service and obeisance to him as unto *Elohiym*.

When *YahuChanan ben Zecharyahu* said in *YahuChanan (John)* 1:28 that he was not worthy to unloose the shoe's latchet of *Yahushua HaMashakhYahu*, he was not only implying his unworthiness in value, but also his immaturity in spiritual power to serve the one who existed before Creation.

If the recruitment of child soldiers in today's wars on earth is repulsive to most peoples' sensibilities, I wonder how we could think the Most High One would recruit teenagers for His army.

At the tail end of the Old Covenant dispensation, comes *YahuChanan ben Zecharyahu*. When he baptized, he did this for matured men of *Yisroel* only.

YahuChanan ben Zecharyahu baptized *Perushim* (Pharisees) professors and *Tzedukim* (Sadducee) philosophers, all with the venom of vipers acquired over many years in them.

He ministered baptism to wicked, extortionist soldiers who would brutalize you when you resisted their efforts to defraud you.

He also baptized matured publican tax collectors who abused their office to exploit the people. *YahuChanan* ministered baptism to mature men who were fleeing the wrath of *Elohiym* which was fast approaching on them.

Yahushua HaMashakhYahu, HaAdon (the Master) and *HaDerekh* (The Way) to *HaAv* (the Father), was baptized at the age of thirty. Was he not setting an example for his would-be followers? At thirty, *Yahushua HaMashakhYahu* was baptized by *YahuChanan ben Zecharyahu* and was declared to be *HaSeh HaElohiym* (the Lamb of *Elohiym*) who had come to take away the sins of the world.

He thereafter went through the mandatory setting apart period of four years—or is it four days?—as the *Pesach Seder* (Passover

Lamb) of *Elohiym* until he was slain at thirty-four—cf. *Shemot (Exodus)* 12:3, 6. That baptism of *Yahushua HaMashakhYahu* by *YahuChanan* was not only to declare and announce him as *HaSeh HaElohiym*, who had come to take the sins of the world away, but it was also Elohiym's manner of commissioning and equiping him for this task.

As evidenced by the scriptures, ministers of the New Covenant faith from its earliest days were led by *Ruwakh HaKodesh* to baptize only matured people for their addition to the Body of *Yahushua HaMashakhYahu*. Starting from the Day of the Outpouring of *Ruwakh HaKodesh* (Pentecost?) in *Yerushalayim*, New Covenant baptism has been for mature people only.

Remember the men from the then Hebrew Diaspora who had come to *Yerushalayim* to celebrate the *Chag Shavu'ot* or Feast of Weeks (Pentecost?), the Ethiopian eunuch, and *Sha'ul* of Tarsus, among many who were baptized in the early days of the New Covenant faith.

All of these men were wayfarers: mature men who could stand up to the dangers of traveling, as were common in those days.

As for *Sha'ul* of Tarsus, there is overwhelming evidence that he was about the age of thirty when he was led to his baptism by *Chananyahu*.

Philippos, who went to *Shomron* to propagate the *Besuras HaGeulah*, baptized only ***"men and women"***—cf. ***Ma'asim (Acts) 8:12***—and was not led by *Ruwakh HaKodesh* of *Elohiym* to consider "boys and girls" as being eligible for baptism into the name *Yahushua HaMashakhYahu*.

When Hebrew ministers of the New Covenant faith ministered baptism to so-called complete Gentile households, as we are told in *Ma'asim (Acts)*, chapters ten and sixteen, for the families of Cornelius and the Philippian jailor respectively, they were not inclusive of any adolescents or toddlers in those families.

The great importance that Hebrew men attached to issues relating to *Elohiym* and to their own spirituality would not permit them to baptize immature members of these households.

We should therefore never think that everybody aged a day and beyond was baptized in the Gentile homes of Cornelius and the Philippian jailor.

It would be wrong for today's salvation seekers of the New Covenant faith to suppose that baptism was ministered to every family member of these men, simply because of the mention of the word "house."

We should not forget that, in both cases, it was only mature people who listened to the word of those who preached—cf. *Ma'asim (Acts)* 10:33; 16:32—and so were the only ones who acted in acceptance and response to the message that was preached by receiving baptism in the name of *Yahushua HaMashakhYahu.*

It is not uncommon today for Gentile teenagers in high school to come home on vacation to tell their parents—who might not themselves know about the salvation of *Elohiym* and how to be born again of water and of *Ruwakh HaKodesh*—that while in school they were born again!

Just what did these teenagers do far away from home to get born again? Invariably, they were led by fellow teenagers, their seniors in higher classes, to recite the *Sinners' Prayer* for that so-called experience that made them born again.

Such teenagers might continue to believe they are born again while growing to be responsible adults as the years roll on. Many still hold onto this faith as they grow to become leaders of flocks in their various Christian denominations.

They become pastors, later on senior pastors, then resident bishops, to archbishops, and all the many other titles many leaders of Christian denominations give to themselves, while in and of this faith. I am scared to the marrow about this. These bishops and archbishops have many followers who were also "born again" in this strange way.

I know of flock leaders who are happy and boastful that they were "called" by *Yahushua HaMashakhYahu* to his service when they were teenagers and in high school. Many of these people claim to have heard the call of *Elohiym* to become ministers of the New Covenant salvation when they were teenagers, and are now leaders who are managing cathedrals, temples, "churches," and whole denominations!

This is sad because, contrary to their claims, I am sure it was not *Elohiym* who they heard call them at that age to be His ministers. At that age, *Elohiym* may only call to caution them to be good boys. Later in life, they could be called to serve Him, but not while they were teenagers.

Yosef, the son of *Ya'akov,* had his dreams at the young age of seventeen—cf. *Bereshis (Genesis)* 37:2. Those dreams announced to him what *Elohiym* would be using him in future to do for His Glory. In the fullness of Elohiym's time, when *Yosef* was aged thirty, he then started to serve as Elohiym's spiritual director to the Pharaoh of *Mitzrayim*—cf. *Bereshis (Genesis)* 41:46.

Hebrew children who had the Word of *Elohiym* washed over them at birth, and continued to regularly receive that washing as they grew up, could only be called to a non-spiritual service at age twenty.

The Levite could be permitted to serve in *Beis HaMikdash* (the House of *Elohiym or Yerushalayim* "Temple") only at age thirty—cf. *Bamidbar (Numbers)* 4:23-40 and *Divrey Hayamin Alef (First Chronicles)* 23:3—after being set apart in preparation for this task at the age of twenty-five—cf. *Bamidbar (Numbers)* 8:24.

By Elohiym's design, *Moshe* was taken from the courts of Pharaoh to be trained in spiritual matters in the desert of *Midyan* (Midian) at the age of forty. At the age of eighty, *Moshe* was ready to act as Elohiym's spiritual representative and a deliverer for His people *Yisroel* in *Mitzrayim*—cf. *Shemot (Exodus)* 7:7 and *Ma'asim (Acts)* 7:23-30.

Caleb had his first spiritual assignment at the age of forty—cf. *Yehoshua (Joshua)* 14:17.

None of the *Shlikhim* of *Yahushua HaMashakhYahu* was a young boy or worse still, a teenager, when they were called and baptized by him or in his name; for, only mature men could be credible witnesses for *Yahushua HaMashakhYahu* and of his resurrection.

For today's Gentiles to be called to serve *HaAdon* (the Master), and to be his witnesses at age sixteen and while in school, after they heard the *Besuras HaGeulah* of the Savior for the first time, whose person, death and resurrection they never saw, is very incredible for me.

For people to hold such a faith, I find it very dangerous. Sadly, that is what some people claim—to have been called to Elohiym's salvation and ministry when they were teenagers. I have fears in these claims.

If teenagers are missing the mark of *Elohiym* and live in error of believing that they were born again at that adolescent age, how about those who claim to have been baptized by the faith of their parents when they were babies?

When such babies grow-up, they believe they were saved when

baptized in their infancy. You will find it extremely difficult to convince such people in their adulthood that they were not born again by that act of infant baptism.

Sadly, the blessings of the sacrifice of *Yahushua HaMashakhYahu*, to the sinner are not reaching a great number of people, particularly those in this group of people who have a false assurance of salvation in infant and teenage baptism.

You can, therefore, see by looking at the world's spiritual landscape that the work of reaching the sinner with the power of Elohiym's salvation has not done much. Is that not sad?

We are only eligible for baptism if we can express faith in the sacrifice of *Yahushua HaMashakhYahu* as the only means to pay the ransom for the sins of mankind and, therefore, the only means by which deliverance from sin, its power, and the grips of the devil over mankind, is obtained.

We are eligible for baptism only if we can repent of our sins, and wish and desire to be delivered of them, so we can avoid the punitive consequences due us from those sins of ours.

We must be able to confess these sins and pledge to forever confess and profess *Yahushua HaMashakhYahu* to be eligible for baptism. We must have the mental acumen, and show our resolve to stay in the Army of *HaAdon* and fight his enemies to the end, in order to qualify to be baptized into his one and only name, *Yahushua HaMashakhYahu*, given by *Elohiym* to mankind by which any sinner may enter His salvation.

We do not serve *HaAdon* in granting baptism to babies, infants, toddlers and teenagers. In fact, anyone who ministers baptism to infants, toddlers and teenagers is neither in Yahushua's workforce and service, nor yet in His salvation and kingdom. This practice of infant and teenage baptism we must stop now.

How to Administer Baptism

It was not intended to have the administration of baptism taught in this book. Because many people administer baptism wrongly, however, I deem it necessary to teach its proper administration. The wrong manner of administering this great ordinance may be due to a lack of understanding of the meaning of the word "baptism".

In my view, many of the misconceptions of how to administer baptism would never have arisen if one little word, **in**, were used in place of another, **with**, in relation to baptism, in some portions of the King James and other popular versions of *The Bible*. May I humbly draw the attention of Bible scholars and translators to the need to look closely at the verses in *Mattityahu (Matthew)* 3:11; *Markos (Mark)* 1:8; *Lukas (Luke)* 3:16; *YahuChanan (John)* 1:26, 31, 33; *Ma'asim (Acts)* 1:5 and 11:16. All these verses of *The Bible* talk about baptism. They talk about *"baptize with", "baptize you with"* or *"baptized you with"*.

I get an irksome feeling in my spirit when I read these. The spirit of the *Holy Scriptures* tells me that we ought to be reading **"baptize in"**, **"baptize you in"** and **"baptized you in"** instead.

Long after *YahuChanan ben Zecharyahu* has excellently executed his assignment as a messenger of *Elohiym* on earth, I am not comfortable when he is quoted as saying, *"I **indeed** baptized you with water"*—cf. *Mattityahu (Matthew) 3:11 and Lukos (Luke) 3:16); "I **indeed** have baptized you **with** water . . ."*—cf. *Markos (Mark) 1:8; "I baptize **with** water . . ."*—cf. *YahuChanan (John) 1:26; "And I knew not: but that he should be made manifest to Yisroel, therefore am I come baptizing **with** water"*—cf. *YahuChanan (John) 1:31; and "he that **sent me** to baptize **with** water . . ."*—cf. *YahuChanan (John) 1:33.*

My spirit is not at peace when I read what *Yahushua HaMashakhYahu* is also quoted to have said, *"For John (YahuChanan) **truly** baptized **with** water, but ye shall be baptized **with** the Holy Spirit (Ruwakh HaKodesh), not many days hence,"*—cf. *Ma'asim (Acts) 1:5, KJV, words in parenthesis are mine;* and these same words repeated in—cf. *Ma'asim (Acts)* 11:16.

The spirit of the *Holy Scriptures* gives me the understanding that it is because of this rendering in translation as **with** water, instead of **in** water, that some people consider it right and proper to pour water on foreheads of people from a cup in their hand in attempts to administer baptism.

Baptism is not administered **with** water but **in** water. Penitent sinners should be baptized, **not with water but in water**. We should look seriously at this inappropriateness in translation, with the view of bringing about the necessary changes so as to portray the correct manner that baptism is administered according to the revelation of the *Holy Scriptures.*

Noach and his family experienced their baptism **in** living waters. The children of *Yisroel* also entered their baptism unto *Moshe* **in** living waters. So did the first entrants into the Promised

Land walk **through a corridor, enveloped by** and in the waters of the *Yarden*, in their baptism unto *Yehoshua*. At Bethabara (Beit-Bar?—House of Cleansing?), the *talmidim* of *YahuChanan ben Zecharyahu* were baptized **in** the waters of the *Yarden*.

When later on *YahuChanan ben Zecharyahu* moved his seat of ministry to a place near *Shalem* (Salim) in the region of *Einayim* (Ænon) in the upper parts of the *Yarden*, he settled in a place where *"there was much water"* so as to make his administration of baptism to his *talmidim* **in** it, meaningful and spiritually beneficial to them—cf. *YahuChanan (John)* 1:28, 3:23. When *Yahushua HaMashakhYahu* was baptized by *YahuChanan ben Zecharyahu*, it was done **in** the waters of the *Yarden*, and not **with** the waters of the *Yarden*. *Philippos* went **into** natural living waters together with the Ethiopian eunuch to perform the act of baptism into the name of *Yahushua HaMashakhYahu*.

From the days of the Old Covenant up until the times of the *Shlikhim* of *Yahushua HaMashakhYahu*, everybody who was baptized, went into living waters and came out of them. Natural living waters were, and still are, the enveloping, surrounding, or immersing media for baptism. Today, our baptism into the name of *Yahushua HaMashakhYahu* must be done by being fully immersed, momentarily, in natural living waters.

We should also understand that our baptism in the name of *Yahushua HaMashakhYahu* is not only an act of identification with him, but is also our participation in his death, burial, and resurrection—cf. *Romans* 6:3-4 and *Colossians* 2:12.

We should, therefore, enter the waters of baptism, die, and be buried there and resurrect from there into a new life. True baptism, in the name of *Yahushua HaMashakhYahu*, is only by immersing the eligible candidate, momentarily, into the medium of natural living waters.

Years ago, I heard of a practice by one Christian denomination where it was its manner and norm to squeeze water from cotton wool and saturate the foreheads of sick and dying persons, supposedly to administer baptism to them for their salvation! The ministration of "baptism" in this ridiculous manner was done in the homes of highly pagan or heathen societies, where the relations or friends of the sick person would not allow their sick to be baptized in the name of *Yahushua HaMashakhYahu*. They themselves did not want to have anything to do with the name *Yahushua HaMashakhYahu*.

Because the sick might be in coma or be so highly incapacitated as to be unable to hear, see or express desire for Elohiym's healing or salvation, this form of "baptism" was so performed just in case the sick would have desired and accepted it, if he were to have been in his right frame of mind!

This kind of "baptism" was termed "maybe baptism" among people who had such a rare kind of "faith" and courage to administer it. Many, "men of God", so-called messengers of *Elohiym*, in their zeal to populate His Kingdom for Him, administered "baptism" supposedly in Yahushua's name in this ridiculous manner.

They camouflaged their intent to minister their kind of "baptism" to the sick and dying by acting as if they were administering medical or nursing care. On their visits to the sick, they would squeeze water from the cotton wool upon their forehead amid the incantation, "I baptize you in the name of the Father, of the Son, and of the Holy Spirit," inaudible to any nearby observers. And this was a practice of people claiming to have been called, taught and sent out by *Elohiym* to minister His salvation to sinners!

The correct and genuine way to administer baptism in the name of *Yahushua HaMashakhYahu*, with the expectation of its accompanying blessings, is to do so in natural living waters. The entire body of the candidate eligible for baptism should be completely immersed, momentarily, in these living waters.

It must be by one single immersion. It is not to be done three times as is the manner of some denominations: one dip for each of the Father, Son and the "Holy Spirit".

The ways of pouring, sprinkling, spraying, or squeezing water from cups and cotton wools are inimical to the norms and practices of the *Holy Scriptures* with regards to how baptism is administered. These practices should be rejected by all salvation seekers.

Just as the issue of baptism **in**, instead of **with**, water was about settled in my spirit, I received some advice from a friend on the issue of how to administer baptism. My friend's advice was for me to look at what the Greek text of the scriptures had to say on the issues of baptism being in water or with water. He believes the New Covenant scriptures were inspired by *Elohiym* and written in Greek (which I am unable to accept, though) and thus might be helpful to examine them.

I considered the advice of my friend even though I believe the New Covenant scriptures were written by Hebrews, originally meant for Hebrews, and, therefore, inspired by *Elohiym* in the same language—Hebrew—by which He inspired holy men for the writing of the Old Covenant scriptures, and never in Greek.

Being a novice in Greek, I immediately visited a local bookshop to see if I could get some help in my quest to further investigate what the spirit of the *Holy Scriptures* had taught me on baptism being *in* living waters, and not *with* water. My visit to the bookshop proved very rewarding. I was blessed to pick up the last available copy of a rare kind of book.

This book was **The New Greek-English Interlinear New Testament,** the UBS 4th Edition or the Nestle-Aland 27th Edition. It contained a Greek text of the *Holy Scriptures* translated into English "As literal as possible, as free as necessary," to follow the maxim of translators, with the two languages placed interlinearly to each other.

I quickly went to the texts of interest about baptism and I was happy to receive confirmation of what I learned from the spirit of the *Holy Scriptures.* In *YahuChanan (John)* 1:26, 31, 33, the Greek words εν υδατι **(en hudati)**, relating to baptism, are correctly translated *"in water".* Again, in *Markos (Mark)* 1:8, the Greek word υδατι is also translated *"in water".*

My joy at this find could not be measured. Even though in *Mattityahu (Matthew)* 3:11, *Lukas (Luke)* 3:16, *Ma'asim (Acts)* 1:5 and 11:16, the Greek word υδατι is translated *"with water",* that did not bother me very much despite my disappointment with these translations. If, in *Markos (Mark)* 1:8, the Greek word υδατι is translated *"in water",* it stood to reason that it ought to have been translated the same in *Mattityahu (Matthew)* 3:11, *Lukas (Luke)* 3:16, *Ma'asim (Acts)* 1:5 and 11:16, and not as *"with water",* at least for the sake of consistency.

Note that *Ma'asim (Acts)* 11:16 is a repetition of *Ma'asim (Acts)* 1:5. Even if the translators had very good reasons for their rendering of **"with water"** and we were to go by a count of **"in water"** against **"with water",** as found in the literal translation into English from those in the Greek text, we would have four counts— as found in *Markos (Mark)* 1:8 and *YahuChanan (John)* 1:26, 31, 33—against three—as found in *Mattityahu (Matthew)* 3:11, *Lukas (Luke)* 3:16, and *Ma'asim (Acts)* 1:5. **"In water"** would then be declared the more appropriate translation by frequency and popularity of usage.

I do not know why Bible translators did not go by their usual maxim, that is, "As literal as possible, as free as necessary," in the translation of the Greek words εν υδατι and υδατι to bring uniformity and consistency in their translation of the Greek "version" of the scriptures to English.

That would have clearly brought out the mode of administration of baptism and saved us the error and confusion of administering baptism with water from vessels, as is done by many. All through *The Bible*, we would then have been reading *"baptize in"* and not *"baptize with"*.

The publishers of the *New American Standard Bible* should be highly commended in this. In three verses of *YahuChanan (John)* 1:26, 31, and 33, they have rightly adopted the literal English translation of *"in water"*, which is heartwarming. I encourage them to go beyond these verses to effect changes in other related verses, notably in *Mattityahu (Matthew)* 3:11, *Markos (Mark)* 1:8, *Lukas (Luke)* 3:16 and *Ma'asim (Acts)* 1:5 and 11:6. For other publishers of *The Bible*, I challenge them to boldly do the same now.

To spice-up this great find in my Greek studies, I chanced upon a tract entitled **What is the "One Baptism"?**, by V. Glenn McCoy, 22470 Mission Hills Lane, Yorba Linda, California, 92687, USA, 714-692-9494. I found in it an interesting piece of information. In that little tract, Glenn McCoy said the English word "baptize" came from the Greek word βαπτιςω **(baptizo)**, meaning to immerse in, as in water.

According to him, the translators of the Greek text to English did not translate *"baptizo."* Instead, it was transliterated when it was anglicized. That is to say, the Greek *"baptizo"* was carried almost whole into the English language in being rendered "baptize," by simply changing the "o" in the Greek to "e." Dear old McCoy says that if the translators had properly translated *"baptizo"* into English, the only word they could ever have come up with would have been "immerse", or "dip."

Ma'asim (Acts) 2:38, for example, would have been more appropriately translated *"Repent, and be immersed in water every one of you in the name of Yahushua HaMashakhYahu, for the remission of sin, and ye shall receive the gift of Ruwakh HaKodesh."* *Markos (Mark)* 16:16 would have read, *"He that believeth and is immersed in water shall be saved; but he that believeth not shall be damned."*

We would then have been unambiguously led to the correct

manner in which to administer baptism. Dear brother McCoy is confident that we would then have been talking of *"YahuChanan the Immerser"* and not "John the Baptist" all these years.

I find it not only amazing but amusing as well that the King James Bible translators did a seemingly better job giving today's readers a clearer understanding of table manners in the days of *Yahushua HaMashakhYahu* than they did of manners associated with baptism at the time. From the Greek text of *Markos (Mark)* 14:20, the translators give us a clear description of a "baptism" of hands at table during the Last Supper.

To me their rendering of the Greek word εμβαπτομενος (*embaptomenos*) as "dipping of hands into a bowl" and not as "baptizing of hands with a bowl" was excellent.

However, I find it strange that they did not seem to find *"baptizo"* in **embaptomenos** so as to follow their own tradition to translate *"baptizo"* as "dip" or "immerse" into water instead of transliterating it as "baptize".

Baptizo should have been translated to the English word "immerse" and should never have been transliterated to "baptize." If *"baptizo"* hadn't been mistakenly transliterated to "baptize", all this confusion in the minds of people today—in pouring, sprinkling, and spraying water on parts of peoples' bodies in their attempts to administer baptism—would never have come into the faith of people seeking the salvation of the Most High One at all.

Maybe it might still be beneficial, if the King James Version of *The Bible* is revised now, with the view to address some of these issues.

In this regard for a revision of the English Bible, I find the work done by Dr. Phillip E. Goble in coming out with the *Orthodox Jewish Bible (OJB)* highly commendable and of such a great blessing to salvation seekers of both Hebrew and Gentile origins that, I suggest all must obtain copies of this book.

Where to Administer Baptism

Let us consider further the issue of where to conduct baptism into *Yahushua HaMashakhYahu*. Of course, from all the foregoing, we can understand that genuine baptism is administered in water; but where should this water be?

Is it alright to administer baptism for kings in their king-sized bathtubs? If baptism is ministered in swimming pools, is it alright? How about those dugout water tanks made in concrete in worship places; are they permissible for baptism?

Is all water, water? Of course, all water is water insofar as it is free of poisonous contaminants and is odorless. The water taken from the Nile that was in the tea kettle, bathtub, and hand-wash bowl of the Pharaoh turned into blood just as the Nile water itself did when *Elohiym* brought a curse on the waters of *Mitzrayim*.

But then, what would *YahuChanan ben Zecharyahu* do if he was sent back to the world today to repeat a dose of baptism for humanity? Where would he be found? Would he stay in the coolness of some cathedral or basilica grounds and have treated water transported via aqueduct over a long distance to him to administer baptism?

What would *Yahushua HaMashakhYahu* himself do if he came disguised to your home and led you to accept the truth of the *Besuras HaGeulah*? Would he order your children to quickly fill up a barrel with water so you could be dipped into it to have him administer baptism for you?

These are questions that need direct answers. We should all be thinking of giving these direct answers to them as we seek to obey the Master's instructions to the letter.

Philippos ministered baptism to the Ethiopian in natural living waters in the desert of Gaza. In Philippi, it was the custom of the *Kehillah*, or Congregation of believers of *Yahushua HaMashakhYahu*, to have their worship meetings on the riverbank upon which the city was built. It would seem safe to believe that Lydia, one of these believers, was baptized in this natural water body when, at worship on a *Shabbat* (Sabbath-day), *Sha'ul* and his company ministered the word of salvation to her.

I would also believe that the jailor in this same city of Philippi was baptized that midnight in this natural body of living waters. It should not be difficult to understand that Crispus was baptized in the sea waters since Corinth was a coastal city—cf. *Ma'asim (Acts)* 18:8. Similarly, with Caesarea being a city on the eastern Mediterranean Sea coast it should not be difficult to understand that Cornelius and his household were marched to the seashore to have baptism ministered to them in the sea, a natural body of living waters.

The puzzle areas are those baptisms that involved *Sha'ul* of Tarsus, the *Shomroni* believers, and the Hebrew Diaspora returnee-

believers on the Day of the Outpouring of *Ruwakh HaKodesh*
(Pentecost?) in *Yerushalayim*. Though there are no references in the
Holy Scriptures to any specific places where these people were
baptized, it would be safe to believe they were baptized in bodies of
natural living waters.

At the time of *Yahushua HaMashakhYahu*, the city of
Yerushalayim was well endowed with natural water resources in
springs, pools, brooks, etc. There was the famous brook *Kidron*
(Cedron) to the east, running roughly north to south, parallel to the
Holy City and about 200metres away from the "Temple". We had
the *Shiloach Berekhah* (Siloam Pool) to the south, about 600metres
away from the "Temple"; and close to *Shiloach Berekhah* was the
Lower Pool. North of the "Temple" were two pools: *Seh Berekhah*
(Sheep Pool) and *Yisroel Berekhah* (Yisroel Pool). *Seh Berekhah* was
about 250metres away, while *Yisroel Berekhah* was less than
100metres away from the "Temple". Besides these was *Nachash
Berekhah* (Serpent Pool) to the southwest, about one kilometre
away, and Tower's Pool about 500metres westward of the
"Temple". Reference: *Thompson Chain Reference Bible*, Fifth
Improved Edition (1988), Map 10.

So, then, on the Day of the Outpouring of *Ruwakh HaKodesh*
(Pentecost?) in *Yerushalayim, Shimon Kefa* and the other *Shlikhim* of
Yahushua HaMashakhYahu did not have any serious difficulties
trying to locate bodies of natural living waters for baptism. We can
safely believe that all their over three thousand converts on this day
were baptized in natural living waters.

But then, if, despite the presence of all these natural resources
of waters in and around the Holy City, *Ruwakh HaKodesh* of *Elohiym*
would only have the *Shlikhim* of *Yahushua HaMashakhYahu*
administer baptism to the over three thousand men in the river
Yarden, which was some 25kilometres away from the Holy City,
then so be it.

It would, no doubt, have been a wonderful event to behold and
capture on film today, these salvation seekers in a happy mood
making a brisk march to the *Yarden*, and of how they swarmed
along its banks for the ritual of baptism to be performed on them by
the *Shlikhim* of *Yahushua HaMashakhYahu*, all of which would seem
reminiscent of the baptism of their ancestors at this same location
in the days of *Yehoshua*. Was this not what happened? I am led to
believe this was what indeed happened.

Obviously, all the accounts of baptisms in the Old Covenant

dispensation reveal they were conducted in bodies of natural living waters like seas and rivers.

I would therefore think that we should follow the tradition of *Elohiym*, the only true conservative being, and administer baptism—in His name, on His behalf, and in His manner—in bodies of natural living waters, be it pools, lakes, or rivers.

We have only one sacrifice to make if we follow His tradition of baptizing in natural living waters—walking or moving to the locations of these bodies of living waters. I am sure this would not seem to be much of a sacrifice for anyone who desires to become eligible to enter the *Malchut HaShamayim* (Kingdom of Heaven).

Those who administer baptism must understand they do so in the stead of *HaAdon*. They must not only strictly copy the manner of its ministration by *HaAdon* himself, but they must do it with his mind and thoughts as well. **"What would *Yahushua HaMashakhYahu* do?"** is the question we should always ask ourselves when we seek to live the life of *HaAdon* or try to do his business for him.

Our conveniences and comforts should be beside our considerations in our labors for *HaAdon*. Our state of modernism should not be a hindrance to our obedience of the Master's will. What would *Yahushua HaMashakhYahu* do? Carry a portable, plastic or inflatable baptistery around town and ask for it to be filled with water for him to administer baptism in anytime he had a willing, repentant and yielding sinner?

Is that what our so-called civilization and modernism are leading us to do? Man is only civilized when he walks in the will of *Elohiym*, and not when surrounded by the beautiful things of the world.

We should, therefore, always seek to do the will of *HaAdon*, irrespective of the inconveniences and discomforts to ourselves. After all, are we not to be working sacrificially, or better still like people who are truly dead to self, for the one who loved us and gave his sinless life as a ransom for our salvation? I think we should walk to bodies of living waters to carry out this great ordinance of *HaAdon* which is baptism.

We should feel more comfortable and secure to have a lasting or perennial place of reference to our baptism than one that can shift itself. It would be more significant and meaningful to say we were baptized in the River Volta, Niger, or Zambezi, than to say we were baptized in a barrel or giant metal basin of water.

Baptism is not to be understood to mean a wash of the body or a bath, in which case a Jacuzzi in a bathroom would have been an appropriate place to administer it.

It would sound absurd for any man of *Yisroel* to say he was baptized in a giant metal basin, but wise to hear him tell of undertaking the rite in the waters of the *Yarden*.

Have we not accepted that baptism means burial of the dead sinner in waters, for the saved righteous to resurrect? Do we carry graves about to bury people anytime or anywhere we find the dead? Again, do we normally go to open up the graves of our buried dead to bury our freshly dead loved ones?

Personally, in consideration of these questions, I think the practice of conducting so-called baptism in portable plastic baptisteries is wrong, just as it is to do so in any man-made tanks or pools.

Throughout Hebrew history there has been a place that seemed to be the ideal location, spiritually and topographically, that was suited for baptism. The baptisms conducted at this site are just too many; occurring so often that one cannot help but acknowledge the sacredness of this baptismal destination. This location is the portion of the *Yarden* that lies opposite *Yericho*.

This is the location where the baptism unto *Yehoshua* was conducted before the conquering of Canaan—cf. *Bamidbar (Numbers)* 22:1 and *Yehoshua (Joshua)* 3:16. It was also the baptismal destination for *Eliyahu* and *Elishah*, two of Elohiym's choicest *neviim* ("prophets") of the Old Covenant period—cf. *Melekhim Bais (Second Kings)* 2:8-14. This same location was the original headquarters for the preaching and baptizing ministry of *YahuChanan ben Zecharyahu*—cf. *YahuChanan (John)* 1:28.

This place named Bethabara, (Beit-Bar?—meaning "House of Cleanness"?), where *YahuChanan ben Zecharyahu* conducted baptism for crowds of repentant Hebrews and also for *HaAdon*, was right across from *Yericho* and on the east bank of the river *Yarden*. Amazingly, "Bethabara" is also said to mean "house of the ford" or "house of passage": A place of passage, indeed, where the performances of rites of cleansing in baptism to pass into a new life were frequently done!!

So does *Elohiym* have a landmark location for baptism? What do you think? I think He does. *Elohiym* does not have a mind of allowing baptism to be conducted just anywhere, shifting from bathroom tubs to metal water tanks placed in some garden and then to tile-lined swimming pools. It must be obvious that we ought to conduct the ministration of baptism in bodies of natural living waters.

Baptism is too important to be done according to the whims and caprices of so-called followers or poor copyists of *Yahushua HaMashakhYahu.*

Let us seek to carry out this ordinance the best way *Yahushua HaMashakhYahu* himself would, if he were here on earth with us. That is the sterling service required of his *talmidim*; he deserves our best. *HalleluYahu, HalleluYahu.*

As I later reflected on these two loud and big *"HalleluYahu"* of the preceding paragraph, it came to me in a strong way that the issue of where to administer baptism, as I have been considering, was not conclusive enough.

I still had a few verses of scripture to consider, to help lay bare the fact that it is wrong to conduct the ritual of baptism in man-made, water-containing structures—so-called *baptisteries.*

From my understanding of the verses of scripture in *Shemot (Exodus)* 20: 25, *Yehoshua (Joshua)* 8: 30-31, and *Ma'asim (Acts)* 17: 24-25, it cannot be acceptable to *Elohiym* that we administer the rites of baptism in man-made, water-retaining structures of any kind for a very obvious reason.

This is because, from all these verses, it is clear that *Elohiym* has no use of man-made things for His Work or Worship, except, of course, for those handiworks of men that He expressly instructed in the Old Covenant times to be made by men He anointed to meet specific purposes.

Let us look at the content of two of the three scriptures referred to earlier here:

"And if thou wilt make me an altar of stone, thou shalt not build it of hewn stone: for if thou lift up thy tool upon it, thou hast polluted it"—Shemot (Exodus) 20:25, KJV.

God (Elohiym) that made the world and all the things therein, seeing that he is Lord of heaven (Shamayim) and earth, dwelleth not in temples made with hands; Neither is worshipped with men's hands, as though he needed any thing, seeing he giveth to all life, and breath, and all things;"—Ma'asim (Acts) 17:24-25, KJV; words in parenthesis are mine.

What can we say in defense of our actions in violating these very clear verses of scripture if we must construct and or fabricate structures to hold water to be used in baptizing people?

Baptism is the number one ordinance for all those who wish to express faith in *Yahushua HaMashakhYahu*. He has instructed it for the observance by all his would-be *talmidim*.

The importance of baptism, therefore, cannot be over-emphasized since it is the bedrock of the faith of all genuine believers in *Yahushua HaMashakhYahu*.

If our understanding of baptism is wrong, then whatever faith and good understanding we may have in the celebration of the *Pesach* (Last Supper?) according to the instructions of *Yahushua HaMashakhYahu*, as the second and last ordinance of the New Covenant faith, cannot bring us any spiritual benefits.

From my knowledge of the tenets of Christianity, it seems to me that this generation has grossly misunderstood the place of baptism in man's salvation and has been misled into doing ridiculous things like ministering baptism in containers made with human hands to hold portable water. We must change this practice now.

Let us consider the issue of where to administer baptism further from yet another angle. Many bible students, Christian clergymen and theologians know that under the Old Covenant, sin in man was disposed of—so to speak—never in homes but outside, far beyond the walls of human habitations.

It is in very much the same vein that garbage disposal sites and cemeteries are never located within built-up areas of human dwellings today, though in later years these sites could be swallowed up by the spread of human settlements.

On *Yom Kippur* of the Old Covenant dispensation, the sins of *Yisroel* were disposed of in the wilderness outside the walls of the Holy City, far away from human settlements.

A *sair l'Azazel* (scapegoat) was always chosen from among two goats for this purpose by the casting of lots. Afterwards, the high priest transferred all the sins of *Yisroel* unto the head of the *sair l'Azazel* by laying his hands upon it and confessing the sins of the nation upon it, after which the goat was sent by the hand of a strong youthful man to be left to eventually die under the burden of sin in the wilderness. Let us quote the relevant verses of the scriptures here:

"But the goat, on which the lot fell to be the scapegoat, (sair l'Azazel) shall be presented alive before the Lord to make

atonement with him, and to let him go for a scapegoat into the wilderness. And Aaron (Aharon) shall lay both his hands upon the head of the live goat, and confess over him all the iniquities of the children of Israel (Yisroel), and all their transgressions in all their sins, putting them upon the head of the goat, and shall send it by the hand of a fit man into the wilderness. And the goat shall bear upon him all their iniquities unto a land not inhabited: and shall let go the goat in the wilderness"—cf. Vayikra (Leviticus) 16:10, 21-22, KJV; words in parenthesis are mine.

As is clearly stated in these verses, sin was disposed of in this manner under the Old Covenant, according to the instructions of *Elohiym*.

As a general rule under the Old Covenant, anybody who showed evidence of sin in his body, which was always a manifestation of sickness in his body, was compelled to vacate camp or leave home, get out into the countryside, and remain there until he was healed before returning to town.

This explains why lepers were always banished from settlements in *Yisroel* and had to stay outside the walls of their cities until they were healed.

When *Yisroel* was bitten by snakes in punishment for sin while they undertook their journey from *Mitzrayim* to Canaan, they had to go outside the camp to be healed, returning to the camp only after their sin and its consequences were removed from their bodies. This we read in *Bamidbar (Numbers)* 21:4-9, the last two verses of which I quote here:

"And the Lord said unto Moses (Moshe), Make a fiery serpent, and set it upon a pole: and it shall come to pass, that every man that is bitten, when he looketh upon it, shall live. And Moses (Moshe) made a serpent of brass, and put it upon a pole, and it came to pass, that if a serpent had bitten any man, when he beheld the serpent of brass, he lived"—cf. Bamidbar (Numbers) 21:8-9, KJV; words in parenthesis are mine.

This miraculous way of receiving healing from *Elohiym* was cited and elucidated by *Yahushua HaMashakhYahu* in *YahuChanan (John)* 3:14-15 during his earthly ministry. In these verses of *YahuChanan*, the Savior teaches why his body must be bruised and disfigured by the stripes that wicked Roman soldiers were later to inflict on him by their whips, and then hung to a pole outside the walls of the Holy City.

The hanging of the Savior, a sacrifice designed by *Elohiym* to be the only means by which sin is taken out of the spirits and bodies of sinful mankind and disposed off, was done outside the walls of *Yerushalayim.*

So, today, anyone who goes out in the spirit to behold the horrible spectacle of the bruised body of the Savior that was hung on a pole, outside the walls of *Yerushalayim* in the year of his sacrificial death, can instantly have his sins forgiven, as well as have the evil consequences of those sins, notably, sickness and disease, removed from his body—that is, if the one would sorrow in his heart, accepting that it was him and his sins that were the reason for all the suffering that the Savior had to bear in his sacrifice.

I do know that in *Bamidbar (Numbers)* 21:4-9, it is not stated that the bronze serpent was hung on a pole **outside** the camp of *Yisroel* at the time they were in the wilderness, and yet my spirit is led to understand that this was so. This is because that event in the wilderness was the shadow to the hanging of the Savior, and their similarities are clear and strong.

It may be helpful to quote *YahuChanan (John)* 3:14-15 here for easy reference:

"And as Moshe lifted up the serpent (nachash) in the wilderness, even so must the son of man be lifted up: That whosoever believeth in him should not perish, but have everlasting life (Chayyei Olam)"—YahuChanan (John) 3:14-15, KJV; words in parenthesis are mine.

Later on in *Hebrews*, we are told that the hanging of the Savior outside the walls of *Yerushalayim* was done so the salvation seeker would have to go out there to receive the blessings of his sacrifice. And so, nobody stays within the city walls to gain the blessings of the Savior's sacrifice. This truth, we read in *Ivriim (Hebrews)* as follows:

"For the bodies of those beasts, whose blood is brought into the sanctuary by the high priest for sin, are burned without the camp. Wherefore Jesus (Yahushua) also, that he might sanctify the people with his own blood, suffered without the gate. Let us go forth therefore unto him without the camp, bearing his reproach"—Ivriim (Hebrews) 13:11-13, KJV; word in parenthesis is mine.

Therefore, we must understand that the administration of baptism is not an indoor, homegrown or intra-city event. The spirit of the *Holy Scriptures*, seen moving from *Bereshis (Genesis)* to *Hisgalus (Revelation)*, gives meaning to this.

We must not minister baptism in man-made, water-holding structures at home or within cities of human occupation. The place to go for baptism is in the natural—the natural bodies of living waters in the world made by *Elohiym* Himself—and not in any other places.

A Definition of Baptism

As we move toward the conclusion of this teaching on the rare truths of baptism, permit me to now attempt a definition of the word **baptism.**

It might seem unorthodox to be defining a word at the end of an exposition on it, but in spiritual matters, there is no difference between *The First* and *The Last,* and so I hope readers will permit my style. He that was *The First* is also *The Last.* He that was *The Beginning* is also *The End.* I hope we can all agree in these regards.

I attempt to define the word baptism based on my understanding of it, from two perspectives. First, baptism is an occasion of saying good-bye forever to a certain relationship, status, lifestyle or environment when someone embarks on a journey, in accordance with the plan and will of *Elohiym* for him, by passing over or through a body of natural living waters.

In passing over the water body, the one on pilgrimage is severed completely and permanently from a certain culture he was previously a participant of and enjoyed. The pilgrim passes over or through the water body from one end to the other, never to return.

Even though many Bible students accept that genuine baptism in the name of *Yahushua HaMashakhYahu* is by immersion, the understanding of the rite as being an in-and-out-of-water situation is thought to be obvious and, therefore, not often stressed or emphasized.

I think we should begin to emphasize this. Baptism is an in-and-out-of-water act or ritual. This we should seek to teach so as to make this important ordinance properly understood.

From a second perspective, baptism is an act of death and burial in natural living waters and a resurrection to life from the same waters.

The candidate for baptism willfully enters the waters to die there, be buried or covered by the water, and resurrect from there, saying an irrevocable good-bye to a previous life, and accepting and living a new one.

Here, too, the in-and-out-of-water situation is often silent, even when baptism is taught from this angle. This, however, ought to be emphasized to bring clarity to the meaning or definition of baptism.

From both perspectives, the role played by natural living waters is very important and, in fact, indispensable. The fact of taking on a new life of better glory, new values, challenges, etc., is also obvious from both perspectives.

So is the fact of the pilgrim, not going back to the previous environment, culture, or lifestyle, also evident in both considered perspectives. The life that one previously lived, and most probably enjoyed and or was enslaved to, now becomes detestable to him after his baptism into *Yahushua HaMashakhYahu.*

Baptism—the passing of man through a body of natural living waters by *Elohiym* or His representative—is the miracle of *Elohiym* that passes man from a base nature to a civilized one. It passes man from an earthly nature to a heavenly one, from being human to being divine, and from sinfulness to holiness, never to return to that lower sin nature.

If we have this understanding of baptism firmly in mind, then we can see its manifestation many times in the *Holy Scriptures*— from *Bereshis (Genesis)* to *Hisgalus (Revelation)*—both in shadow and real forms. New life has always come to man through baptism.

Where the word "baptism" is used in any context devoid of waters, it is only in a figurative sense and does not rightly lead us to the actual meaning of the word.

Even in the figurative usage of the word "baptism", the same ingredients of passing from a certain place, situation, or life to a better and more glorious one are always present.

When *Yahushua HaMashakhYahu* talked to his *talmidim* about his then fast-approaching affliction, grief, and vicarious death as being a baptism in suffering, he was alluding to a passing over from a lower state to a more glorious one, never to return to the lower— cf. *Mattityahu (Matthew)* 20:22-23, *Markos (Mark)* 10:38-40, and *Lukas (Luke)* 12:50!

Let me state here that whatever phenomenon or spiritual experience that some people consider as a "baptism in the Holy Spirit" is, in fact, no baptism at all.

If we look at this strange spiritual phenomenon of a so-called "baptism in the Holy Spirit" critically, within the definition of the word "baptism" as being an in-and-out-of-water (or some medium) situation, this strange spiritual experience does not qualify to be termed baptism for obvious reasons.

Obviously, *Ruwakh HaKodesh* (same as this Holy Spirit?) is the personality of *Elohiym* and not a medium or a visible confine into which one can deliberately walk and come out of anytime and anywhere.

Even if this experience is an enveloping, gripping or engulfing feeling of the presence of "the Holy Spirit" (Note: Holy Spirit may not be same as *Ruwakh HaKodesh* of *Elohiym*), it is one that comes to the person who experiences it and not as a result of the person willfully, deliberately, and conscientiously walking into and out of it.

The opposite of all known types of baptism—shadowy, real, or figurative—is what we see in this so-called "Holy Spirit baptism". Instead of the salvation seeker walking into "the Holy Spirit", it is rather "the Holy Spirit" that comes to the salvation seeker to envelope him.

The term "Holy Spirit baptism" is therefore a misnomer of what any salvation seeker might experience of a genuine and spectacular enveloping presence of *Ruwakh HaKodesh* of *Elohiym*.

This term we should desist from using since nowhere in Elohiym's Holy Word are we taught or permitted its usage. Its continued use will only prolong our confusion, delay bringing salvation seekers to the ways of *Elohiym* through which the power of *Ruwakh HaKodesh* will come to dwell within their hearts, and take us away from the fact that baptism in water, in the name of *Yahushua HaMashakhYahu*, is the only way to make this happen.

We must understand that a genuine enveloping presence of *Ruwakh HaKodesh* of *Elohiym* on His people occurred many times in the Old Covenant past. It is remarkable to note that, in that dispensation, it was never termed a baptism. In all those occurrences of this phenomenon, they were described as *Ruwakh HaKodesh* coming upon the holy men who experienced it and not as a baptism.

What happened in the upper room on the Day of the Outpouring of *Ruwakh HaKodesh* (Pentecost?) in *Yerushalyim*, can, in my view, be more appropriately described as the coming of *Ruwakh HaKodesh* upon the heads and into the hearts of the *talmidim*, rather than a semblance to any kind of baptism, whether real, shadowy, or figurative.

Of course, the letter—mind you, not the spirit—of *The Bible* accounts of *Ma'asim (Acts)* 1:5 and 11:16 seem to describe the events in the upper room on the Day of the Outpouring of *Ruwakh HaKodesh* (Pentecost?), as a "baptism with the Holy Ghost". That assertion is attributed to *Yahushua HaMashakhYahu* himself by bible translators!!

Those accounts, however, are puzzling to me and no doubt puzzling to any student who considers the letter of these verses against the spirit of the whole New Covenant revelation.

Why did *Yahushua HaMashakhYahu*, in all his days during his teaching ministry before his death, never mention a "baptism with or of *Ruwakh HaKodesh* (Holy Ghost?)", as a pre- or post-salvation experience meant for all his *talmidim*?

In my view, *Yahushua HaMashakhYahu* did not teach this as a doctrine because, in the mind and wisdom of *Elohiym*, there is no such thing as a "baptism with, of, by or in *Ruwakh HaKodesh* (Holy Spirit?)".

It would seem strange to many for *Yahushua HaMashakhYahu* to be using the words ". . . ye shall be baptized with the Holy Ghost (*Ruwakh HaKodesh*?)", after his resurrection, when all through his teaching and healing ministry he never used them.

Throughout his teaching on earth, *Yahushua HaMashakhYahu* used words that could only be translated as, ***"I will send you Ruwakh HaKodesh"*** and ***"Ruwakh HaKodesh shall come upon you"***. Why would he, after his resurrection, be talking as to "baptize with the Holy Ghost (*Ruwakh HaKodesh*?)"?

Again, why would the Master at this time tie the descent of *Ruwakh HaKodesh* into the hearts of his *talmidim* to the baptism of *YahuChanan ben Zecharyahu* and not even to that of his own, which he ministered to them himself?

Was YahuChanan's baptism more relevant to the receipt of *Ruwakh HaKodesh* than that which *Yahushua HaMashakhYahu* ministered to his followers? I do not think so; in fact, it is not so.

In any case, were **all** of the Savior's followers or *talmidim* also baptized by or in the name of *YahuChanan ben Zecharyahu*? No. Why then would he be referring to YahuChanan's baptism, and making a link between it and their receipt of *Ruwakh HaKodesh*?

Is it not obvious that the word "baptized," used in the context of these verses of *Ma'asim (Acts)* 1:5 and 11:16, is contrary to the manner of describing the descent of *Ruwakh HaKodesh* throughout the Old Covenant dispensation and is also against the spirit of the teachings of *HaAdon*?

In the Old Covenant dispensation, all the accounts of people coming into the phenomenon of an enveloping presence of *Ruwakh HaKodesh* of *Elohiym* were never said to be baptisms.

Ruwakh HaKodesh, in all of those instances, was said to have come upon those blessed to experience the phenomenon, as seen in *Bamidbar (Numbers)* 11:25, 24:2, *Shofetim (Judges)* 3:10, 6:34, 14:6, *Shmuel Alef (First Samuel)* 10:10, 16:13, and *Lukas (Luke)* 2:25.

We must find good reasons why the words of *Ma'asim (Acts)* 1:5 which are repeated in *Ma'asim (Acts)* 11:16 stand the way they are, different from the whole revelation of the *Holy Scriptures* about how *Ruwakh HaKodesh* is received throughout all dispensations. It is very important we find these reasons.

Until we find them, it might not be beneficial to take these verses to mean a postulation of a so-called *"Baptism with the Holy Spirit Doctrine,"* simply because of the mention of the word "baptized" in these verses. *HalleluYahu!*

A Conclusion

Elohiym has designed for sinful man to receive His *Ruwakh HaKodesh* in only one way: that is, by the obedience of His Word. The Word of *Elohiym* instructs the salvation seeker to receive baptism in living waters in the name of His Son, *Yahushua HaMashakhYahu*, after repenting of his sins, on accepting the message of the *Besuras HaGeulah*, so he can be born again and then receive *Ruwakh HaKodesh* to dwell within his heart.

Baptism in the name of *Yahushua HaMashakhYahu* leads one to obtain remission of sin, which further leads one to receive the gift of *Ruwakh HaKodesh*—cf. *Ma'asim (Acts)* 2:38-39. No other baptism "with, by, or in the Holy Spirit" (*Ruwakh HaKodesh?*) exists after this one and only baptism in water, ministered by ministers duly sent by *HaAdon*, which brings about the descent of *Ruwakh HaKodesh* into the hearts of men. *HalleluYahu!*

My dear reader, we must strive to understand baptism, so as to reap its blessings. We understand easily that water is life, since it is indispensable to both animals and plants. We should also understand that water is life spiritually since, without waters for baptism, the spirit of man is dead in trespasses and in sin. Baptism brings the life of *Elohiym* to unite with the spirit of man, making him eligible to spend eternity in *Shamayim* with the angelic host,

Yahushua HaMashakhYahu, the Creator and only begotten Son of *Elohiym*, and *Elohiym*, the Most High One, Himself.

There are only two ordinances instructed by *Yahushua HaMashakhYahu* for the strict observance of all his *talmidim*. Baptism is one; the other is the Last Supper memorial. Baptism however precedes the Last Supper; baptism makes people qualified to observe the Last Supper ordinance. Yet we have missed this significance of baptism? What is gained in the celebration of the Last Supper by a people whose understanding of baptism is messed up and highly poisoned?

I wonder what our lot would have been if we had about ten ordinances of *Yahushua HaMashakhYahu* to observe. Maybe, it would then have been pardonable if we brought errors and misconceptions into them, since we could claim they were too many. As it is, we have only two of them. We are supposed to study to understand and obey them to the letter for our own gain. What our problem or difficulty is in this regard I do not know.

We have allowed laziness and gullibility of our minds to deal treacherously with us. Our faith is that baptism into *Yahushua HaMashakhYahu* is a mere formality; we are saved in some *Sinners' Prayer* recitals in theatrical fashion after some "man of God", and go for baptism later on as a cooler!

Not even knowing how best to cool the body, we are sprinkling, pouring, and spraying water on parts of the body to administer baptism! As if these errors are not enough, we are even baptizing Gentile babies, infants, toddlers, and teenagers, thinking to, by our will, qualify them to enter Elohiym's salvation in *Yahushua HaMashakhYahu*, the Service of *HaAdon*, and the *Malchut HaShamayim,* by such erroneous faiths!

Why do we allow the devil to deal with us so wickedly? Why do we allow him to confuse our faith in the value of baptism to the extent that we are denied its blessing of salvation? How do we enter the *Malchut HaShamayim* without heeding the warning of *HaAdon* to *Nakdimon*? **"Omein, omein, I say to you: unless someone is born of mayim (water) and of Ruwakh HaKodesh, he is not able to enter the Malchut HaElohiym (Kingdom of Elohiym)"** cries *HaAdon* to *Nakdimon* and to all who seek his salvation. Do we not hear Him? If we do, can we not obey Him?

The devil knows what baptism is meant to do for the sinner; sadly, we do not. He has introduced many misconceptions into our faith in it so that he can deny us its benefits. At the end of the day, we realize too late that we have been made tares, the devil's counterfeit wheat. May we beware of this and steer our spiritual lives to the obedience of the instructions of *HaAdon*, so that we can avoid the snares of this enemy.

The time has come for all to look at what they have done in pursuit of Elohiym's salvation. We are saved through repentance from sin and baptism into the name **"Yahushua HaMashakhYahu"**. There is no other way taught in the Word of *Elohiym* by which the sinner can be saved. We should beware of this and avert our courses, which we have made by our recitals of a so-called *Sinners' Prayer* or *Prayer for Salvation*, which are leading us to an undesirable destination. May *Elohiym*, be with us in this. *HalleluYahu*!

After all this rather lengthy teaching on a Greek-based word, "baptism", I would like to conclude this chapter by using this same word as an example, to explain why I said earlier in this book that I am always reluctant to use words of Greek origin in my expositions on the salvation message of *Elohiym*— a message He revealed in the Hebrew tongue, through Hebrew messengers He inspired, and principally, for Hebrews.

Interestingly, *Elohiym* has always spoken His Word only in Hebrew and so wants to be heard and understood in Hebrew! This may be why *Elohiym* has said in His revealed Word, that, **"...Yahushuat Eloheinu (salvation of our Elohiym) is from the Yehudim (Hebrews)"—cf. YahuChanan (John) 4:22, Yeshayahu (Isaiah) 2:3, Romans 9:3-5; OJB, words in parenthesis are mine.**

It is for two reasons that I choose the word "baptism" to explain my reluctance to use Greek-based words to teach a Hebrew message. The first reason is because "baptism" is a very popular word among the target audience of this book. My copious use of the word, therefore, seemed inevitable if my teaching was to be easily followed. That notwithstanding, my use of the word has been with much reluctance!

The second is because, even as "baptism" is a popular word among salvation seekers, a lot of misunderstandings and bad practices have crept into our quest for Elohiym's salvation through it. These misunderstandings could have been avoided if only we had strained our ears to hear *Elohiym* speak to us in Hebrew, instead of listening to Greek-speaking folks who claim to have heard and understood Him in Hebrew, and who then tried to lead us to understand Him, in and by their word "baptism", derived from the Greek **"baptizo"**.

You see, in almost all instances when *Elohiym* speaks to mankind with regards to His instructions on "baptism", He always uses certain key Hebrew words to make Himself clear and easily understood. These key words are: **teshuva, mayim, mikveh,** and **tevilah.**

Now, *teshuva* means "repentance" from sin; *mayim* means "water"; *mikveh* means a natural place of a "gathering of waters" as in a river, lake, or pool; and *tevilah* means "dipped himself" or "immersed himself" into water.

So then, what English Bible translators have termed "baptism" after being taught *"baptizo"* by Greek-speaking theologians is, in fact, *"tevilah";* and this **tevilah,** from the perspective of Elohiym's revelation in Hebrew, must be done within the context of repentance from sin *(teshuva)*, in a place of naturally gathered waters *(mikveh mayim)*, and by being fully immersed or dipped momentarily in these waters, for only those people who have repented of their sins upon receiving the *Besuras HaGeulah.*

If Gentile seekers of Elohiym's salvation in *Yahushua HaMashakhYahu* were to understand the born again doctrine in the light of the meanings of *teshuva* and *tevilah* in a *mikveh mayim*, all the misconceptions so prevalent among them about the initiation rite into or of this rebirth and into the Name and Body of *Yahushua HaMashakhYahu* would have been avoided.

Unfortunately, because, most Gentiles are without the meaning and appreciation of the value of these Hebrew words in relation to the born again experience, they are often misled into doing ridiculously weird things such as "baptize" babies who, obviously, are unable to do *teshuva*—repent of sin. These weird things include the dripping of a few drops of water on the foreheads of such babies from a cup in the hand of some "priest" amidst the incantation, *"I baptize you in the name of the Father, and of the Son, and of the Holy Spirit"* as their method of carrying out Elohiym's instructions on *tevilah*!!

Because of the obvious risk of killing these babies, even if they were momentarily immersed in waters, in *tevilah* in a *mikveh mayim*, this has led to the general adoption of the norms of sprinkling, pouring, or spraying of water on parts of even adult peoples' bodies, purporting to be the administration of *tevilah* to them; away from the command of *Elohiym* to fully dip or immerse the salvation seeker in natural living waters in the performance of the rite of *tevilah* ("baptism").

At the end of it all, what blessings *Elohiym* has purposed to dispense to salvation seekers in and by their understanding and submission to undergo *tevilah* in *mikveh mayim*, after *teshuva*, are denied them through these erroneous practices in "baptism".

Missing the blessings of *Elohiym*, due to ignorance and or misunderstanding of His Hebrew-revealed Word is common, especially to the Gentiles. For instance, the Hebrew city-name *"Beit-Lechem"* means "House of Bread". However, English Bible translators have in their work rendered *Beit-Lechem* as "Bethlehem" (resulting from a corruption in pronunciation?), thus, simply making their version (or is theirs a perversion?) of this city-name devoid of any meaning and spiritual value!

And so, whereas Hebrew-speaking people can very much appreciate and be awed by the wisdom of *Elohiym* displayed in His Son, *Yahushua HaMashakhYahu*, as being the "Bread of Life" begotten as a matter of course in *Beit-Lechem*, the Bread City, the Gentile is denied any fascination or thrill in this display of wisdom by the Almighty!! The English Bible scriptures in this regard are simply dry and abstract to any Gentile!

Similarly, the great Hebrew title *"Melekh-Tzedek"*, for *Yahushua HaMashakhYahu*, means "King of Righteousness" and carries a deep meaning and value to the Hebrew-believer of the Hebrew *Holy Scriptures* about the righteous works done and continuously being done by the Savior for sinners, which Gentile believers of *The Bible* are unable to fully comprehend!

The illegal and ridiculous English rendering of *Melekh-Tzedek* as *"Melchizedek"* has, indeed, made it meaningless to Gentile seekers of Elohiym's salvation, and therefore denies them almost all of what was intended for them by *Elohiym* in *Melekh-Tzedek*!!

So, what wisdom *Elohiym* has clearly revealed in *tevilah* in a *mikveh mayim* for those who have done *teshuva* of their sins, is denied non-Hebrews because of their many misconceptions and wrong rituals on "baptism" that are brought to them through Greek thought and teaching.

In view of the misunderstanding of the *Holy Scriptures* that have come to Gentile believers of the English Bible because they are ignorant of Elohiym's intent in His Hebrew-revealed Word, one can only advice Gentiles to be more forceful and diligent in their search for His salvation that is in *Yahushua HaMashakhYahu.*

Those who read *The Bible* with Gentile eyes need to take a more serious look, time and again, at the faith they profess, in order not to be misled and taken away from the truth. In all of this, I say, with all of my best wishes, *Shalom Aleikhem*—Peace, be unto you.

Chapter Four

Facts of the Sinners' Prayer Laid Bare

Long before *Yahushua HaMashakhYahu* went to *Gulgotha* to deliver salvation to mankind, he had cause to worry about the menace of false teachers and prophets. He knew all the sacrifices he was making for the redemption of mankind would be rendered unbeneficial if his teaching on how man was to receive or enter this great salvation was tainted in even the smallest way with falsehoods in doctrine and teaching.

Yahushua HaMashakhYahu therefore prepared his *talmidim* to be very vigilant in looking out for false teachers or prophets, and to deal with them, so that their influence did not bring to naught his redemptive work. False doctrines or teachings have a great propensity of not only denying people desiring to enter the salvation of *Elohiym* in *Yahushua HaMashakhYahu* the opportunity of securing that entry, but also of bringing back even the saved to the very place they were before their salvation.

On many occasions, *Yahushua HaMashakhYahu* taught his *talmidim* that for a doctrine to be useful and beneficial for the salvation of mankind, it had to be of *Elohiym* and not of men. He taught them the true doctrines of *Elohiym* and, in many instances, pointed out to them how important it was for him to follow the doctrine of *Elohiym, HaAv*. His *talmidim* were to obey the doctrines that he taught them if they were to be effective and successful in the business of winning souls, for which assignment he was training them to be in charge after his ascension to *Shamayim*.

In *Mattityahu (Matthew)* 7:13, this is what we read from the admonition of *Yahushua HaMashakhYahu* concerning false prophets:

"Beware of false prophets, which come to you in sheep's clothing, but inwardly are ravening wolves"—Mattityahu (Matthew) 7:15, KJV.

False doctrine teachers always use this strategy to disguise themselves as cunningly as possible. Their greatest weapon, however, is the word they speak. In *Mattityahu (Matthew)* 24:24, the issue of false prophets assumes a more alarming and menacing dimension. Apart from what they say, with their intent to deceive, false prophets attempt to confuse the people of *Elohiym* by the miracles they perform. Shall we read this verse?

"For there shall arise ... false prophets, and shall shew great signs and wonders; insomuch that, if it were possible, they shall deceive the very elect"—Mattityahu (Matthew) 24:24, KJV.

The only way the people of *Elohiym* were to survive this onslaught of His enemies was to stick to true doctrine and to be vigilant in looking out for such wreckers of their salvation. As long as the *talmidim* tenaciously adhered to the doctrines of *Elohiym* as were taught them by *Yahushua HaMashakhYahu*, they would be safe and successful.

After all, if they did that, they could be said to be acting in Elohiym's stead, and success would never elude them. If they, however, out of complacency, lack of vigilance, and or compromises in any form or amount diluted the pure, holy, powerful and saving Word of *Elohiym*, then, it would lead to failure and disaster for them and for all seekers of the salvation of *Elohiym* as well.

The enemies of *Elohiym* struck the Flock not long after *Yahushua HaMashakhYahu*, the *Ro'eh HaTov* (Good Shepherd) of the Flock, had physically departed from this world. Though false prophets were largely unsuccessful in their enterprise during the days of the *Shlikhim* due to their vigilance, they remained persistent and adamant in their resolve to wreak disaster among believers of *Yahushua HaMashakhYahu*; they disguised themselves at every turn to look like people of *Ohr HaAmitti* (The True Light). It was, therefore, not long before their determination started to yield dividends for them.

Gradually and steadily, the enemies of *Elohiym* pushed their agenda forward through propaganda of falsehoods, and today it is as if the people of *Elohiym* have been reintegrated into the world.

The teaching of a particular wrong doctrine is one big blow dealt by the enemies of *Elohiym* against mankind's quest for His salvation in *Yahushua HaMashakhYahu*. This doctrine has been so designed as to keep many people from taking the genuine steps to enter the salvation of *Elohiym*. The born again experience, which the doctrine of *Elohiym* teaches to be the means of entering His salvation, has been contaminated and polluted by these enemies of *Elohiym*, to the extent that mankind's understanding of it has become very distorted and confused.

Many people have, therefore, been misled into doing wrong things in their pursuit of becoming born again. Many people have done this unconsciously and do not know that they have been deceived into acting inappropriately and contrary to the instructions of *Elohiym* which He gave to lead mankind into His salvation in *Yahushua HaMashakhYahu*. Many have not obtained what they went out seeking to achieve as a result of this.

As to how sinful man can get to enter the salvation of *Elohiym*, the *Holy Scriptures* show only one clear and foolproof way. This is because when one enters into it, one connects into the power, nature, and resources of *Elohiym*. Therefore, the only way to enter the salvation of *Elohiym* is based on His plan and His clear and simple instructions.

Anything genuine can be counterfeited, so we can understand that, even though Elohiym's plan for the salvation of the sinner is a sure and genuine one, the devil has been able to counterfeit it. For anybody familiar with currencies of exchange, a counterfeit bank note is often made to look very much like the real or genuine one.

In fact, the counterfeiting can at times be so expertly done in the hands of a master craftsman that the fake currency becomes almost impossible to detect and expose. This is exactly what the devil has succeeded in doing with the plan of *Elohiym* for the salvation of the sinner.

We should always keep in remembrance the *Parable (Marshal) of Wheat and Tares*—cf. *Mattityahu (Matthew)* 13:24-30, 36-43—so we can wise up to its meaning and intrigue. Tares are the invention of the devil, a counterfeit product made to look like wheat.

The devil is such a great craftsman that he has been able to perfect a false plan of salvation to look true. Simple and unsuspecting people have accepted it as true and live in the belief of having been saved from the influence of the devil when, in reality, they still remain in his grips.

There exists a large army of zealous, sincere, and dedicated teachers of this contaminated and polluted born again doctrine, ignorant that it is wrong and has no power to save the sinner.

The wicked devil has seen the ease with which gullible mankind has accepted his falsehood, and is intensifying its propagation to frightening limits. The devil is all too happy if the deceived believe they are saved when he knows they are not.

Paradoxically, the people who are easily deceived by this doctrine are the ones who pride themselves as strong adherents to the true doctrines of *Elohiym*.

They are those who belong to the fast-growing denominations of people that claim to be *talmidim* of *Yahushua HaMashakhYahu*. And yet, they live in error of how sinful man must enter the salvation of *Elohiym* in the born again experience. This is very frightening.

A deception of the devil as to how the sinner enters the salvation of *Elohiym* arises from a certain popular doctrine by which people are led to pray that "Jesus Christ" (*Yahushua HaMashakhYahu?*) enter their hearts for them to become born again.

The teaching of this doctrine is structured on some great verses in the *Holy Scriptures*. Through these verses, a message is developed and guided responses are taught.

Because of the profuse use of verses taken from the *Holy Scriptures* in the development of the doctrine, many simple-minded people become victims, easily accepting this falsehood. At the core of this doctrine are the following verses of scripture:

"For all have sinned, and come short of the glory of God (Elohiym)"—Romans 3:23, KJV; word in parenthesis is mine.

"For the wages of sin is death; but the gift of God (Elohiym) is eternal life (Chayyei Olam) through Jesus Christ (Yahushua HaMashakhYahu) our Lord"—Romans 6:23, KJV; words in parenthesis are mine.

"And as it is appointed onto men once to die, but after this the judgment..."—Ivriim (Hebrews) 9:27, KJV.

"Behold, I stand at the door, and knock; if any man hear my voice, and open the door, I will come in to him, and will sup with him, and he with me"—Hisgalus (Revelation) 3:20, KJV.

A message is developed with these verses at the core. The state of the sinner and his ultimate doom are taught. A measure of hope for the sinner is given by the proponents of this doctrine when they get to quote *Hisgalus (Revelation)* 3:20. The sinner, as this doctrine teaches, can enter the salvation of *Elohiym* and receive deliverance from His judgment at the end of the world if he would respond to His invitation in this verse of scripture.

When it comes to deception and counterfeiting, the great ingenuity of the devil is at play here. He puts together these genuine scriptures to bring about a falsehood, which leads many from the truth. Many people, including the learned teachers of this doctrine, fall into his trap of deception simply because the scriptures he uses in his strategy come out clean from the *Holy Scriptures*.

They forget the devil is a deadly wolf that very often takes on sheep's skin, easily transforms itself into an angel of light, and very skillfully misuses Elohiym's Word. Many do not know that the strategy of the devil has always been to use the Word of *Elohiym* to subvert His plans and deceive His people.

This has been his strategy since the fall of man in the *Gan Eden* (Garden of Eden) recorded in *Bereshis (Genesis)* 3:1-5. Since his success in deceiving man in the *Gan Eden*, the devil has been emboldened to perfect his art of causing man to act inappropriately on the Word of *Elohiym*. By this, he ensures that man does not get to obtain the blessings of Elohiym's Word promised to him, particularly the blessing of man's deliverance from the devil's dominion and power through the born again experience.

When *Yahushua HaMashakhYahu* emerged on the spiritual scene of Planet Earth, the devil once again adopted his strategy in trying to tempt him to sin just before the beginning of his earthly ministry. When he failed in his bid to cause *Yahushua HaMashakhYahu* to sin by tempting him to act inappropriately on the Word of *Elohiym*, we are told that he left him for a season—cf. *Mattityahu (Matthew)* 4:1-11 and *Lukas (Luke)* 4:1-13.

During that interlude, the devil went to deal with the logic and thinkings of the *Perushim* (Pharisees), *Sofrim* (scribes), and the then leaders of *Yisroel*. All he did was to lead them to the available truths in the *Holy Scriptures*; that, up until the coming of *Yahushua HaMashakhYahu*, no *navi* ("prophet") had ever come out of *Galil* (Galilee).

He, thereby, skewed the minds of the spiritual leaders of *Yisroel* into believing that *Yahushua HaMashakhYahu* could not be a messenger from *Elohiym*, simply because he was, apparently, to many of them, a native of *Galil*—cf. *YahuChanan (John)* 7:50-52). The Hebrews' rejection of *Yahushua HaMashakhYahu* as a messenger of *Elohiym* was the result of this vile propaganda of the devil using Elohiym's Word to achieve his ambitions.

Salvation seekers should have, by now, been aware of all the wiles of the devil. We ought to have wised-up by now to his cunning ways of using the Word of *Elohiym* to confuse us, which ultimately deny us His salvation.

How could the devil be so successful in leading us away from the salvation of *Elohiym* in *Yahushua HaMashakhYahu*, by taking us speedily to the end of the *Holy Scriptures—Hisgalus (Revelation)* 3:20—to postulate a kind of salvation doctrine for humanity? How could we so gullibly accept this bait and deception? May we find courage and wisdom in our generation to destroy this doctrine of the devil!

In concluding the message as outlined, the preacher instructs for all in the assembly to bow down their heads and to shut their eyes. He further instructs those who, in his words—*"want to accept 'Jesus Christ' (Yahushua HaMashakhYahu?) as their Lord and personal Savior or to give their lives to him"* to stick up their right hands.

Those with their hands up are told to stand on their feet; then, they are told to walk up to the preacher at *"the altar"*. At *"the altar"*, these salvation seekers are led through what the proponents of the doctrine call **The Sinners' Prayer** or **The Prayer for Salvation** by the preacher leading the service. The salvation seeker is led to recite this prayer after him.

Basically, the *Sinners' Prayer* is one asking "God" (*Elohiym?*) for forgiveness of sin. It includes a denunciation of the devil and his cohorts and a pledge to "God" (*Elohiym?*) and "Jesus Christ" (*Yahushua HaMashakhYahu?*) to be with them forever thereafter.

The salvation seeker is led to pray that "Jesus Christ" (*Yahushua HaMashakhYahu?*) would enter his heart and come into his life, purporting to mean a compliance with *Hisgalus (Revelation)* 3:20. All the while, the rest of the congregation must keep every eye shut and every head bowed down, while hymns are sung softly and tenderly.

Before the salvation seekers return to take their seats among the congregation, the preacher prays for them. The preacher's prayer for those who were not long ago considered to be sinners, but now are believed to be saved and born again, is one of thanksgiving to *Elohiym* for receiving them to Himself.

Elohiym is entreated in the prayer to keep them forever, and also thanked for a supposed jubilation in *Shamayim* among the *malakim* (angels) as a result of the "salvation" of these sinners! As these salvation seekers return to their places in the congregation, their faith is that they have become born again!! They believe that they are now the children of *Elohiym*, are now in the *Malchut HaElohiym*, and have had their names written in *HaSefer HaChayyim* (the Book of Life)!!

This doctrine, by which people are taught to receive the

salvation of *Elohiym* through prayer, is spread through many media. This is done through printed pages, radio, television, the Internet, and one-on-one contact in auditoria and crusade grounds across the world. The acceptance and response to this teaching is, sadly, phenomenal.

People have knelt before radio and television sets and, while listening to some preacher in their bedrooms, have prayed that "Jesus Christ" (*Yahushua HaMashakhYahu*?) would enter their hearts. Many of such people have been instructed to place their hands on these radio or television sets, ostensibly as points of contact between them and the preacher, and to say the so-called *Sinners' Prayer* after these preachers for salvation!

Coming out of bedrooms, thereafter, they proclaim to all who would listen to them how they have become born again! Many have come back home from attending some mass crusades or meetings to tell of how they were led to accept "Jesus Christ" (*Yahushua HaMashakhYahu*?) as their "Lord and personal Savior" by the crusader, and how, in praying the *Sinners' Prayer*, they have become born again.

For me, this is the most glaring anti-scriptural act for anyone to ever do in his quest to enter the salvation of *Elohiym*. Sadly, just by being told by "men of God" that this act of prayer made in the name of "Jesus Christ" would make them become born again, many people have expressed a very strong faith in it.

When they have so matured in it, they go to all lengths to defend this faith and practice. Nothing could be sadder than for people, in their ignorance, to believe and defend this falsehood, unaware of the disappointment that awaits them because of it.

It is surprising that people could hold such beliefs that are not taught by the *Holy Scriptures*; yet, this has been the practice and faith of these erring denominations, even long before I came to know and to be associated with this doctrine around the mid 1980s. At times, the only slight modification to their practices, in these regards today, is their skipping of the walk to the pulpit area by salvation seekers when invited to receive "Jesus Christ" (*Yahushua HaMashakhYahu*?) into their hearts as their "Lord and personal Savior".

For those people seeking the salvation of *Elohiym* today, the current practice allows them to stay in their seats or stand in front of them while they are led to pray "Jesus Christ" (*Yahushua HaMashakhYahu*?) into their hearts, and they are then prayed for by those leading them to their so-called salvation of *Elohiym*.

The propagation of this doctrine, with its attendant characteristic of being easily accepted by a great many simple-minded, unsuspecting and ignorant people, has led many to live in delusion of being saved when they are not.

Once they believe they have assurance of being saved in this fashion, they shut their minds to reason, taking a hardened stand against the real truth when they are later confronted with it.

In recent times, the proponents of this doctrine have sought to add credence to their message by bringing into their teaching two very popular verses from *Romans*. The addition of these verses of scripture to the teaching of their doctrine has made their message seem convincing and more acceptable to a lot more people who desire the salvation of *Elohiym*. Let us look at these particular verses of scripture from *Romans*:

"That if thou shalt confess with thy mouth the Lord Jesus (Yahushua), and shalt believe in thine heart that God (Elohiym) hath raised him from the dead, thou shalt be saved. For with the heart man believeth unto righteousness; and with the mouth confession is made unto salvation"—Romans 10:9-10, KJV; words in parenthesis are mine.

These teachers teach their listeners that if they would simply obey the instruction of these two verses of scripture they will be saved! That is, if their listeners would give mental acceptance to these verses and verbally confess them, they would become born again instantly!!

Once they have made a one-off confession of these verses, their faith is that they have become born again. How fallacious this is! Yet, many simple-minded people have accepted this deception as the truth and live in the false belief of being in Elohiym's salvation when they are not.

The teachers of this doctrine draw a lot of their strength, faith, and convictions from *Romans*. However, this book is not a revelation to people who want to become born again. The book of *Romans* is a revelation to people who have already gained the new birth.

It is clearly addressed to holy men ("saints"), and not to sinners desiring entry into the *Malchut HaElohiym*. Let us read the following from *Romans* 1:7:

"To all that be in Rome, beloved of God (Elohiym), called to be saints (holy people); Grace to you and peace from God

(Elohiym) our father, and the Lord Jesus Christ (Yahushua HaMashakhYahu)"—Romans 1:7, KJV; words in parenthesis are mine.

Fact is, all those who are beloved of *Elohiym*, called to be holy, and can call *Elohiym* "Father", are the ones in the salvation of *Elohiym* in *Yahushua HaMashakhYahu*. The entire book of *Romans* is addressed to born again people who were in Rome.

Today, however, the whole of *Romans* is intended to teach members of the Body of *Yahushua HaMashakhYahu* everywhere and to help them understand better the expression of their faith in the salvation of *Elohiym*.

While *Ma'asim (Acts)* teaches and demonstrates how to bring sinners into Elohiym's Kingdom, *Romans* adds explanation to these teachings of *Ma'asim (Acts)*.

The deceiver, therefore, purposely leads salvation seekers to wander through *Romans* and, in the end, causes them not to see Elohiym's instructions for the born again experience.

The instructions for the new birth of the sinner are in the books of *Mattityahu (Matthew), Markos (Mark), Lukas (Luke), YahuChanan (John)*, and *Ma'asim (Acts)*. These are the places the salvation seeker must be roaming in search of how to become born again.

Sha'ul, the writer of *Romans*, was not led into the salvation of *Elohiym* by any of the verses in this book. He entered the salvation of *Elohiym* without *Romans*.

In fact, *Sha'ul* did not have knowledge of any one verse of *Romans* before, or at the point of, his new birth. Yet he could be saved and born again!!

Sha'ul, therefore, could not be leading today's salvation seekers to act on any verse of *Romans* for entry into the new birth. These verses of *Romans* are not intended to lead us into the born again experience.

If, indeed, these verses are meant to bring us into the born again experience, as many people claim they do, then the message of the *Besuras HaGeulah* in *Yahushua HaMashakhYahu* and the directives on how to enter it must have changed, since *Sha'ul* and all other *talmidim* of *Yahushua HaMashakhYahu* accepted and were born again through them.

Nevertheless, the message of the *Besuras HaGeulah* cannot and has not changed, so we are mistaken if we take these verses of *Romans* to mean a directive into the born again experience.

The issue of how to enter the *Malchut HaElohiym* or become

born again was settled in the books of *Mattityahu (Matthew)*, *Markos (Mark)*, *Lukas (Luke)*, *YahuChanan (John)*, and *Ma'asim (Acts)*. The doctrines of *Yahushua HaMashakhYahu* in these books teach to explain how the sinner is born again.

If we miss or ignore, willfully or unknowingly, these teachings of *Yahushua HaMashakhYahu* about how one is born again, we cannot receive the new birth in any other way.

We should therefore search these five books of the New Covenant *Holy Scriptures* to get to know and fully understand the doctrine of *Yahushua HaMashakhYahu* on how we are to be born again, if ever we are to be.

All the books of the *Holy Scriptures* that follow *Ma'asim (Acts)* are meant to educate all believers of *Yahushua HaMashakhYahu*, or those of us who are born again, on the meaning of our expression of faith in *Yahushua HaMashakhYahu*.

These books teach us the way to live to the fullest our new life in *Yahushua HaMashakhYahu*. They teach our status, responsibilities, rights, and privileges, etc. They teach our authority, transformation, and our rewards at the end of time. They teach our final destination in our walk with *Yahushua HaMashakhYahu*.

They do not teach us to replace what we learned and did to obtain the new birth in accordance with the doctrines of the first five books of the New Covenant teachings with these subsequent revelations of *Elohiym* to *Ma'asim (Acts)*.

All the books of the *Holy Scriptures* that follow *Ma'asim (Acts)* teach us what we should continuously do, to obtain that final salvation which we embarked on pilgrimage at our new birth to receive. All these books teach on our progressive salvation, not the instantaneous one that brought us the new birth.

Salvation is both instantaneous and progressive. At the point of entry into the *Malchut HaElohiym* is the born again experience. This is instantaneous salvation.

On receipt of this instantaneous salvation, we are to progressively grow and mature in it through a daily process of sanctification by the Word of *Elohiym* until we attain the full stature of *Yahushua HaMashakhYahu*.

One of the ways that *Romans*, chapter ten in particular, advises that we can be successful in our progressive salvation is for us to forever keep in mind our faith in the new birth.

The truth that leads us to become born again is that about the death, burial, and resurrection of *Yahushua HaMashakhYahu*. This truth we should constantly keep in our human spirits through a lifestyle of faith and confession, until we exit this world.

If we adopt a lifestyle of faith and confession of all that we are in *Yahushua HaMashakhYahu*, and particularly of our participation in the death, burial, and resurrection of our Savior, we shall always remain focused on our calling and appreciate the value of the sacrifice offered for our redemption.

Then, by being so focused all the time, we can live this new life in *Yahushua HaMashakhYahu* in such a way that we are able to obtain that final salvation we seek.

Romans 10:9-10 is not telling any sinner to do a one-off confession of these verses to become born again. That would contradict all that we ever learned from *Mattityahu (Matthew)* through to *Ma'asim (Acts)* about the doctrine of being born again of water and *Ruwakh HaKodesh* of *Elohiym*.

These verses of *Romans* are instructing the born again person to make his faith in the Word of *Elohiym* and the confession of it, particularly that of the death and resurrection of *Yahushua HaMashakhYahu*, his daily, hourly and all-time lifestyle.

That lifestyle would bring to the born again person the final salvation he set out to obtain in the new birth. This is all *Romans* 10 is teaching.

Romans 10 teaches the holy elect of *Elohiym* the great value of the principles of faith and confession to them reaching their destination. Faith and confession should be to the born again person as the compass and rudder of a ship, respectively, are to the sailor.

This is all *Romans* 10 is teaching us. *Romans* 10:9-10 is simply reminding us and emphasizing what the *Holy Scriptures* seek to teach us in *Devarim (Deuteronomy)* 30:11-14 and *Yehoshua (Joshua)* 1:8.

The sinner cannot enter Elohiym's Kingdom by just zealously and passionately confessing *Romans* 10:9-10. No matter how many times and how loudly he confesses these verses, he cannot become born again in that act of confession. These verses are not intended to get the sinner born again.

To be told by anyone to make a one-off confession of these verses, claiming that in so doing one can become born again, is a complete deception. Do not let anybody teach you to confess these verses in your quest to become born again. Please do not allow this.

Any people that will teach *Romans* in such a way that it

overshadows the first five books of the New Covenant teachings, namely, *Mattityahu (Matthew), Markos (Mark), Lukas (Luke), YahuChanan (John)* and *Ma'asim (Acts),* will bring confusion into the faith of true believers in *Yahushua HaMashakhYahu.*

The book of *Romans* is intended to add light and meaning to these five books, and not to overshadow them. We must understand that *Romans* was not revealed by *Elohiym* to us so we could do away with the instructions given in these five books about how we are to be born again.

For the proponents of this strange doctrine on salvation to dwell on *Romans,* and try to teach the salvation of *Elohiym* in *Yahushua HaMashakhYahu* as they do, is to attempt to write another *Besuras HaGeulah.* This strange teaching is not in tune with the spirit of the New Covenant teachings and should not only be rejected but also opposed.

Many questions must be asked about this strange doctrine of how one is taught to enter Elohiym's salvation based on so-called *"altar calls",* Sinners' Prayer recitals, and praying for *"Jesus Christ"* (*Yahushua HaMashakhYahu?*) to enter hearts.

The first question is: Who in the accounts of the *Holy Scriptures* was saved in this manner? Secondly, where in the *Holy Scriptures* do we find such a doctrine? Thirdly, before Elohiym's revelation of *Romans* 3:23; 6:23; 10:9-10, *Ivriim (Hebrews)* 9:27 and *Hisgalus (Revelations)* 3:20, which are cited in attempt to give strength and meaning to this doctrine, were sinners ever saved; and if they were, by what foundational scriptures were they led into this salvation? Lastly, if *Sha'ul,* the writer of *Romans,* was saved before being used by *Ruwakh HaKodesh* to write this book, what scriptures led him into his born again experience?

By the time we obtain answers to these questions, we will find out that this doctrine, which the sinner is taught to enter the salvation of *Elohiym,* by praying for "Jesus Christ" (*Yahushua HaMashakhYahu?*) to enter into his or her heart in a so-called *Sinners' Prayer* recital, is wrong.

Our great question comes to mind once more. ***Did you, in praying the Sinners' Prayer, do as they did for salvation?*** *They,* refers to those saved in the accounts of *Ma'asim (Acts).* You accepted and acted on a deception and are therefore living in delusion of being born again if you prayed, no matter how sincerely and fervently, that "Jesus Christ" (*Yahushua HaMashakhYahu?*) enter your heart to stay.

Why do we not imitate the obedience of *Yahushua HaMashakhYahu* to the doctrines of *HaAv* by obeying his instructions on how one is born again? Why do we choose some other ways—of *Sinners' Prayer* recitals and of praying for "Jesus Christ" (*Yahushua HaMashakhYahu?*) to enter hearts—which are doctrines of men?

While preparing to write this book, I came across and read some teachings espoused by two of my countrymen on the born again doctrine.

The first was from a pamphlet-typed book, entitled **Born Again** written by Heward-Mills, in which he makes the following statements that I not only disagree with, but also find very strange:

HOW TO BE BORN AGAIN

What I must do? If you want to be Born Again, you must do two important things. You must first believe in Jesus Christ as the son of God.

Whosoever believeth Jesus is the Christ is born of God: ... 1 John 5:1

Secondly, you must ask Him to come into your heart or life. The spirit of God will come upon you and into your heart. Then the inner part of you will be *born or produced again.*

God gives you a new heart and spirit altogether.

With your new spirit, you become a **New Man** or a **New Creature**, and are ready to live a **New Life. This new life is possible because you are actually a new person with a new heart.** To be Born Again is as simple as that. People want to do complicated things. But becoming Born Again is very simple!

Believe in Jesus. Ask him into your heart. Confess him as Lord. And you will be Born Again. **(2005, pp. 21-22).**

With great pain and sadness in my heart, I say that the teachings of the writer on how one is born again stand contrary to that of the *Holy Scriptures* on the matter. What did *Yahushua HaMashakhYahu* teach *Nakdimon*, and, for that matter, all of us, about how to be born again? What we are taught by *Yahushua HaMashakhYahu* in *YahuChanan (John)* chapter three should be the foundation upon which any minister of the New Covenant salvation doctrines should attempt to teach people how they can be born again.

When the early ministers of the New Covenant doctrine on the salvation of *Elohiym* in *Yahushua HaMashakhYahu*, like *Shimon Kefa, Philippos, Chananyahu, Sha'ul,* etc., had to teach the manner that salvation seekers can enter the *Malchut HaElohiym*, this teaching of *Yahushua HaMashakhYahu* to *Nakdimon* was their inspiration. Let us capture here this teaching of *Yahushua HaMashakhYahu* on how one can become born again or get to enter the *Malchut HaElohiym*:

> **"Omein, omein, I say to you: unless someone is born of mayim (water) and of Ruwakh HaKodesh, he is not able to enter the Malchut HaElohiym (Kingdom of Elohiym)"—YahuChanan 3:5, OJB; words in parenthesis are mine.**

You can literally feel the loud cries and emphasis in the words "omein" (verily), "omein" (verily) of the Master. In these words of *Yahushua HaMashakhYahu* in *YahuChanan (John)* 3:5 and *Markos (Mark)* 16:16, he set the parameters within which any sinner could ever enter his salvation.

These parameters do not seem negotiable to me. Why do we choose to ignore them in trying to teach how one is born again?

A quotation from the KJV of *The Bible* of *YahuChanan (John)* 3 in the very first page of Heward-Mills's cited book promised some great revelations and spiritual insights. Unfortunately, in his exposition on it, he dwelt on only a portion of this great teaching of *Yahushua HaMashakhYahu* to *Nakdimon* and ignored the most crucial part of it.

The most crucial part of the teaching of *Yahushua HaMashakhYahu* to *Nakdimon*, in my view, concerns how we are to be born again. This is in *YahuChanan (John)* 3:5. In this verse, we are told we can only be born again of **water** and of *Ruwakh HaKodesh*. However, the author ignored this part of the teaching of *Yahushua HaMashakhYahu* to *Nakdimon* and then went on to teach how we could become born again in his own way, which he claims to be by prayer, contrary to that shown by *HaAdon*.

As said earlier on, if the born again experience could come to us by prayer of any kind we would have been told so by *HaAdon*, and he would have given us the substance of such a prayer. *HaAdon* did not teach us this and, therefore, we pray amiss if we do so in the manner that Heward-Mills has taught in his cited book.

Verily I say to you, no matter how many days of fasting and fervent praying we do asking that we be born again, we cannot get born again by that prayer. This is one prayer that is not in the plan of *Elohiym* and we therefore pray outside and against His will—amiss—if we pray in the manner the writer teaches.

The will of *Elohiym* is for **water** and *Ruwakh HaKodesh* to do the work of the new birth or the born again experience. This is His will in the lives of all men, from the day *Ruwakh HaKodesh* was first outpoured upon men in *Yerushalayim* to commence the New Covenant era till the end of this Age. Elohiym's way is not going to change for any people.

It remains the same for all people, in all places, through all seasons and times of the Grace Dispensation. It is therefore only when we move toward natural bodies of living waters in obedience to the instructions of *Elohiym* to be baptized in the name of *Yahushua HaMashakhYahu* that we can hope to become born again to enter His Kingdom.

Elohiym is only too happy with us when we do things according to His clear, simple, and easy instructions. Come to think of it, even though Heward-Mills says in his book that praying for "Jesus Christ" (*Yahushua HaMashakhYahu*?) to come into your heart for you to be born again is simple and without complication, I find this to be the contrary in comparison with Elohiym's instructions on the issue. To me, Elohiym's way is the easiest; any other is impossible. Elohiym's way is for you to repent of your sins and be baptized in the name of *Yahushua HaMashakhYahu* to become born again.

Elohiym never leaves important matters to man to do as he chooses or pleases. *Elohiym* instructs in fine detail and empowers man in the execution of all matters that concern man and also His Kingdom work. Every messenger of *Elohiym* that was successful on his errands, missions, and assignments knew the importance of clearly hearing Elohiym's instructions and obeying them to the letter. So must today's errands men of *Elohiym* learn to carry out, to the letter, His instructions to them.

When *Elohiym* decided to preserve the lives of righteous *Noach* and his family through a flood brought about by forty days and nights of torrential rain, He directed in every detail how *Noach* was to make an ark of gopher wood to ensure the preservation of their lives. According to *Bereshis (Genesis)* 6:22 and 7:5, *Noach* did all that *Elohiym* commanded of him.

The obedience of Noach to these directives of *Elohiym* brought excellent results: an ark that stood the test of the storms, torrential rain, and the barraging waves for those forty days and nights, and one hundred and fifty days of turbulent sea-wave bashing thereafter—cf. *Bereshis (Genesis)* 7:17-24 and 8:1-3.

Your guess about what could have happened to the plan of *Elohiym* to preserve the lives of *Noach* and his family is as good as mine, if *Noach* chose to construct an ark in a way that he fancied, throwing away Elohiym's detailed instructions.

Yet, this is what many are doing with the instructions of *Elohiym* for the salvation of the sinner—throwing them overboard while substituting them with their own. This is not obedience to *Elohiym* and is certainly a far cry from the character of *Yahushua HaMashakhYahu*, who obeys to the minutest detail all what *Elohiym* instructs him.

One of the most accomplished acts of Elohiym's deliverance for mankind was executed at the hand of *Moshe* in *Mitzrayim*. This was during the first *Pesach* (Passover?), in which *Elohiym* delivered all first-born children of *Yisroel* and also all their first-born livestock from death. Details of this event can be found in *Shemot (Exodus)* 12:1-14, and 46.

Please read these verses before continuing with your reading of this book so as to go along smoothly with me as I attempt some exposition of these verses. *Shemot (Exodus)* 12:1-14 and 46 contain the details of some stringent instructions of *Elohiym* to *Yisroel*, obedience of which manifested one of the greatest acts of deliverance by *Elohiym* of a people in terrible bondage.

These instructions of *Elohiym*, given to *Moshe*, were meant for strict obedience and compliance by the people of *Yisroel*. They were to be obeyed without question, wholly and completely, devoid of any variations, alterations, or deviations whatsoever. Shall we run through these clear and simple instructions designed in the mind and wisdom of *Elohiym*, obedience of which yielded this great deliverance?

Every household of *Yisroel* living in Goshen, *Mitzrayim*, was to make a selection out of their flocks of sheep or goats one animal, in the first month, *Aviv* (Abib), of the Hebrew calendar, and on the tenth day of this month. The animal had to be male, not more than one year old and without blemish or defect of any kind.

It had to be tethered or set apart from the flock to be slaughtered at sun down, timely enough for its *cadavre* to be within their homes at the start of the sunset-hour that commenced the fourteenth day of *Aviv*, for the commencement of *Pesach*, an event instructed by *Elohiym* to forever be an annual, night, indoor, family feast.

The blood of the slain animal was to be applied to the external parts of the three pieces of wood that formed the front entrance doorframes of their houses. The meat of the animal was to be roasted on an open fire. No other means of cooking were permitted. They were not to boil steam, or fry the meat. Neither was any part of the meat to be eaten raw.

They were to eat the meat indoors in the night, in haste, in readiness to travel at the break of dawn. They also had to be dressed in the appropriate clothes and footwear as of one on a journey. Besides unleavened bread and bitter herbs, they were not to eat this grilled meat with any other foods. There were to be no leftovers of this meal of mutton or goat meat unto daylight.

If anything remained, it was to be burned early in the morning. In *Shemot (Exodus)* 12:46, the people of *Yisroel* were further instructed not to bring any of the grilled meat outside of their homes. They were also to ensure that no bone of the *Pesach* lamb was broken as they prepared or ate it.

These were the instructions of *Elohiym* given to *Moshe* for strict compliance and obedience by the people of *Yisroel*. This, as you can see, was a tall order, when you come to understand the ease with which the children of *Yisroel* often walked in disobedience and intransigence before *Elohiym*. Yet *Moshe* and *Aharon* (Aaron) had between the tenth and fourteenth day of *Aviv* to teach *Yisroel* to comply fully with these instructions of *Elohiym*.

All along, the people of *Yisroel* had watched their leaders— *Moshe* and *Aharon*—obey the instructions of *Elohiym*, and had seen how that obedience brought about all those miracles in *Mitzrayim*. The people of *Yisroel* had played no role in bringing about the miracles galore seen in *Mitzrayim* before their departure for the Promised Land. They had all along been passive.

Elohiym now demanded their obedience of these instructions to bring about this act of deliverance from death. What were *Moshe* and *Aharon* to do if some stiff-necked children of the house of *Yisroel*, who were not used to obeying to the letter the instructions of *Elohiym*, decided to do something else contrary to any of these instructions?

If, for example, some stiff-necked children of *Yisroel* decided that it was not really important how many days the *Pesach* lamb was set apart awaiting its fate, and went to their flocks for the selection of the appropriate lamb or goat on, say, the twelfth day of *Aviv*? How about if some households decided to select a bull or a lamb of three years old, so they could have more meat and fat to eat instead of doing as instructed by *Elohiym* through His servants?

What if some overzealous son of *Yisroel* decided to paint the rooftop of his house, instead of his wooden doorframes, with the blood of the *Pesach* lamb, hoping that the visiting angel of *Elohiym*, when descending from *Shamayim*, would see his house before everyone else's?

Since *Elohiym* and his angels knew very well that this and every man of *Yisroel* and their families resided in Goshen, an exclusive residential area of *Yisroel* and far away from any son of *Mitzrayim*, why would any angel need an identification of his house, through a paint of goat blood on a wooden doorframe, just to bring him deliverance?

He might in his mind think to please *Elohiym* to a point by painting the inside parts of the doorframe with the blood of the lamb, instead of the external part. Then he could claim before *Elohiym* that he did so to be sure that the bloodstain would be there and that some enemy neighbor he sometime ago quarreled with at work could not get to wipe or wash it off, which he could if put on the external part of the frame.

How about if some lovers of the onions, garlic, and leeks that were in abundance in *Mitzrayim* decided to steam their *Pesach* meat in some big cooking pots with these spices in plentiful supply, in their cooking of the *Pesach* lamb, instead of obeying the instruction to roast it on fire?

What were *Moshe* and *Aharon* to do to stop any revelers of the *Pesach* meal from getting out of their houses with chunks of grilled meat, running across the street to friends and kinsmen in excitement, under moonlight, contrary to Elohiym's instruction? What were poor *Moshe* and *Aharon* to do to ensure that all of *Yisroel* obeyed these instructions of *Elohiym* on this first *Pesach* to the letter?

You can appreciate the task of these already tired octogenarians in bringing *Yisroel* to obey these instructions of *Elohiym*. At the end of the day, no first-born member of the house of *Yisroel* died, and neither did any first-born of their livestock, meaning that *Yisroel* complied with the instructions of *Elohiym* on the *Pesach* to the letter.

You should have been there in *Mitzrayim* to congratulate *Moshe* and his brother *Aharon* for exhibiting rare skills in cajoling, teaching, and communication to bring this about.

If the obedience of Elohiym's instructions brought absolute deliverance to *Yisroel* in *Mitzrayim*, we ought to learn to secure our entry into the new birth by obeying Elohiym's instructions to the letter.

Moshe taught us in all what he did for and by *Elohiym* in *Mitzrayim*, and in the wilderness journey to Canaan, what we can gain by obeying Elohiym's instruction to the letter, without asking questions or trying to rationalize them.

Moshe made one error, maybe in anger and frustration, and struck the rock with his rod, instead of speaking to it as instructed by *Elohiym*, and, for this, he was punished by not being allowed to set foot into the Promised Land—cf. *Bamidbar (Numbers)* 20:1-13 and *Vayikra (Deuteronomy)* 32:48-52.

Do we not have anything to learn from the obedience of *Moshe* to the instructions of *Elohiym*? Our attitude towards the instructions of *Elohiym* should be as that of *Moshe*. We should seek to hear Elohiym's instructions clearly and zealously obey them to the letter.

Oh, how wonderful it would be if *Moshe* could surface in some of our congregations of religious folks to teach us the importance of obedience to the instructions of *Elohiym*.

He would chastise us for our error in praying with hands raised as if in surrender to *Elohiym* in *Shamayim*, asking to be born again, instead of obeying His instructions on how to obtain this.

I am sure many of today's people would have been quick to condemn and to call any children of *Yisroel* in Goshen names, if they failed to observe any of the instructions of *Elohiym* in the first *Pesach* and brought death to their families. People today would call such people of *Yisroel* foolish, faithless, and uncircumcised in their hearts and minds.

Yet, are we not rather the foolish, faithless, and disobedient people in not accepting Elohiym's instruction for repentance and baptism into the name of *Yahushua HaMashakhYahu* for our salvation? Are we not the unwise, absurd, and ridiculous lot who choose to disobey Elohiym's clear instructions for repentance and baptism into the name of His Son by praying to be born again?

I thank *Elohiym* that none who believe strongly that people today can become born again through the recital of a so-called *Sinners' Prayer* lived in Goshen at the time of the first *Pesach*.

They would have contaminated the faith of these children of *Yisroel* living in Goshen in their attempt to carry out the instructions of *Elohiym* by urging them to adopt the line of prayer instead.

They would have suggested and taught those children of *Yisroel* to pray to *Elohiym* asking for the deliverance of their first-borns from death, rather than obey Elohiym's instructions, simply because *Elohiym* hears and answers prayer! They would have been so zealous in spreading their faith in the power of prayer that they would surely have confused some of those Goshenites.

In their confusion, many would have been misled into setting aside the instructions of *Elohiym* for the deliverance of their first-borns from death, and to instead wax strong in prayer. I am sure, in the state of being misled and confused, that they would have brought death into their homes.

Today, anybody who is led to believe in toeing the line of prayer, as is strongly advocated by many to be the means to entering the salvation of *Elohiym*, will definitely fail to gain the new birth.

Nobody who sets aside the strong and unambiguous warning of *Yahushua HaMashakhYahu* to *Nakdimon* in *YahuChanan (John)* 3:5 or his instruction in *Markos (Mark)* 16:5-16 meant for every salvation seeker to, instead, toe the line of saying a prayer for salvation or to be born again, can ever enter the *Malchut HaElohiym*.

Nobody who fails to obey the only one and all-time regulation set by *Elohiym* for any person's entry into His salvation, as laid bare in *Ma'asim (Acts)* 2:38-39, can ever enter the born again experience. The born again experience will come to only those people who express faith in the instructions of *Elohiym* to repent from sin and to be baptized in, and into, the name of *Yahushua HaMashakhYahu*.

We should never forget that *Yahushua HaMashakhYahu* is the writer of the script that we are to act on the world stage to bring about the salvation of the sinner.

We therefore have to hold tenaciously to that script and act it out with *Ruwakh HaKodesh* as Director-Producer, as of a movie-making company, so we obtain good results.

Shimon Kefa, Philippos, Chananyahu and others all had the right attitudes in this regard and so were able to lead sinners perfectly, genuinely, and smoothly into the salvation of *Elohiym* in *Yahushua HaMashakhYahu*.

Please, we need to learn from those who were called to the faith and ministry of the New Covenant doctrines before us, if our roles in leading people to become born again are to be beneficial to salvation seekers and worthy of commendation by *HaAdon*.

The second teaching on the born again doctrine, which I came across while preparing to write this book, is very much the same as the one taught by Heward-Mills, in that it also approaches the issue of being born again into the salvation of *Elohiym* in *Yahushua HaMashakhYahu* from an angle of prayer.

The second teaching raises quite a number of issues that are of importance in preparing the sinner with information about the salvation plan of *Elohiym*, and that could aid him make up his mind to receive it.

However, the conclusions drawn from these discourses, and the directives given by the writer to the salvation seeker to enter the born again experience, are what I would be drawing my focus on since I find them incongruent with teachings in the *Holy Scriptures* on the issue.

Once again, I do this with a lot of pain in my heart. That notwithstanding, woe is me, if I do not bring this erroneous teaching to light for the warning of humanity.

In this second teaching, Otabil, in his pocket-sized book, ***How to be Born Again***, writes the following:

Accepting God's Free Gift

No one has the power to save you from sin except Jesus Christ, the crucified and risen Messiah. If you realise that you need him, come, just as you are, with no strings attached.

So what must you do to be saved?

To be saved, you must turn away from your sins, believe in the death and resurrection of Jesus, and receive him as Lord and Saviour of your life. Here is a step-by-step process:

a) Acknowledge that you are a sinner. Most people recognize that already and know that they need help.

For all have sinned and come short of the glory of God; Romans 3:23

b) Realise that the penalty for your sin is death. Had He not died, we would have had to die for our own sins.

For the wages of sin is death, but the gift of God is eternal life in Jesus Christ our Lord. Romans 6:23

c) Repent of your sins. You must consider your life and turn away from everything that is contrary to what God wants. This turning away from selfishness and towards God is called repentance.

d) Believe that Jesus died and has already paid the price for your sin.

But God demonstrates His own love towards us, in that while we were still sinners, Christ died for us. Romans 5:8

e) Openly declare Him as your Saviour and Lord.

That if you confess with your mouth the Lord Jesus and believe in your heart that God has raised Him from the dead, you will be saved. For with the heart one believes unto righteousness, and with the mouth, confession is made unto salvation. Romans 10:9-10

This gift of God is for anyone who accepts it. You may be a pastor, thief, politician, porter, hawker, or doctor; you may be a black man, white man, American, Chinese, or Indian. Whosoever believes in Him will have everlasting life.

The Bible says many that received Him were given the power to become the children of God (John 1:12). When you open your heart and receive Him, He comes into your heart—your inner person—through his Holy Spirit, and He begins to live His life in you. **From that point, it is your privilege to call yourself a child of God.**

To allow Christ into your life and be Born Again, kindly pray this simple prayer:

Your Prayer (to receive Salvation)

Heavenly Father, today, I come to you just as I am. I am a sinner. I have sinned against you and turned away from you. I have lived my own way but today, I ask you to give me a new life. Forgive me, of all my sins, cleanse me and wash me in the blood of Jesus. Come into my heart. I receive forgiveness of sins, I receive salvation, I receive new life in Christ Jesus today. I declare today that I have left my sins and the world to follow Jesus and His Word. From now on, I belong to Jesus. I am a child of God and am not turning back. Thank you, Father, for accepting me in Jesus Name.

If you prayed this prayer sincerely, you have come to Christ and he will give you abundant life. He'll draw you closer to Himself and protect you from the storms of life. I would like to pray for you as well.

My Prayer for You

Father I pray for these ones who have run to you today. I pray Lord that they will find comfort and newness of life in you; that they will find sustenance and renewal and the remission of sins in you today. I pray Lord that their lives will be made new, that they will discover true live in Christ Jesus. Thank you, Father, for the free gift of salvation. Amen. **(2006, pp. 45-50).**

The two sentences in the above quote, which have been underlined, are so identified by me to help readers take particular note of them.

My understanding of the *Holy Scriptures* gives me the conviction that the **step-by-step** process taught by the writer, intended to lead sinners to the salvation of *Elohiym* in *Yahushua HaMashakhYahu*, does not seem to have any scriptural basis, support, or authorization. Nowhere in the *Holy Scriptures* are we mandated to teach the way into the salvation of *Elohiym* in this manner or process.

Apart from Otabil's teaching on c) **Repent of your sins**, in the quotation above, being scriptural and crucial to our entry into the salvation in *Yahushua HaMashakhYahu*, his other teachings based on quotations from *The Bible*, all of which incidentally are from *Romans*, do not bring us to the point of entry into the salvation of *Elohiym* in *Yahushua HaMashakhYahu*. It has already been explained elsewhere in this chapter why this overdependence on *Romans* in the teaching of the born again doctrine does not lead sinners to become born again.

Let me say again that before *Romans* came, we had the complete revelation of *Elohiym* about how to enter His salvation or become born again. Let us therefore not look to *Romans* in our pursuit to be born again into Elohiym's Kingdom.

The faith of the author, which he seeks to impart to humanity, is that if you prayed after him as he led, and if he prayed for you thereafter as he did, then you became born again and a child of *Elohiym*!

This doctrine is flawed on many grounds. The first is that nobody in the New Covenant teachings ever got saved in this manner, and neither do the *Holy Scriptures* teach the born again doctrine in this way. You do not get to be born again, become a child of *Elohiym*, or enter the salvation of *Elohiym* in *Yahushua HaMashakhYahu* by simply saying that you have, of your own volition or due to your affirmation of it, when you have not been directed by *Elohiym* to do so.

Secondly, it is not forgiveness of one's sins *per se* that will enable one become born again. Rather, you need to get remission of your sins if you are to be saved. You should not therefore pray asking for the forgiveness of your sins if you want to be born again. You should seek to obtain remission of your sins according to the instructions of the *Holy Scriptures*, if you want to enter the salvation of *Elohiym* in the born again experience.

Thirdly, nobody ever got remission of sins by his or someone else's prayer. Remission of sin is obtained by faith in baptism into the name of *Yahushua HaMashakhYahu* after genuine repentance from sin, and not by a prayer of any sort.

The only way to obtain remission of sins is through one's faith in, understanding of, and sincerity in receiving the baptism into the name of *Yahushua HaMashakhYahu* after one has repented of one's sins upon hearing the *Besuras HaGeulah*. I suppose you had a firm grasp of these truths from the earlier teachings on forgiveness and remission of sin in Chapter Two of this book.

It is alarming and very sad to count the number of people who have believed this wrong doctrine of offering and receiving salvation through prayers, by asking "Jesus Christ" (*Yahushua HaMashakhYahu?*) into hearts. The number continues to increase daily through radio and television programs and by other equally powerful means of mass communication. The extent of damage done to the quest for salvation of people by this incorrect teaching is unimaginable. This is very sad indeed.

I am sad every time I watch some preachers on television. Though they preach thought-provoking messages and expositions on stories and events of the Old and New Covenant eras, they always leave a sour taste in my mouth at the end of every program. The sourness comes when they attempt to lead sinners into the *Malchut HaElohiym*. They do this in exactly the same manner as taught in the books **Born Again** and **How to be Born Again** cited in this teaching—that is, through prayer.

With regards to the preaching of issues relating to the *Holy Scriptures* on Ghanaian television and radio, I must say I have some preachers that I admire in a way, but I get lost and out of touch with them every time they try to lead sinners to the salvation of *Elohiym* in *Yahushua HaMashakhYahu*. This they all do by leading salvation seekers to recite the *Sinners' Prayer* or the *Prayer for Salvation*.

I have always felt *Yahushua HaMashakhYahu* sorrowing in his heart when the rituals of *Sinners' Prayer* recitals are done on television, day by day, instead of teaching the truth of his Word about how the sinner gets born again through repentance from sin and baptism into his name. It is no doubt as a result of this heartache that I have been burdened and commissioned of *Ruwakh HaKodesh* of *Elohiym* to undertake this book project to teach the truth of how one is born again.

In *Mishle (Proverbs)* 14:12, we read the following, which I believe is meant to be a warning against what many people believe in and do in trying to get born again.

"There is a way which seemeth right unto a man, but the end thereof are the ways of death"—Mishle (Proverbs) 14:12, KJV.

There are obviously many ways that may seem right to man, concerning how man can enter the salvation of *Elohiym* in *Yahushua HaMashakhYahu*. These might include praying for "Jesus Christ" (*Yahushua HaMashakhYahu*?) to come into the hearts of repentant sinners in their quest to enter Elohiym's Kingdom!

However, since the manner of praying for "Jesus Christ" (*Yahushua HaMashakhYahu*?) to enter the hearts of penitent sinners is not the way *Elohiym* instructed for man to pursue entrance into His Grace and salvation, this could be one of the ways that might seem right in the eyes of man but could ultimately lead to death.

From where and by whom did man come to be misled into believing that when one prays a so-called *Sinners' Prayer*, asking that "Jesus Christ" (*Yahushua HaMashakhYahu*?) forgives him of his sins and come to take control of his life, he would become born again? The originator of such a teaching has done one of the greatest disservices to the human race that has ever been done since the resurrection of *Yahushua HaMashakhYahu*.

The gullibility of mankind has allowed the perpetuation of this falsehood from the times of its origin to the present. It is now time we critically examined this doctrine, identified the obvious falsehoods in it which are against the true Word of *Elohiym*, and corrected it.

This wrong teaching must end now. It must not be allowed to continue to endanger the salvation of people desiring to reconcile with *Elohiym* and to qualify to spend Eternity with Him at the end of time.

All of us claiming to be doing the work of *Elohiym* should seek to understand what *Yahushua HaMashakhYahu* has said in *Mattityahu (Matthew)* 7:21-27, meant to be a warning to us. In this scripture in *Mattityahu (Matthew)*, this is what *HaAdon* says:

"Not everyone that saith unto me, Lord, Lord, (Adoneinu, Adoneinu) shall enter the kingdom of heaven (Malchut HaShamayim); but he that doeth the will of my Father (Abba) which is in heaven (Shamayim). Many will say to me in that day (Yom HaDin), Lord, Lord, (Adoneinu, Adoneinu) have we not prophesied in thy name? And in thy name have cast out devils (shedim)? And in thy name done many wonderful works? And then will I profess unto them, I never knew you: depart from me, ye that work iniquity. Therefore, whosoever heareth these sayings of mine, and doeth them, I will liken him unto a wise man, which built his house upon a rock: And the rain descended, and the floods came, and the winds blew, and beat upon that house; and it fell not: for it was founded upon a rock. And everyone that heareth these sayings of mine, and doeth them not, shall be likened unto a foolish man, which built his house upon the sand; And the rain descended, and the floods came, and the winds blew, and beat upon that house; and it fell: and great was the fall of it"—Mattityahu (Matthew) 7:21-27, KJV; the words in parenthesis are mine.

In these verses, *Yahushua HaMashakhYahu* tells us that not everyone who says to him *Adoneinu, Adoneinu,* casts out devils, performs miracles, or prophesies in his name will enter *Shamayim* at the end of time. According to him, many people today who perform miracles of healing, cast out devils from people, or even preach in **his name**—but obviously without his bidding, authorization, anointing—will be considered workers of iniquity at the end of time.

The boldness of these workers of iniquity, arguing their eligibility to enter *Shamayim* by saying on *Yom HaDin* (the Day of Judgment) that they addressed "Jesus Christ" (*Yahushua HaMashakhYahu*?) as *Adoneinu*, casted out devils and preached in the name "Jesus Christ", gives the impression that these workers of iniquity were sincere and certain in their commitment to what they engaged in as unto *HaAdon* himself. Yet, they are judged to be wrong and are labeled workers of iniquity.

We should be sure who the true *HaAdon* is and what kind of work we do for him, so we do not join this large group of surprised workers of iniquity on the day of reckoning, arguing in vain with *Yahushua HaMashakhYahu* to be given entry into *Shamayim*.

We should ensure that our names are written in *HaSefer HaChayyim* (the Book of Life), from which the roll call will be made for those qualified and eligible to enter *Shamayim* to file in, to the thunderous applause of the angels of *Elohiym*. Oh, what a day it will be. Let us ensure that we so run the race as to be in the winning team.

If you obey the instructions of *Elohiym* concerning how to be born again, you would be the wise man that built on the rock—this rock is *Yahushua HaMashakhYahu*, Elohiym's dependable, powerful, wise, saving, and beautiful Word—whose building withstood and survived the floods and winds that sought to bring it down. You are sure of being in Elohiym's salvation if, and only if, you acted with understanding, sincerity, and in accordance with Elohiym's instructions for repentance and baptism into the name of *Yahushua HaMashakhYahu*. This is the only way of *Elohiym* directing the sinner into His salvation.

Please, let the accounts on the salvation of people in the *Holy Scriptures* become the guide and inspiration to your own salvation. Otherwise, you might believe in vain some doctrine that was not taught in the New Covenant doctrines for the salvation of humanity, and be living in delusion of being saved. My dear reader, reexamine your faith in the born again doctrine, and please seek to advise yourself in the light of the revelations of Elohiym's Word and what is taught in this book for your salvation.

Please do this in a state of urgency to avoid any disappointment at the *Sha'arei HaShamayim* (Gates of Heaven) when time would have ended for Eternity to begin, and when it would then be too late to go for the right doctrine of *Elohiym* for your born again experience,—the new birth, your foremost qualification and requirement to enter *Shamayim*.

Before we bring this chapter to a close, let us look at the lives of people who respond in seriousness and sincerity to so-called *"altar calls"* and *Sinners' Prayer* recitals. Many of those who sincerely desire and are determined to live holy lives, and respond to invitations to recite the *Sinners' Prayer*, may show changed lifestyles thereafter.

Many of such people succeed in doing away with sins that easily beset them. They manage to live in obedience to many commandments of *Elohiym*. Serious and determined people, who desire to be saved but are misled into responding to so-called *"altar calls"*, may develop some kind of seriousness in fasting, prayer, giving, and service, etc.

They may change, for the better, their attitudes to the worship of and their commitment to the issues and things relating to their Maker. Their trust in Him may increase and they could have some manifestations of blessings in their lives in answer to prayer or the exercise of their faith.

In fact, for most of those who are serious in their responses to the *"altar call"*, you will most likely see a change in their lifestyles, faith, and attitudes. Simply put, they bear the fruit of repentance. This is all well and good.

That does not mean, however, that as things now go well for them they are born again and in the family of *Elohiym*. Fact is, many people who make resolutions to change their sinful ways for the better—not necessarily in response to *"altar calls"*—do get a lift in life, if they are able to stick to their resolutions.

The response to an *"altar call"* may make people express belief in "Jesus Christ" (*Yahushua HaMashakhYahu*?) mentally. They may give mental accent to all what *Yahushua HaMashakhYahu* ("Jesus Christ"?) stands for and did for humanity in his sacrifice. But the manner of making that response, in the saying of a *Sinners' Prayer*, so-called, does not make them act in a way corresponding to the teachings of the *Holy Scriptures* for salvation.

Faith in *Elohiym* always has to go with the appropriate corresponding actions, in order for it to be beneficial or bring to manifestation His promises. If you believe in the work of *Yahushua HaMashakhYahu* done for humanity to be saved, then, go further to act on his instructions on repentance and baptism in his only one true name for your salvation.

Your faith in the work of *Yahushua HaMashakhYahu* for the salvation of mankind should lead you to act in the right and corresponding manner for your salvation. The only corresponding action in this regard is to accept repentance of sin and baptism in the name, *Yahushua HaMashakhYahu*.

You see, long ago, at about the time the faith in *Yahushua*

HaMashakhYahu began to spread in *Yisroel*, our now all-too-familiar Cornelius of *Ma'asim (Acts)*, chapter ten precisely, decided to be radical with sin and to get it out of his life. He sought to know *Elohiym*, the Most High One, who *Yisroel* worshipped. He himself was a Roman, a Gentile, and knew at that time and season that he could not enjoy life like any righteous person of the house of *Yisroel* to whom the promises of *Elohiym* were given.

But he knew he could enjoy life on the fringes of Yisroel's blessing. He therefore set himself on a course to please *Elohiym* in word and deed. He might have said a prayer asking for Elohiym's help in this, and perhaps in a manner similar to what people do in their recitals of the *Sinners' Prayer*. By dint of determination and zeal, he managed to worm himself into the heart of *Elohiym* through a very rewarding friendship with Him.

Though not in the family of *Elohiym*, because he neither belonged to the house of *Yisroel* nor as yet born again of water and of *Ruwakh HaKodesh*, he was loved of *Elohiym* and greatly blessed by Him in many ways. He was blessed even above many of those that were in Elohiym's family—in the house of *Yisroel*—because of his zeal and commitment in worshipping *Elohiym*, who he had chosen to always worship, even without being called by Him.

You could say, from the accounts about him in *Ma'asim (Acts)*, that, Cornelius constantly lived in the presence of *Elohiym*. But he was not as yet born again of water and of *Ruwakh HaKodesh* until *Shimon Kefa* was sent to him.

People who respond to *"altar calls"*, and go on to recite the *Sinners' Prayer* in a quest for salvation, do not get to enter the family of *Elohiym* by that response. And yet, they can have their prayers heard and answered, just like Cornelius before he was born again. They can get deliverance from sickness and diseases for themselves or others in answer to prayer. They might experience financial break-throughs in reward for their changed lives. But they, like Cornelius, still need a visit from a *Shimon Kefa* to teach them the way to be born again, by which birth they get their names written into *HaSefer HaChayyim*.

All the many people who have responded to *"altar calls"*, recited the *Sinners' Prayer*, and live in assurance of having entered Elohiym's salvation will have to ask themselves what *Shimon Kefa* went to the home of Cornelius to do for him and his household to get saved or born again.

Was it even necessary for *Shimon Kefa* to visit Cornelius with the message of the *Besuras HaGeulah* and for him to work to lead Cornelius to respond to it in the only appropriate manner of baptism into *Yahushua HaMashakhYahu*, considering the very high spiritual level of the man before the visit?

When such *"altar call"* and *Sinners' Prayer* faithful get to know the answers to these questions, they should go and get them fulfilled in their own lives. That fulfillment would no doubt get them born again and put them legally on the way to spending Eternity in the presence of *Elohiym* in *Shamayim*.

That realization will bring to their hearts the filling of *Ruwakh HaKodesh*, and will stamp them with the seal of *Ruwakh HaKodesh* as Elohiym's own in this world, making them eligible to enter the *Sha'arei HaShamayim* (Gates of Heaven) upon their departure from this world.

People who are serious in their response to *"altar calls"*, and to the recitals of *Sinners' Prayers* in their search for the salvation of *Elohiym* in *Yahushua HaMashakhYahu*, may, like Apollos, gain great zeal for *Elohiym*, knowledge of the scriptures, eloquence, and dedication in preaching Elohiym's Word, but will still not be born again. Evidently, Apollos was not born again, while he displayed all the charisma that he had, before being taught the perfect way of salvation by Aquila and Priscilla. People who believe they have assurance of salvation by their recitals of *Sinners' Prayers* must look back on the error of Apollos and take a lesson from that account of scripture in *Ma'asim (Acts)* 18:24-26.

When, in *Ma'asim (Acts)* 19:1-7, *Sha'ul* met his twelve friends in Ephesus, they looked like born again *talmidim* of *Yahushua HaMashakhYahu* to people in their neighborhood. To the immature and undiscerning subscriber to the New Covenant faith, they could even pass as born again people since they looked like saved *talmidim* of *Yahushua HaMashakhYahu*.

They professed and confessed *Yahushua HaMashakhYahu* with their mouths, as many of today's believers in the *Sinners' Prayer* do. They claimed loyalty to *Yahushua HaMashakhYahu*, obviously hated and denounced sin and the devil, and were regular in attendance to meetings or services with true believers. They even might have portrayed some kind of joy and liberty in spirit of a newfound peace with *Elohiym*—even though they were not yet born again.

Their names were not yet written in *HaSefer HaChayyim*. This is because the initiation rite of baptism into *Yahushua HaMashakhYahu* for the born again experience was unknown to them, they having not been taught to receive it. They did not know this great ordinance of *Yahushua HaMashakhYahu* commanded the obedience of all his *talmidim* to bring them the born again experience and the blessings that would come with this new birth in baptism into his name.

People who respond to *"altar calls"* in all seriousness might just be like any one of those twelve *"talmidim"* that *Sha'ul* met in Ephesus, who believed that they were born again when they were actually not. At the time, those Ephesians had no knowledge of the baptism into *Yahushua HaMashakhYahu*! For those who believe in and respond to *"altar calls"* today, theirs is not ignorance of baptism *per se;* it is ignorance of the value of baptism, the true name of the Savior one must be baptized into, and the blessing that one obtains by accepting baptism in faith and understanding. The blessing of baptism, as the rite that puts one into *Yahushua HaMashakhYahu*, into the new birth experiences, and into the *Malchut HaElohiym*, is denied people who respond to *"altar calls"* and believe they are saved or have become born again by that response before they go to be baptized.

You can only be born again of water and of *Ruwakh HaKodesh*. You are born again through repentance from sin and baptism in natural living waters into the name of *Yahushua HaMashakhYahu*. When you understand and accept this fact, and obey Elohiym's Word in this way, then can you be born again of water and of *Ruwakh HaKodesh* in the eyes of *Elohiym*! Otherwise, you are still unsaved, your sins being unwashed with the blood of the Savior. Please be warned in this, and seek the salvation of *Elohiy*m for your soul in the right way.

Being born again will transfer the person who responds to an *"altar call"* from a life beside or with "Jesus Christ" (*Yahushua HaMashakhYahu?*), to one **in** *Yahushua HaMashakhYahu*. A life **inside** *Yahushua HaMashakhYahu* is the ultimate of all our relationships with him. It is only when we are born again through repentance from sin and baptism into his name that this can be established. No matter what good spiritual experiences the person who says the *Sinners' Prayer* may have, it is all because he or she **may** be living beside or with *HaAdon—Yahushua HaMashakhYahu*—but not **inside** him.

I am, of course, very much aware that many who say the *Sinners' Prayer* and express their faith in it, believing it brings them into the salvation of *Elohiym* in *Yahushua HaMashakhYahu*, get baptized afterward. As a preparation for their baptism, they go through weeks of teaching, supposedly to equip them with the truths of baptism.

Students of these classes are made to believe that, even though they are "saved" in their recitation of the *Sinners' Prayer*, they still need to undergo baptism for some important reason. Baptism, for them, then becomes a post-salvation ritual.

In these supposed post-salvation teachings for baptism, the salvation seeker is made to believe that baptism is a sign of his conversion or salvation that took place inside of him. Baptism is taught to be the outward sign of an inward work of "Grace"—a rare kind of "Grace" unknown to many people—which brought salvation to them through their recitals of *Sinners' Prayers*!

Unfortunately, we cannot find anywhere in the New Covenant teachings that baptism is taught to be a post-salvation rite or a sign to or of anything. Today's baptism in the name of *Yahushua HaMashakhYahu* is the reality of that which was a sign or a shadow in the Old Covenant past. Yesterday's baptisms unto *Noach, Moshe, Yehoshua*, and unto *YahuChanan ben Zecharyahu* were signs to the baptism into the name of *Yahushua HaMashakhYahu* today.

Elohiym used those events to teach and keep reminding us that a time was coming when their reality would come about or manifest. Now they are all evident in *Yahushua HaMashakhYahu*. And we still call baptism a sign? When will the real baptism come to bless mankind, and for such people, in particular, who believe baptism is a sign? No wonder some people are still awaiting the advent of *HaMashakhYahu*. It is sad that we have been deceived into believing baptism is a sign in this age and time.

Our baptism into *Yahushua HaMashakhYahu* today is the manifestation of the sign or coming into being of that shadow of the past; ours into *Yahushua HaMashakhYahu* is the reality. You will not benefit from the baptism into *Yahushua HaMashakhYahu* if you hold the belief that you subscribe to it to show or demonstrate it as a sign to your salvation.

You render baptism into *Yahushua HaMashakhYahu*, which is the ordinance for Elohiym's initiation of the sinner into the new birth, null and void if you hold the belief that it is an outward sign of an inward work of grace in your inner being, or that it is simply a post-salvation rite.

Many "men of God" teach those who respond to their *"altar calls"*, and to their commands of the recitations of so-called *Sinners' Prayers,* to believe and hold the view that baptism is a public and open declaration of one's profession of the Savior as being one's *"Lord and personal Savior"*. These "men of God" teach that baptism is supposed to be an open declaration of one's intention and resolve to follow the Savior!

Sadly, nowhere in the New Covenant teachings are we told that baptism should be a public act or an advertisement to the world of one's being in the Savior or of one's intention to follow him. On the contrary, many baptisms in the true name of the Savior—*Yahushua HaMashakhYahu*—were administered very privately.

There were no requirements for even so-called *"God-parents"* to be present at baptisms in the New Covenant teachings, as is the practice of many Christian denominations today. If you make a public show of your baptism, that is your own matter; but it is not meant to be done as any kind of fanfare or for public view. Maybe, somebody wanting to advertise his ministry or missionary work might want baptism publicized to relish in some vainglory.

Did the Ethiopian eunuch have witnesses to his baptism in the desert of Gaza in order for it to be meaningful and beneficial to him? Of course not! He got the descent of *Ruwakh HaKodesh* into his heart in the privacy of the desert, in his baptism into *Yahushua HaMashakhYahu*, and went away rejoicing in the power of the dwelling presence of *Ruwakh HaKodesh* within him.

Did *Sha'ul* call witnesses to his baptism into *Yahushua HaMashakhYahu*? No, he did not. He would have scared away everybody if he had tried calling witnesses to his baptism. I hope you know why.

Baptism neither has to be public to be meaningful or beneficial, nor does it have to be a demonstration to the world that the one who subscribes to it is serious with the Savior. Please let us understand that our advertisement of our newfound salvation in *Yahushua HaMashakhYahu* starts from our functioning as the salt of the earth and as the light of the world, when any changes inside us are then visible to the world. Baptism is not proof to the world that we are new or changed men.

Again, those who believe that they are saved in their recital of the *Sinners' Prayer* are taught to undergo baptism **"to fulfill all righteousness"** as a follow-up to their so-called salvation! This is about the most popular reason why those who express confidence in *Sinners' Prayer* recitals for salvation are ever baptized at all.

When *YahuChanan ben Zecharyahu* resisted the demands of

Yahushua HaMashakhYahu to baptize him, *Yahushua* pleaded with him to go ahead to baptize him **"to fulfill all righteousness".** Of course, *Yahushua HaMashakhYahu* had no sin to wash away in the baptism, but he had to go through the rite of baptism to meet the demands of *Elohiym.*

Righteous acts are done to meet the demands of *Elohiym.* They are done in obedience to His instruction. *Yahushua HaMashakhYahu* was simply telling *YahuChanan ben Zecharyahu* that he had to receive his baptism to meet the instructions of *Elohiym* to him (*Yahushua HaMashakhYahu*).

Maybe, the route by which *Elohiym* was to anoint *Yahushua HaMashakhYahu* for the work before him was through his humble submission to be baptized by *YahuChanan ben Zecharyahu*. Why can we not think so? Why, with all the opening up of the heavens, the visible overhead presence of *Ruwakh HaKodesh*, and the thundering voice of *Elohiym*, the Most High One, announcing *Yahushua HaMashakhYahu* as His only begotten Son immediately after he had received his baptism from *YahuChanan ben Zecharyahu*—cf. *Mattityahu (Matthew)* 3:13-17, *Markos (Mark)* 1:9-11, and *Lukas (Luke)* 3:21-20—would we not believe this to be true?

Not long after this act of baptism, *Elohiym* spoke to mankind in other places of scripture in a manner similar to how He spoke at the baptism of *Yahushua HaMashakhYahu*—cf. *Mattityahu (Matthew)* 17:5, *Markos (Mark)* 9:7, and *Lukas (Luke)* 9:35—urging mankind to listen to His only begotten Son.

What are we mortal sinners to hear from the one *Elohiym* has sent to us to bring us His salvation? Of course, we are to hear, before anything else, the very elementary doctrine of how sinful man is born again through the powers of living waters and of *Ruwakh HaKodesh* acting in unison. We are to hear of the Son of *Elohiym* how repentance of sin and baptism in his name act together to bring salvation to anyone desirous of it.

By submitting to the baptism of *YahuChanan*, *Yahushua HaMashakhYahu* did not only obey the instruction of *HaAv* in *Shamayim*, but he also established the rite for all his followers. He set an example by his obedience to the will of *HaAv* that all his followers should obey *Elohiym* and go through the rite of baptism with understanding, so as to reap its benefits of *Chayyei Olam* (Everlasting Life) while on Earth.

No instruction of *Elohiym* is casual or ordinary. This is because

Elohiym is not ordinary. Every instruction of *Elohiym* is His deepest thought. Elohiym's instruction is His wisdom. All of Elohiym's instructions to man are meant to meet man's needs. They are meant to meet the needs of sinful man for the restoration of him to a life he lost through the First Adam to the devil in *Gan Eden*. No instruction of *Elohiym* is casual or superfluous.

Many simple-minded people are taught to believe that baptism is a superfluous rite! They are made to believe that baptism does not add to or takeaway from their salvation, which they claim to have received in their recitals of *Sinners' Prayers*; you are born again without it, you will not enter life in, by, or with it, and neither will you fail to enter life without it. Now, these are shocking ideas to hear anyone teach.

What is baptism to these people? Is it simply an act to fulfill all righteousness? That is fine. Just as *Yahushua HaMashakhYahu*, who had no sin-nature or sins to shed-off in baptism, went ahead and received one at the hand of *YahuChanan ben Zecharyahu*, we too do the same, thinking we are made sinless in our recitals of the *Sinners' Prayer* before being baptized.

Well, it is good to follow *Yahushua HaMashakhYahu*, but be sure you follow him with understanding. Please, never follow *Yahushua HaMashakhYahu* without faith in his Word and obedience to his commands. You might end up like *Yehudah ben Shimon* from *K'riot* (Judas Iscariot, son of Simon). Follow *Yahushua HaMashakhYahu* with understanding, and in faith. That is the only way to get your blessing. Never follow *Yahushua HaMashakhYahu* casually or halfheartedly.

In **The Voice of Truth International**, Kyle (n. d.) in his article, **"Are You Walking in the Truth?"** asks the following questions, which I am sure, if you answer sincerely, will help you see the great importance of baptism to the salvation of the sinner:

"If Christ [I suppose he intended to mean *Yahushua HaMashakhYahu*, not Christ] stood before you right now and said directly and personally to you, as he did in his instructions to his apostles, 'He that believeth and is baptized shall be saved,' (*Mark* 16:16), what would you do? If the Lord will save us without baptism, why did Peter command it (*Acts* 10: 47- 48)? If the Lord promises salvation without baptism, why did Peter say it saves (*First Peter* 3:21)? If we can receive remission of sins without baptism, why did Peter say baptism is for the remission of sins (*Acts* 2: 38)? If we get into Christ [*Yahushua HaMashakhYahu*?] without baptism, why did Paul say we are baptized into Christ [*Yahushua HaMashakhYahu?*] (*Galatians* 3:27 and *Romans* 6:3)? If we get into the body of Christ [*Yahushua HaMashakhYahu?*] without baptism, why did Paul say we are baptized into the body (*First Corinthians* 12:13), since the Bible teaches that the **body** and the **church** are the same (*Colossians* 1:18)? If Jesus Christ [*Yahushua HaMashakhYahu,* not Christ] grasped your hand and said, 'If you love me you will keep my commandments,' (*John* 14:15; 15:14), would you love and obey?" **(p. 33). Please note: All the words in square brackets in this quote are mine.**

Your acceptance of the instructions of *Elohiym* to you, as not being casual, ordinary, or superfluous, but needful to your very being, would always bring you to His mysteries and miracles. When you obey with faith and understanding any of His instructions, you walk in the realm of the extraordinary, of the miraculous, and in His awesome presence.

You should therefore understand the baptism into *Yahushua HaMashakhYahu* and apply your faith to it. You will then know the joy of being born again. Then would you experience a huge flood of *Ruwakh HaKodesh* of *Elohiym* rushing into you to dwell within your innermost parts. That is the blessing of being born again. *HalleluYahu!*

For sinful man turning to be a *talmid* of *Yahushua HaMashakhYahu*, it is his faith in understanding and accepting baptism in his name that washes away his sins. No sins are washed away in the reciting of a so-called *Sinners' Prayer* after some preacher, since *HaAdon* has not commanded his followers to pray for salvation.

We therefore hear the voice of a stranger-shepherd when we are told to pray to become born again. We should not follow this shepherd if we want to avoid the disaster of arriving at an undesirable destination.

Let us yet again read *Ma'asim (Acts)* 22:16: **"And now why tarriest thou? arise, and be baptized, and wash away thy sins, calling on the name of the Lord".**

It is only in our coming to the point of repentance from sin, and our faith in and acceptance of the baptism in the name of *Yahushua HaMashakhYahu*, that our sins are washed away. I think we adopt a holier-than-thou attitude, if we do not blaspheme outrightly, when we hold the view that we come on level ground or equal status with *Yahushua HaMashakhYahu* before his baptism by *YahuChanan ben*

Zecharyahu in our saying of the *Sinners' Prayer*, or that we are sin-free before our acts of baptism and only need to go through it, like *Yahushua HaMashakhYahu*, simply *"to fulfill all righteousness."*

It seems to me that the seeds sown by the bishop who said he was first born again—according to him, of prayer and not of water—and later baptized to fulfill all righteousness, and those sown by people of like-faith, have begun to bear bad fruits, and these might have corrupted our faith in and understanding of baptism.

By this corruption of faith, we have come to lose the power and value of baptism into *Yahushua HaMashakhYahu* as the rite of initiation into the *Malchut HaElohiym*, the born again experience, and the salvation of *Elohiym* in *Yahushua HaMashakhYahu*. We also seem to have no understanding of the doctrine of baptism as the only ordinance of *Elohiym* that saves the sinner in today's Dispensation of Grace.

Lastly, people who subscribe to recitals of the *Sinners' Prayer* as the means of becoming born again are led to undergo baptism as a condition for their membership to the Christian denomination that led them to their so-called salvation. You cannot be a registered and good-standing member of their denomination if you are not baptized in accordance with the tenets of their doctrines on baptism.

How do you reconcile this state of inconsistency? When one is saved in the real sense, scripturally, one becomes part of the Body of *Yahushua HaMashakhYahu*—the True Vine. So, since these people who say the *Sinners' Prayer* are supposed to be saved, or to be in *Yahushua HaMashakhYahu* by saying that prayer, are they not supposed to be automatically made co-joined members of the Body of *Yahushua HaMashakhYahu*—the True Vine—by *Elohiym* Himself?

Why then would any denomination say one has to be baptized, even if saved in the recitation of the *Sinners' Prayer*, before one can be admitted in membership into it? Is it that such a denomination is terribly confused about baptism or that it is not really a part of the Body of *Yahushua HaMashakhYahu*—the True Vine—to which all true saved people are joined automatically by *Elohiym*, the Most High One, Himself?

In all these post-*Sinners' Prayer* teachings for baptism, the true meaning and significance of baptism in the name of *Yahushua HaMashakhYahu* cannot be found. As a result, even though people

239

who respond to *"altar calls"* and go on to say the *Sinners' Prayer* do go through baptism later on, it brings them no benefit at all.

Their faith in it is misguided, not being based on the *Holy Scriptures*. It therefore makes baptism a mere sign, an ordinary and unnecessary witness to the world, an issue wrongly believed is supposed *"to fulfill all righteousness"* and a ritual performed to enable one gain membership into a Christian denomination, and not necessarily into the Body of *Yahushua HaMashakhYahu*—the True Vine.

Let me say it again that it is our faith in, understanding of, and sincerity towards our baptism into *Yahushua HaMashakhYahu* following repentance from sin which saves, and not the recitals of some *Sinners' Prayer* and the praying of some "Jesus Christ" into hearts.

Many people have terribly confused the issue of baptism into the name of *Yahushua HaMashakhYahu*. In their confusion, they have placed the cart before the horse. Instead of baptism leading us to the salvation of *Elohiym*, it is rather their "salvation" that leads them to their kind of baptism!

What benefit do we gain in baptism by acting from such a position? We are baptized for and into salvation, and not saved for baptism. Baptism is meant for spiritually dead people, and it makes them alive in a resurrection with *Yahushua HaMashakhYahu* by their faith in it.

Baptism has always been the rite that separates the saved from the unsaved—that is, setting aside those delivered from the wrath of *Elohiym* from those who perish by Elohiym's wrath. As baptism was in the days of *Noach* and of *Moshe*, so shall it forever be in the days of the son of man. Baptism into (or in) the name of *Yahushua HaMashakhYahu* is the rite that separates the righteous from the wicked.

Come to think of it, *Noach, Moshe, Yehoshua, YahuChanan ben Zecharyahu*, and *Yahushua HaMashakhYahu* were all "Baptizers", if you will. Their messages, which were accepted and obeyed, brought their followers baptism, thus separating or setting them apart unto life, unto *Elohiym*, while those who did not receive their message and could not come to receive their baptism died or stood in danger of death.

Yahushua HaMashakhYahu, the "Baptizer", separates unto himself for a life with him those who understand and accept baptism into his name. All who want to be *talmidim* of *Yahushua HaMashakhYahu* must be taught to understand that a decision for baptism in the name of *Yahushua HaMashakhYahu* is one to receive *Ruwakh HaKodesh*—the Life-type, *Chayyei Olam* (Everlasting Life), that is in *Elohiym*—into their lives.

You are joined to *Yahushua HaMashakhYahu*, the True Vine, as a branch in him in baptism. You become a partaker of Elohiym's Divinity in baptism—cf. *Kefa Bais (Second Peter)* 1:4. Please do not take the issue of baptism into *Yahushua HaMashakhYahu* lightly. The ministration of baptism into the name of *Yahushua HaMashakhYahu* is of Elohiym's Ministry of Water, Fire, Power and *Chayyei Olam*.

If you were baptized with the belief that baptism is a post-salvation rite, then you missed the blessing of baptism entirely. This means that, before *Elohiym*, you are not baptized. You are therefore not in the Body of *Yahushua HaMashakhYahu* and are without *Chayyei Olam* dwelling in your body. You have needs to be properly baptized and into the only saving name—*Yahushua HaMashakhYahu*.

You must have the right faith and understanding of what baptism entails and brings to the repentant sinner. If your faith was not right at your first baptism, you must seek a correction of this faith and be baptized anew by a genuine messenger of *Elohiym* so that you can enter Elohiym's salvation in *Yahushua HaMashakhYahu*. This is your obligation and duty to your good self.

Permit me to give you a revelation. *Elohiym* wants us to understand that for us to receive the born again experience He speaks to our mind for the response of the body. *Elohiym* speaks His Word to the mind, so that the body can respond to this information from the mind by obeying it.

The obedience of the body to the information in the mind must be in accordance with the instructions of *Elohiym* that the mind receives. This act of synergy between mind and body ignites the rebirth of the human spirit.

It is rightly understood by many that it is the spirit of man that is made anew and alive in the New Birth. Many do not know, however, that it is the body of man acting in obedience to the instructions received by the mind from *Elohiym* that brings about the born again experience.

The fact is that if there is no body or flesh to obey the instructions of *Elohiym* received through the mind, the human spirit cannot become born again. In other words, you cannot short-circuit the body to reach the spirit with the wisdom of *Elohiym*, His Word and power for the recreation of the human spirit.

A short-circuiting of the body, if attempted, will be outside the design of *Elohiym* for our salvation. If short-circuiting the body, and thereby making it redundant in the plan of *Elohiym* for the recreation of the human spirit were permitted, then *shedim* (demons) could also act on this plan and be reborn.

The only difference between man and *shedim* or the fallen angels is that man has a body; angels do not. Man and angels— whether these angels are loyal to *Elohiym* or have fallen from His Grace—have two things in common: mind and spirit.

If the mind of a man alone can act on the Word of *Elohiym* for the new birth of his spirit, then the fallen angels can act on what they know to be the truths of *Elohiym* in their minds for the rebirth of their spirit. We are told in *Ya'akov (James)* 2:19-20 that the fallen angels know in their minds and tremble at the thought that *Elohiym* is forever the One on the *Kes HaMisphat* (The Judgment Seat) in *Shamayim*.

That knowledge, however, cannot bring them the rebirth of their spirit for their salvation. Why? Because they do not have flesh or bodies with which they can act on this knowledge of *Elohiym* for their rebirth. Salvation therefore eludes them forever simply because salvation or becoming born again is not a mind-only issue.

Anybody who would short-circuit his body, in attempt to receive the new birth, will forever remain unsaved. If there is no body, or if it is there but is not involved in the obedience of the word of instruction of *Elohiym*, there will never be the rebirth of the spirit. The born again experience is the design of *Elohiym* to reach man, a tripartite-being, as the execution of His redemptive plan to save the spirit of man.

In that design, the body of man plays the crucial and indispensable role of obedience to bring about the fulfillment of His redemptive work. Let nobody teach you that you can be born again using your mental faculties when you only hear the Word of *Elohiym*. Do not be misled into reciting a so-called *Sinners' Prayer* or fervent and zealous confession of *Romans* 10:9-10 in your quest to become born again.

Someone might teach you into believing that the role to be played by your body to obtain the new birth of your spirit is to exercise your lips and vocal chords in the recitals of the *Sinners' Prayer*, confession of "Jesus Christ" (*Yahushua HaMashakhYahu?*) as the resurrected "Savior", and or zealous and loud vocalizing of *Romans* 10:9-10. That, however, is an inappropriate and ridiculous response to the instruction of *Elohiym* to become born again.

This is because I have read many times in the *Holy Scriptures* about *shedim* confessing willingly with their mouths during the days of the Savior that he is indeed *HaMashakhYahu* and yet they still ended up remaining *shedim* which can not be saved. *Shedim* accept the truth that *Yahushua* is *HaMashakhYahu*, and confess this truth sincerely in fear and trembling, and yet they are not saved by that sincere confession.

Check out this fact in *Mattityahu (Matthew)* 8:29, *Markos (Mark)* 1:24; 3:11; 5:7; *Lukos (Mark)* 4:41; 5:33-43, and 8:28. *Shedim* oftentimes act to deceive people, even the elect people of *Elohiym*, that, they are angels of light, and they do easily confess *Yahushua as HaMashakhYahu* in parrot fashion. The fact is, simply confessing *Yahushua* as *HaMashakhYahu*, even in all sincerity of heart, by any being, human or angelic, cannot bring the born again experience to that being.

The only appropriate response of the body to the instructions of *Elohiym* is for all men seeking the salvation of *Elohiym* to walk into the waters of baptism and have the entire body, not just a part of it, immersed in natural living waters in obedience to the command of *Yahushua HaMashakhYahu*. That is how one is born of water and of *Ruwakh HaKodesh*. There is no other way.

Saving-faith is initially directed at the mind, but it is meant to bring change or transformation to the spirit of man through the appropriate obedience of the human body. After the new birth of the spirit comes about, the body and mind are gradually and progressively redeemed through knowledge and obedience of the New Covenant teachings in fellowship with *Ruwakh HaKodesh*.

The re-born human spirit then takes Elohiym's Word, discerns its meaning and values, and then passes on the meaning to the mind, which in turn compels the body to act appropriately for the blessing promised by *Elohiym*.

This is our struggle in our walk with *Yahushua HaMashakhYahu*. It is those who know this who are on pilgrimage to *Shamayim*. We struggle to get our recreated human spirits to accept the truth and value of Elohiym's Word as His only wisdom and power to bring us the blessings He has promised us.

When our spirit gains this acceptance, it passes this meaning and value to the mind. The mind also undergoes a process speeded up in oral confession, meditation, contemplation, and deep thought to understand what the human spirit passed to it.

When the mind is satisfied with and fully persuaded by what the spirit of man brought to it, it is ready to send a command to the appropriate part of the human body to act in the corresponding way for the promised blessing. When the body receives the command of the mind, it must act in an appropriate manner to the mind's order.

To have a smooth interplay in the functions of the spirit, mind, and body, all three natures have to be renewed. This starts in the born again experience where the human spirit is recreated and enabled to gain insight and understanding of the Word of *Elohiym*. The mind follows suit, and is gradually renewed as it feeds on the Word of *Elohiym* sent to it by the re-born spirit.

The flesh, which before the born again experience was the most active part of tripartite man—though in an unholy, irrational, and impulsive way—undergoes processes aimed at its self-control through the influence of the renewed mind giving instructions to it. This is supposed to go on continually and constantly until the point is reached where the body-flesh is sensitive enough and able to obey the Word of *Elohiym* by the powers exerted on it by the spirit and mind.

This is what our progressive salvation, which we ought to work out in fear and trembling, is all about. The interferences of the Deceiver in this enterprise are the things that make the walk with *Yahushua HaMashakhYahu* a big struggle, one needing the continuous touch of *Ruwakh HaKodesh* for us to be successful to the end.

During a radio program one day, while striving to make known my faith and understanding of baptism into the name of *Yahushua HaMashakhYahu*, as being the one and only rite which—when received in faith, understanding and sincerity of heart, and performed by any servants of *Elohiym* duly commissioned by *Ruwakh HaKodesh*—brings sinners into the salvation of *Elohiym*, I faced the stiff and contrary opinions of three Christian clergymen on the program who referred me to *Ephesians* 2:8-9.

All three clergymen belonged to the same denomination of the Christian faith and insisted that baptism was an act of works; whereas, according to them, the revelation of *Ephesians* is that salvation is by grace only and not by works of any sorts.

To help these clergymen deliver themselves from their wrong

understanding that baptism into the name *Yahushua HaMashakhYahu* is an act of works, I led them to the many teachings in the *Holy Scriptures* on the issue—by *Yahushua HaMashakhYahu* himself in his final instructions to his *Shlikhim* on soul-winning in the Great Commission—and the practices of these same loyal *shlikhim* in leading sinners into the salvation of *Elohiym*, but all to no avail. I then had to ask them one simple question, which was: If baptism is indeed works, is it the one who receives the administration of baptism who works for salvation or is it the servant of the Most High One elected to minister the rite who works, or both of them? I would be delighted to have someone give me a simple answer to this question.

The obedience of the instructions of *Elohiym* for one's salvation as in *Mattityahu (Matthew)* 28:19-20, *Markos (Mark)* 16:16, *YahuChanan (John)* 3:5, *Ma'asim (Acts)* 2:38, 22:16, etc., all of which hinge on baptism, cannot be said to be acts of works outside the will of the Most High One, and thus can not be taken to mean an individual's personally motivated effort to gain the salvation of *Elohiym* by any means outside the revelation of the *Holy Scriptures*.

I believe that we are in the error of *Sinners' Prayer* recitals for salvation for two reasons. The first is our complete misunder-standing of Elohiym's doctrine for the born again experience.

This is all what I have been laboring in this book to teach humanity. Our faith in *Sinners' Prayer* recitals for the born again experience is simply misplaced and out of step with the doctrine of *Elohiym* for our salvation in *Yahushua HaMashakhYahu*.

The second reason lies in our neglect of the instruction of *HaAdon* on the manner of winning the world for him. He has developed a strategy for us to follow in our mission to bring sinners to accept the *Besuras HaGeulah*.

While the Master instructs us to wage this war of winning the world in the strategy of an infantry battalion, we have disobeyed him and seek to do so as long-range missile-launchers. The Master has developed a strategy of person-to-person combat for his loyal and obedient forces to bring the sinner into his salvation.

He said we should first conquer *Yerushalayim*, then, go on to tackle *Yahudah* (Judæa), and then *Shomron*, before reaching the uttermost parts of the world. This gives the picture of an infantry brigade that rakes all in its way into its power while advancing tactfully.

This is like a force in wave-motion. It is like the force of ripples spreading out when a pebble is dropped into still waters. Presenting salvation to the sinner is effective only in person-to-person physical contact, because that is the wisdom and strategy of *HaAdon*.

But what have we done? We have sought to contact the sinner from afar by remote control, through the magic of light and sound waves. We believe wrongly that if salvation seekers can hear and see us through modern technological media of communication, then they can receive the salvation of *Elohiym*. We think it is not necessary to be physically present with the sinner to offer him the salvation of *Elohiym*.

We believe wrongly that insofar as our prayer can reach the sinner through radio, television, printed paper, etc., the sinner can respond for his salvation. We launch a war by throwing missiles at intended targets instead of going directly to hit them.

You see why we have missed the targets by this approach at sending Elohiym's salvation to the sinner through missile launching? How can our feet gather the much-needed dust to be used in testimony against unbelieving cities—cf. *Mattityahu (Matthew)* 10:14, *Markos (Mark)* 6:11, and *Lukas (Luke)* 9:5—by this missile-launching approach?

Our approach to offering Elohiym's salvation to the sinner is wrong in practice. When we have sent the word of salvation through the electromagnetic spectrum to viewers and listeners, which people are at the end-point to minister baptism to viewers who accept our message to bring them the fulfillment of *Mattityahu (Matthew)* 28:19, *Markos (Mark)* 16:16 and *Ma'asim (Acts)* 2: 38-39? Let us never forget that *HaAdon* has **sent** us to physically be with salvation seekers to offer them his salvation, which is only receivable after preaching and baptizing.

I am particularly delighted by the record in *Ma'asim (Acts)* 20:20 of how *Sha'ul*, a *Shliakh* of *Yahushua HaMashakhYahu*, went about spreading the message of the *Besuras HaGeulah*. He went from **"house to house"** in every city that he entered to preach *Yahushua HaMashakhYahu*. If we are to be successful in executing our task in the Great Commission of *HaAdon*, we should go from **door to door** propagating the message of salvation.

I find it difficult to comprehend why many "men of God" of this generation are so preoccupied with getting salvation seekers to recite after them the *Sinners' Prayer* for a claim to the born again experience. Since my youthful days, I have known many globe-trotting *"evangelists"* who have made stopovers in my country

Ghana to spread their understanding of the message of the *Besuras HaGeulah*. They have come from Europe, the USA, and, in lesser numbers, the African continent. They come in chartered aircrafts loaded with high-powered electronic equipment and gadgets to organize loud, giant, open-air crusades.

Their purpose in organizing these crusades is to get salvation seekers to recite after them the *Sinners' Prayer*. Thinking to make people accept into their hearts "Jesus Christ" (*Yahushua HaMashakhYahu?*), "as their Lord and personal Savior", so to speak, is the reason for all the sweat and investment toward the organizing of these crusades. The climax of the crusade is their success in getting as many salvation seekers as possible to rush to the pulpit area and act their decision to *"receive Jesus Christ into their hearts"* through recitals of the *Sinners' Prayer*.

Immediately after chalking their successes in this regard, these globe-trotting *"evangelists"* move on to other destinations, confident in having carried out an errand for *HaAdon* in his commission to his genuine *talmidim* to spread the message of the *Besuras HaGeulah* to the world!

To these *"evangelists,"* they have carried out the Great Commission of *HaAdon*. But, is that really true? Have they carried out in full the Great Commission of *HaAdon*? I very much doubt that. Without coming close to any natural body of living waters, to conduct the rite of baptism, I wonder what service was rendered to the kingdom of *HaAdon* and to salvation seekers in these prayer-for-salvation practices.

The usefulness or otherwise of whatever service these globe-trotting *"evangelists"* render to the *Malchut HaElohiym* can be seen if we critically examine the Great Commission instructions of *HaAdon* found in *Mattityahu (Matthew)* 28:18-20, *Markos (Mark)* 16:15-16, and *Lukas (Luke)* 24:46-48 against their work.

For all who are conversant with the operations of these itinerant *"evangelists,"* there is always some unfinished work left to be done after the crusade by the host "Man of God." This work is considered secondary and consequential to the feat accomplished at the crusade, where thousands were deemed to have become born again in their recitals, enbloc, of the *Sinners' Prayer*.

The work left to be done by host "Man of God" of these itinerant *"evangelists"* involves counseling and teaching, in four to fourteen weeks for "new convert" salvation seekers, in preparation for them to be baptized in water. Their baptism is considered of secondary need or necessity to a so-called born again experience that came to them through a *Sinners' Prayer* recital. But then, does the *Holy Scriptures* teach all this kind of stuff? No, it does not!

I think it is absolutely important for all salvation seekers to critically examine many of today's practices among people professing to be championing the cause of *Yahushua HaMashakhYahu*. We must be sure the faith we uphold today is exactly what all genuine followers of *Yahushua HaMashakhYahu* of the first century subscribed to under the leadership of the *Shlikhim* of *HaAdon*. Otherwise, we could place our quest for the salvation of *Elohiym* in great jeopardy.

As a messenger of *Elohiym* commissioned to teach His true salvation, I act in love to bring you this teaching. My alarm and sadness of heart, when I see people teach the wrong doctrine of *Sinners' Prayer* recitations for salvation, has given me the energy and commitment to bring to you the true doctrine of Elohiym's salvation.

It is purely in love that I do this work, citing people who express faith in this wrong doctrine. My love for *Yahushua HaMashakhYahu*, in appreciation of his sacrifice of atonement for sin and the blessings arising thereof for me, gives me the zeal to do this teaching.

It is my love for the teachers of a wrong doctrine, one that has the effect of keeping many a salvation seeker away from the *Sha'arei HaShamayim* (Gates of Heaven), which drives me to do this work of the *Malchut HaElohiym*. It is still the love in my heart for all the simple-minded people, who have been misled from the path to Eternity with *Elohiym*, which causes me to teach in tears the genuine doctrine of Elohiym's salvation. The love I have for you, dear reader, is what burns in my heart and causes me to labor in this teaching, until *Yahushua HaMashakhYahu* is fully formed and become clearly visible in you.

May *Elohiym* bless all who see no malice in my bringing to light, the many people who teach this wrong doctrine of *Sinners' Prayer* recitals for salvation. May the followers of these teachers, see no ill-motive in my (and Yahushua's) contrary teaching to that of their icons; otherwise, they will not get the intended blessing meant for them in this work I do, my labor of love for them. My joy is in the delivering of a heavy blow at the Deceiver of men, which blow brings deliverance and illumination to the minds of many people he has held captive in a wrong doctrine for salvation for so long.

Let us look at the *Mashal (Parable) of Wheat and Weeds (Tares)* in *Mattityahu (Matthew)* 13:24-30, 36-43 closely. In this parable, you can see the wisdom of the devil. He made a counterfeit product to look very much like the genuine.

His ability shown in making a replica of wheat, in his invention of tares, should alarm all pursuers of the salvation of *Elohiym*. The ability of the devil in his intent to deceive mankind, all the way till the harvest time, as we are warned of in this *mashal (parable)*, must be a wake-up call to every salvation seeker to diligently search for the truth of Elohiym's salvation.

I shudder to think of what fate could have befallen Cornelius, Apollos, and the twelve *"talmidim"* Sha'ul met in Ephesus, if they did not receive the interventions they did in the ministries of *Shimon Kefa*, Aquila, and *Sha'ul* respectively, before arriving at paradise or the *Sha'arei HaShamayim*.

These people would have been living their spiritual lives in the beliefs of being saved when they were not. They looked to me then very much like tares living beside wheat. Strangely, many of their observers did not see these fervent and zealous people—followers of *Elohiym*?—any differently from the true and genuinely saved people of *Yahushua HaMashakhYahu*.

These people took nourishment from common "soil," which was the Word of *Elohiym*, as the saved also did. They confessed the same words as the true children of *Elohiym* did. They did most of what true children of *Elohiym* would do: they loved and served Him, praised and worshipped Him, prayed and fasted regularly, witnessed the love of *Elohiym* for others, showed love and concern to the poor in their communities, etc.

They seemed to be bearing the fruit of *Ruwakh HaKodesh*, and yet they were not born again of natural living waters and of *Ruwakh HaKodesh* into the *Malchut HaElohiym*. Now that alarms me, and you ought to be alarmed also.

You see, once upon a time, many people from *Ashur* (Assyria) found themselves as an occupation "force" deployed by their king in a part of *Yisroel* called *Shomron* (Samaria). Then they fell in love with the spiritual worship of true Hebrews, and for many centuries, did as devout children of *Yisroel* were doing. They, thus, evolved to be called *Shomronim* (Samaritans)—a changed people who were neither Assyrians any longer nor of biological Hebrew identity.

After imitating the Hebrew faith for all those centuries, however, they wrongly considered themselves to be the children of

Avraham, and of *Ya'acov*. They lived in delusion of having Elohiym's salvation since they did not come out of the loins of father *Avraham*!

Many people today also hold on to the recitals of *Sinners' Prayers* for salvation, wrongly touting their claims of being the children of *Elohiym*. These are the modern-day *Shomronim* in today's spiritual *Yisroel*, who believe wrongly that their copying of the faiths and practices of the true children of *Elohiym* makes them His children too! This is a sad error of faith that is leading many a salvation seeker to disappointment and doom.

Do you remember the love and devotion Cornelius had for the Hebrew faith? He lived in daily confession of his sins and acts of good deeds to the poor. Even in that devotion to holy living however, he was not in the family of *Elohiym*. He was neither a child from the loins of *Avraham* nor one born of natural living waters in baptism into *Yahushua HaMashakhYahu*. In this condition, he needed help from *Elohiym* as far as salvation was concerned.

Elohiym made sure Cornelius and his family—and later on, Apollos and Sha'ul's twelve friends of Ephesus—were not to be disappointed at the harvest time. He sent to them help and direction onto the right path, which is that all-time narrow way on which very few mortals tread.

They were humble enough to receive correction. I am sure they would be given the honor by *Elohiym* to welcome some of us latter-day servants of *Elohiym* to His Abode amid the melodious trumpet sounds of archangels.

Oh, what a destination that awaits the few that find and tread the narrow and slippery way faithfully to the end. What starting point shown by *HaAdon* to takeoff from onto this glorious destination. What glorious and sure instruction of *HaAdon* to obey, so as to embark on this blessed pilgrimage to Elohiym's Abode.

Yahushua HaMashakhYahu, HaAdon, said we would not be there, in Elohiym's Abode, without being born of water and of *Ruwakh HaKodesh*. He said if we receive His Word of instruction, repent of our sins, and are baptized in his name, we would be saved and set on this pilgrimage that promises a happy ending.

Do not doubt his instruction. Repent of your sins and be baptized in his name for the remission of your sins. Then, you shall receive the power of *Ruwakh HaKodesh* into your heart to fuel and power you to the end of this pilgrimage, so you can arrive in the bosom of *Elohiym*.

Please do not be content and hopeful that your fervent and sincere recitals of *Sinners' Prayers* would lead you to *Shamayim*. No evidence exists in the *Holy Scriptures* that any past pilgrims ever said this prayer and gained the power to become born again. The *Sinners' Prayer* is a cunning deception of the devil to make you a tare, a product of his wicked machinations against the commandments, instructions, and will of *Elohiym* for you to become born again into His kingdom.

May your spirit and mind, receive the illuminations of the *Holy Scriptures* so you escape the destruction of the devil. His diabolical enterprise and resolve to bring you to the place of disappointment and doom is exposed in this teaching. Please wise up to it so you can escape the catastrophe that awaits many at the harvest time of *Elohiym*, when they are gathered up as tares and thrown into a lake of unquenchable fire.

The devil has no respect for personalities or title bearers. He only respects those who know the Word of *Elohiym* and zealously obey it. He does not care if you are happy with the appellations of high priest, senior pastor, general overseer, bishop, or archbishop by people. If you are known and honored by men to be in these positions and do not know how to rightly divide the Word of Truth, he will mess you up and send you to live with him in hell.

You see how wickedly he dealt with *Anan* (Annas) and *Caiapha*, (Caiaphas) high priests of *Yisroel* in the days of *HaAdon*, who were in direct succession to *Aharon*. These people had their gold-finished residences in *Shamayim* booked for them long before becoming *kohen gadol* (high priest) due to their ancestral lineage, but the devil did not respect that and, because they did not have thorough knowledge of the scriptures, he messed up their faith.

The devil has more sinister tricks up his sleeve for those who are at the forefront trying to bring sinners to *Yahushua HaMashakhYahu*. If he is able to make you a tare, when you believe you are wheat, then he succeeds in getting you and all your followers to his side.

By now the devil is beating his chest boastfully in what he has achieved in this *Sinners' Prayer* deception of his. This doctrine looks too good to be wrong. Many scriptures are drawn to embellish it to the extent that the simple see in it a sure way to become born again.

Please believe only what *Yahushua HaMashakhYahu* tells us. *Yahushua HaMashakhYahu* has said: ***"Omein, omein, I say to you:***

unless someone is born of mayim (water) and of Ruwakh HaKodesh, he is not able to enter the Malchut HaElohiym (Kingdom of Elohiym)"—YahuChanan 3:5, OJB; words in parenthesis are mine.

Do you believe that? If yes, then blessed are you. If not, then you need to believe him now without further delay.

Yahushua HaMashakhYahu is *HaDerekh* (The Way), the door, and the key to the born again experience. If you do not do as he teaches, be prepared for your punishment on doom's day. I hope I have warned you enough.

May the Word of *Elohiym* in the lone chapter of *YahuChanan Bais (Second John)* 1:9-11, sound a loud warning to anyone who would believe the word of preachers without making sure what was taught him was indeed the Word of *Elohiym*. Shall we read these verses?

"WHOSOEVER TRANSGRESSETH, (or whosoever believeth a false teaching), AND ABIDETH NOT IN THE DOCTRINE OF CHRIST (Yahushua HaMashakhYahu), HATH NOT GOD (is neither known by Elohiym, nor has any knowledge of Him). HE THAT ABIDETH IN THE DOCTRINE OF Christ (Yahushua HaMashakhYahu, not Christ), HATH BOTH THE FATHER AND THE SON. IF THERE COME ANY UNTO YOU, AND BRING NOT THIS DOCTRINE (of Yahushua HaMashakhYahu), RECEIVE HIM NOT into your house, neither bid him God speed (farewell in the name of Elohiym); FOR HE THAT BIDDETH HIM GOD SPEED (or wishes him well in the name of Elohiym) IS PARTAKER OF HIS EVIL DEEDS"—cf. YahuChanan Bais (Second John) 1:9-11, KJV, caps and all the words in parenthesis are mine.

We are responsible for what we believe. *Elohiym* will hold us to it. When we believe a doctrine which is false, we shall be judged by *Elohiym* in the same manner as the one who preached it, deliberately or out of ignorance, is to be judged.

This is because by accepting a false doctrine we encourage and even commend the teacher of it. In accepting a false doctrine, we share or partake in the harm caused by the teacher of it and should take blame and punishment with him—*Yechezkel (Ezekiel)* 14:10.

If I were you, I would seek to have the spirit of the early followers of *Yahushua HaMashakhYahu* in Berea and double-check all what preachers tell me before imbibing them as the holy truths of *Elohiym*.

Today, we have ready access to both the Old and New Covenant teachings—typically, the *Orthodox Jewish Bible*—in print and electronic forms, unlike in the days of the Bereans when they had very scarce hand-written copies of only the Old Covenant teachings.

We therefore have no explanation to give *Elohiym*, why we believe false doctrines taught by some preachers when His Word, the *Holy Scriptures* in book and electronic forms, are readily available to us for studying.

Maybe what we see as a disadvantage to the spiritual awareness of the Bereans, in not having both the Old and New Covenant teachings in their hands, was actually a blessing in disguise. They had no options but to live in close study of the Old Covenant scriptures they had in hand-written form, matching its types and shadows to those of the New Covenant revelations and truths, which *Sha'ul* and others verbally taught them.

They could easily accept and live by the New Covenant teachings they received at the hand of *Sha'ul* anywhere and anytime they saw in them the Old Covenant types and shadows manifesting in reality. It was easy for them to accept whatever realities of the New Covenant doctrines on Elohiym's salvation *Sha'ul* taught them, because they could see their types and shadows in the Old Covenant scriptures.

If the Bereans envied those of us who live in today's times where both Old and New Covenant scriptures are readily available for study, understanding, and discernment of the values of our salvation, then they envied us in vain.

For while they desired and yearned to have both Old and New Covenant teachings for critical and careful study for reconciliation between them so they could rest their salvation in *Yahushua HaMashakhYahu* on firm foundation, we are indifferent and lazy about this.

That which would have been a great blessing to them, we have spurned and treated very lightly. May *Elohiym*, help us see the value in having His Word, readily, in our hands. May we be inspired to study it in all diligence!

I know that for many, accepting this true teaching on the born again doctrine will be hard since, for a long time, they have become used to the false teaching on the *Sinners' Prayer* in which they express faith in the name "Jesus Christ" as the way to become born again. They should imbibe this true teaching, a bitter pill, and yet the remedy to their need of salvation. Please swallow this pill in all humility and courage of heart, and you will be blessed with the opportunity of spending Eternity in the presence of *Elohiym*.

You are a true and genuine **royal** of the *Malchut HaElohiym*, a **precious one** in the sight of *Elohiym*, **a conqueror** in *Yahushua HaMashakhYahu*, a **victor** over sin, **a winner** in all situations and circumstances, **an over-comer** of the wiles of the deceiver, **an ambassador** of *Yahushua HaMashakhYahu*, and a real **man of action**, only when you are in *Yahushua HaMashakhYahu*.

Your ability to enter *Yahushua HaMashakhYahu*, and be fully encapsulated in him, is made possible only in your faith in *YahuChanan (John)* 3:5, *Markos (Mark)* 16:16, *Ma'asim (Acts)* 2:38-39, *Romans* 6:4-7, *Galatians* 3:27, *Kefa Alef (First Peter)* 3:20-21, etc. and in your obedience of them to the letter, and not in the recitals of some *Sinners' Prayers* in the name "Jesus Christ" after some "men of God".

This plain truth is that which you must be told by somebody who truly loves you and cares about the destiny of your soul. *Elohiym* bless you, dear reader, for your humility and courage in receiving this teaching. *Elohiym* bless you the more for not taking offence at this teaching. *HalleluYahu*!

Chapter Five

Some Last Words

As said somewhere in this teaching, it is dangerous for anybody to teach his personal experiences in spiritual issues. This is because it is not all spiritual experiences or manifestations that are genuine or from *Elohiym*. Where spiritual experiences are taught in place of doctrine, deceptions can result and deny people the salvation of *Elohiym* they seek.

Nevertheless, permit me to talk a little about my personal experiences. I promise you this is not related to any doctrine and should not endanger your faith.

In the early days of my search for spiritual renewal, I would often go for services or prayer meetings anywhere I could find them. At almost all of these meetings, we sang hymns, psalms, and hot spiritual songs.

A particular one that I loved to sing with all the zeal, passion, and life in me, was about prayer being the key. Its lyrics went like this: *"Prayer is the key. Prayer is the key. Prayer is the master key. Jesus started with prayer, and ended with prayer. Prayer is the master key. Jesus started with prayer and ended with prayer. Prayer is the master key."*

As we sang it in our meetings, my conviction that prayer in the name "Jesus Christ" was the only key into the blessings of *Elohiym* grew stronger and stronger by the day. We all lived in the thought that everything could be sought from *Elohiym* in prayer. We never thought we could exercise faith for any of Elohiym's many blessings promised us; all was about prayer being the key.

We prayed fervently for everything. We prayed for our daily bread, healings from diseases, financial breakthrough, employment, and success in exams, but we also prayed for "Holy Spirit" fire and power to come into our hearts.

You should have been there to see how we prayed for this fire and power to descend into our hearts. We would always end by leading some repentant sinners to recite the *Sinners' Prayer* for them to become born again, never forgetting to thank "God" for souls "won". Prayer was our one and only key to and for every need.

Looking back on those prayer meetings I can see how much of our zeal was misplaced. We had a great amount of zeal but very little or no knowledge.

I can now see *Yahushua HaMashakhYahu* did not start with prayer: He started with baptism. He started obeying the will of *HaAv* in the baptism he received at the hands of *YahuChanan ben Zecharyahu*. We, however, can infer that he went into prayer in the wilderness after the baptism.

Did *Yahushua HaMashakhYahu* end in prayer? I am not sure about that. When he finished all he had come to do on earth by obeying the will of *HaAv*, he concluded by announcing to *Shamayim* and Earth in his last statement, *"It is finished"*—cf. *YahuChanan (John) 19:30*. Now that was not a prayer; it was an announcement. *Yahushua HaMashakhYahu* did not end his time on earth in prayer.

I am not sure if prayer is the master key. Prayer is a key, no doubt, but the master key is obedience to the instructions of *Elohiym*.

The obedience of the word of instruction of *Elohiym* will always bring us into His blessings. Obedience is the master key into *Chayyei Olam*. It is the master key to the born again experience. We can only enter the *Malchut HaElohiym* by obeying what *Elohiym* tells us in the *Holy Scriptures*. There is no other way.

When we pray, it is primarily because we are obedient to the instruction of *Elohiym* to pray, so prayer does not precede obedience. Rather, obedience leads prayer, and therefore, the master key is obedience and not prayer. This truth we must keep in our spirits throughout our pilgrim journey from Earth to *Shamayim* if we are to arrive there.

Ever since I came to the conviction that prayer was not the master key, I have decided to look critically at the many beliefs, dogmas, and doctrines of people today who claim to be followers of *Yahushua HaMashakhYahu* (Christians?). It is amazing to me how many practices of Christianity are neither even biblical, nor of the faith of the *Shlikhim* of *Yahushua HaMashakhYahu*. The recitation of so-called *Sinners' Prayers* in the quest of sinners for salvation is one of such wrong practices of Christianity.

I would encourage everybody in search of Elohiym's salvation to go into serious study of the *Holy Scriptures* before upholding the faiths and practices of today's Christianity as if they were the unblemished faith of the *Shlikhim* of *Yahushua HaMashakhYahu*. The sure foundation of our faith, practices, and way of life is in our instructions received from the Word of *Elohiym*, and not the word of preachers.

As for me, I have gone beyond living like the Bereans of *Ma'asim (Acts)*, chapter seventeen fame, to more serious study of the Holy Word of *Elohiym*. I now study the Word as the Constitution of the *Malchut HaElohiym*.

The First Constitution of *Elohiym* is called **Tanakh** which comprised the **Torah** (the *Law* of *Moshe*), **Neviim** ("Prophets") and **Ketuvim** ("Prophetic" Scriptures) of the Old Covenant scriptures. *Elohiym* ordained for this constitution to govern the lives of only the people of *Yisroel* among all the nations of the Earth while it remained legal. The *Tanakh*, however, stood as a surety to and the vitual image or shadow of a better constitution that was to come about in and through the sacrificial death and resurrection of *Yahushua HaMashakhYahu*, which would also then be beneficial to any people in all nations of the Earth who exercised faith in his death, resurrection and true name.

This First Constitution, the *Tanakh*, ceased to be in force on the Day of Outpouring of *Ruwakh HaKodesh* in Yerushalyim, (Pentecost?), giving way to a second.

The Second Constitution is the final and current one and is known as **Beyrit Chadasha**. It comprises the parts of the *Torah* which continue to be obligatory to salvation seekers even after the sacrifice of *Yahushua HaMashakhYahu* fulfilled a large portion of it, together with the *Neviim* and the *Ketuvim* of the First Constitution; and together with the teachings and works of *Yahushua HaMashakhYahu* and his *Shlikhim* as well. The **Beyrit Chadasha** defines the way of life of *Yahushua HaMashakhYahu* as portrayed by his teachings, doctrines, and ordinances, which all his *talmidim* must emulate and live by.

It is this constitution that was bequeathed as a Will to all seekers of Elohiym's salvation in *Yahushua HaMashakhYahu*. All followers of *Yahushua HaMashakhYahu* are advised to be knowledgeable and conversant with the scope and content of this Second Constitution, so that they are able to live by it without fault.

This constitution also defines and charts what is, in fact, known as **"HaDerekh"—"The Way"**—cf. *Bereshis (Genesis)* 3:24, *Shemot (Exodus)* 32:8, *Devarim (Deuteronomy)* 9:16, 11:28, *Shofetim (Judges)* 2:17, *Yirmeyahu (Jeremiah)* 7:23, **Malachi 2:8**, *Ma'asim (Acts)* 9:2, 18:25-26, 19:9, 23, 22:4, 24:14—which every salvation seeker must live by to be sure of being given a warm reception at the *Sha'arei Shamayim* upon exiting Earth.

In this second constitution are various articles, clauses, and sub-clauses. There are articles pertaining to membership of earthlings to the *Malchut HaElohiym*. These are further broken down to include clauses and sub-clauses dealing with son-ship and adoption.

If you know all these articles and clauses, you will easily see *Sinners' Prayer* recitals for salvation as unconstitutional and denounce the practice.

If you study this constitution, you will know your standing before *Elohiym* and His Son, *Yahushua HaMashakhYahu*. If, however, you do not know this constitution, you will be happy with the deception that somebody or some people are higher than you in some kind of spiritual order; people to whom you must pay tribute and royalties.

There is no hierarchy in son-ship in the *Malchut HaElohiym* according to this constitution. Everybody who gains membership to the *Malchut HaElohiym* is a royal priest reporting directly to *Kohen Gadol* (High Priest) *Melekh-Tzedek—Yahushua HaMashakhYahu*. This Constitution spells out to the student of it, in very clear and no uncertain language, the status, responsibilities, privileges, code of conduct, etc., of its members.

What joy to study this constitution to know when you can call for angelic reinforcement of your bodyguard corps! What joy to know how to fly back to *Shamayim* where your papers of accreditation as an ambassador to Earth were signed and put into your hand for healing from any diseases, if for any inexplicable reason, you ever fell sick on Earth while *Chayyei Olam* (the Eternal or Everlasting Life) of *Elohiym* is dwelling in your body!!

Simply report to the Mighty Healer of *Shamayim*, *Yahushua HaMashakhYahu*, for cost-free, drug-free, and perfect healing. The place for you to be healed under this Constitution is not some medical center on Planet Earth. Do not make the mistake of King Asa seen in *Divrey HaYamim Bais (Second Chronicles)* 16:12, in ignoring *Elohiym* to seek help from earthly physicians.

Study the *Holy Scriptures* as Elohiym's only pathway to *Shamayim*. Your resolve should always be to know what *Elohiym* teaches mortals in His Holy Word to do to get to *Shamayim*. Let it be in you at all times of your study of Elohiym's Word to ask yourself the question: *"What did Elohiym say I should do?"*

You must always be of this critical mind so that when you hear some preacher man giving out unconstitutional instructions and directives to any people to recite after him some *Sinners' Prayer* to gain membership to the *Malchut HaElohiym*, you can help him out by leading him to the appropriate clauses or articles of the constitution on membership.

The pathway to *Shamayim* is charted for you in this Constitution. Do not turn to unauthorized pathways: They will send you to the wrong destination where you will be greatly shocked.

Please get serious in the study of Elohiym's constitution. You will be blessed by it. You will be tested by it. You will be judged by it. It is your very life, so do not play with it. I have spoken out my heart to you, dear reader, and I hope you receive my words as such.

Please, permit me to put on the mantle of a *navi* (seer, *"prophet"*) and foretell of days to come. I know that a true *navi* is one who hears clearly the Word of *Elohiym* and speaks it out unadulterated to others who must hear it. I am, therefore, careful to have *Ruwakh HaKodesh* of *Elohiym* lead me in this.

Please listen to Elohiym's Word: ***"For as in the days of Noach, thus will be the Bias HaMashakhYahu, the Coming of the Bar Enosh."—Mattityahu (Matthew) 24:37-39, OJB.***

In Noach's days, salvation came by water baptism—cf. *Kefa Alef (First Peter)* 3:20-21—so it must be that salvation will come by water baptism in the name of *Yahushua HaMashakhYahu* when the son of man returns.

Before that day of Yahushua's return, *Eliyahu HaNavi* comes first—cf. *Malachi* 4:5-6. The latter-day *Eliyahu* is *YahuChanan ben Zecharyahu*, the known forerunner of *Yahushua HaMashakhYahu*. Therefore, before the return of *Yahushua HaMashakhYahu*, *YahuChanan ben Zecharyahu* must first come. This we are told in *Mattityahu (Matthew)* 17:10-13.

When *Eliyahu*, in *YahuChanan ben Zecharyahu*, returns, he will not land on *Har HaCarmel* (Mt. Carmel), where centuries ago he performed the rite of symbolically baptizing the twelve tribes (twelve-stone altar?) of *Yisroel*—cf. *Melekhim Alef (First Kings)* 18:31-35. Rather, *Eliyahu*, in *YahuChanan ben Zecharyahu*, will surface in the wilderness about the *Yarden*, precisely Bethabara.

Bethabara (*Beit-Bar?*—House of Cleansing?) is where the children of *Yisroel* on many occasions, over centuries, have been known to cross the fords of the *Yarden* in the purification rites of baptism on their way to the "Promised Land".

YahuChanan ben Zecharyahu, in *Eliyahu*, is coming to complete his truncated ministry of teaching and administering to his fellow

Hebrews the baptism for the remission of sin. This truth of *Elohiym* I speak to you in the spirit of a *navi.*

What began the New Covenant dispensation on the Day of the Outpouring of the *Ruwakh HaKodesh* (Pentecost?) in *Yerushalayim*—the administration of mass baptisms to Hebrews— will be the same that will end it.

You see, very soon, the current Age of *Goyim (Gentiles)* will come to an end to give way for the Age of *Yisroel* to begin—cf. *Romans* 9:1 to 11:36. When the Age of *Yisroel* begins, it will be one of the signs of *Yahushua HaMashakhYahu's* imminent return—cf. *Romans* 11: 15. Not long into the Age of *Yisroel, Yahushua HaMashakhYahu* shall show Himself in the skies, and then the end of all things will come.

Therefore, be assured of this: Before *Bar Enosh* (the Son of Man) returns, *YahuChanan ben Zecharyahu* in the spirit of *Eliyahu HaNavi* will be back to minister mass baptism to repentant Hebrews. *YahuChanan ben Zecharyahu*, in the spirit of *Eliyahu*, will return to earth to prepare the last crop of Hebrews in readiness for the coming of *Bar Enosh.*

We cannot be ignorant of this, since we are told in Elohiym's Word as a confirmation that *Yahushua HaMashakhYahu*, the King of kings, will return in a manner reminiscent of the days of *Noach*. The return of *Yahushua HaMashakhYahu* will not only be a surprise in its timing, as was the coming of the flood of *Noach*, but it will be the same as in those days to take away those saved in, of, and by water in the baptism in Living Waters. *HalleluYahu!*

In conclusion of this whole enterprise of teaching how to enter the salvation of *Elohiym*, let me say that *Elohiym* has clearly taught us from His Word how we can be born again or how we can enter the *Malchut HaElohiym*. In the mind and wisdom of *Elohiym*, we are born again of water and of *Ruwakh HaKodesh.*

This might be a mystery to man, but it is Elohiym's clear and simple truth. It is our faith in the combined powers of living waters and *Ruwakh HaKodesh* that brings the sinner into the state of being born again. When we express faith in the ability of living waters and of *Ruwakh HaKodesh* to bring the sinner to the born again experience, then can we be seen to be agreeing with *Elohiym* in what He says.

We act contrary to the revelation of *Elohiym* to us, if we think it is by **prayer** and *Ruwakh HaKodesh* that the sinner becomes born again. In fact, our posture that we can become born again by prayer brings us on a collision course with Elohiym's Word. We therefore seem to be fighting *Elohiym*.

It is not just simple disobedience, but it is rebellion against *Elohiym*, His will, power, and Word. We may not be aware of our rebellion but that ignorance will lead us to the hot and unproductive argument to be allowed to enter *Shamayim* at the end of time, when many of us are denied the chance to enter by *Yahushua HaMashakhYahu*.

From the *Beyrit Chadasha* teachings, we understand that the salvation of the sinner is serious business. We are safe in our beliefs and practices for salvation if and only if they are in harmony with the teachings of the *Holy Scriptures*. For this reason, we should always seek to reconcile whatever we are taught by our spiritual leaders with what is in the *Holy Scriptures* in order to be safe.

The Great Commission and its realities must be understood by all salvation seekers and preachers. In *Mattityahu (Matthew)* 28:19, the command of *Yahushua HaMashakhYahu* is for his *talmidim* to teach and administer baptism for the salvation of souls. It is explicitly stated in *Markos (Mark)* 16:16 that salvation comes through baptism in the name of *Yahushua HaMashakhYahu*.

If we understand the value and true significance of baptism into the name of *Yahushua HaMashakhYahu*, as the ordinance of *Elohiym* for the initiation of sinners into His salvation, we could rightly teach the sinner how to walk into this salvation. This understanding of baptism into the name of *Yahushua HaMashakhYahu* will take us away from the errors of reciting so-called *Sinners' Prayers* for salvation.

In *Lukas (Luke)* 24:47 we are told that repentance and remission of sins, obtainable only through baptism in the name of *Yahushua HaMashakhYahu*, should be preached to bring salvation to mankind. Let us therefore not confuse the salvation issue by preaching that **repentance and forgiveness of sin** will bring it about. This cannot do so, but rather leads us to teach the error of praying a prayer of confession of sins and a request for forgiveness in our quest to become born again.

The teaching by the *talmidim* and *shlikhim* of the first century on salvation is centered on the person and mission of *Yahushua HaMashakhYahu*, repentance from sin, and baptism into the name of *Yahushua HaMashakhYahu*. This is evidenced from *Ma'asim (Acts)* and the *Iggrot Kodesh (Holy Letters)* of the *Shlikhim* of *Yahushua HaMashakhYahu*. All through the *Beyrit Chadasha* scriptures, this has been the teaching of the *Shlikhim* of *Yahushua HaMashakhYahu* and does remain the only true doctrine for us today that will bring any sinner into the salvation of *Elohiym* in the born again experience.

In the light of the teaching of the *Shlikhim* of *Yahushua HaMashakhYahu* on how to enter the salvation of *Elohiym*, the doctrine of praying some *Sinners' Prayers* as the way to enter Elohiym's salvation is manifest to be deceptive, false, counterfeit, and fraudulent. It defrauds many of the salvation of *Elohiym* in *Yahushua HaMashakhYahu*.

It is therefore the duty of all enlightened messengers of *Elohiym*, who have rightly divided *HaDevar HaEmes* (the Word of Truth), to rise up against this falsehood with the mission of dismantling it. For sure, *Sha'arei Sheol* (the gates of Hell) cannot prevail against the will of *Elohiym* and genuine believers in, and of, the Body of *Yahushua HaMashakhYahu*—the True Vine.

While we fight this falsehood, we ought to be wary of the wiles, cunning ways, and preaching prowess of the enemy, the devil. We should understand that he works like modern-day terrorists who hijack airplanes of their enemies and fly them into buildings belonging to these same enemies, killing them in the end.

The devil similarly hijacks Elohiym's Word, packages it to achieve his intent of deception against Elohiym's own people and, in many instances, succeeds in his enterprise due to the ignorance and gullibility of those professing to be the elect of *Elohiym*. What a sad situation arising from the laziness of the salvation seeker in researching Elohiym's Word.

One last scripture I wish to leave with you to chew on is one that talks about three things that bear witness on Earth. These, we are told, are *Ruwakh HaKodesh*, the water, and the blood. Shall we read from *YahuChanan Alef (First John)* about this: ***"And there are three that bear witness in earth, the Spirit (Ruwakh HaKodesh), and the water, and the blood: and all these three agree in one"—*** **cf. *YahuChanan Alef (First John)* 5:8, *KJV*; words in parenthesis are mine.**

It is obvious what ***"Ruwakh HaKodesh"*** and ***"the blood"*** are and stand for. Unfortunately, we seem to neither know nor understand what ***"the water"*** is or stands for. Dear precious reader, it might be that *Elohiym* is waiting for you to seek from Him insight and wisdom on this issue of the perfect corroboration between *Ruwakh HaKodesh*, the water, and the blood. Please do share what

Elohiym tells you in the privacy of your closet with humanity, concerning these three witnesses that are in agreement in the earth.

I would be most grateful to anybody for sharing *Ruwakh*-revealed information in this regard because nobody can claim to have all knowledge. Not even the "wise" philosopher of secular knowledge, Socrates (469-399 BCE), or the greatest expositor of the New Covenant realities, *Sha'ul*, could say they were totally full of knowledge.

Listen to Socrates: *"One thing that I know and that is that I know nothing".* This is for you to ponder over. Was Socrates not by this expression indicating a yearning for the true knowledge of *Elohiym* long before the coming to Earth of the greatest Teacher to sinful mankind—*Yahushua HaMashakhYahu*—the Son of *Elohiym*?

What did *Sha'ul*, a *Shliakh* of *Yahushua HaMashakhYahu*, conclude in this matter after all the many revelations he received from *Elohiym*? Hear him: *"For we know in part, and we prophesy in part. But when that which is perfect is come, then that which is in part shall be done away with. For now we see through a glass, darkly; but then face to face: now I know in part; but then shall I know even as also I am known"*—cf. *First Corinthians 13:9-10, 12, KJV.*

So I also say *I know nothing until you, my dear reader, will lead me to the hidden truths of Elohiym's Word.* Of course, I do know that a lie repeated many times over centuries gains some credibility, as is the case in the belief that a so-called *Sinners' Prayer*, loudly and sincerely recited many times over will make one become born again, which has gained phenomenal credibility by many simple-minded people in our generation!

May *Elohiym* richly bless you and may His peace and mercies be yours in abundance. *Shalom Aleikhem*—Peace of *Elohiym*, be unto you.

THE END

Author's Letter to All Readers

Dear Reader,

Thank you for the time and your effort in reading this book and for the money spent on its purchase. I believe they have been rewarding.

I write to seek your assistance toward enriching future editions of this book. I would be most grateful to you, and delighted, to receive your comments, suggestions, questions, reservations, etc., on any of the issues raised in this teaching. May you also please share with me your knowledge of sources of any available literature along the lines of teaching in this book, that you may know of—information like book titles, authors, periodicals, journals, magazines, etc.—and that could be of benefit to me in developing a textbook edition of this teaching.

If you have been inspired and challenged by the message of this book, and would wish to have some interaction personally or in a group with me, I will be delighted to arrange one such meeting for a memorable get-together. Do not delay in sharing the revelations of this book with friends, family, workmates, etc., even as you make plans for a group interaction with me.

Toward these ends, please send me an e-mail or post me a letter through the following:

E-mail address: chrisbapuohyele@yahoo.com
Postal address: P. O. Box CT 6282, Cantonments-Accra, Ghana.

Also, would you please provide a short review of the book at Amazon.com if you love it and drop me a hint on this through the Publisher/Author website address on the back cover?

Yours affectionately,

NngmingBongle Bapuohyele

Glossary

Beis HaMikdash: The *Yerushalayim* Temple.

Besuras HaGeulah: The Good News of Redemption for mankind in the sacrifice of *Yahushua HaMashakhYahu*; also known as the "Gospel".

Beyrit Chadasha: The New Covenant scriptures.

Chag Shavuot: Feast of Weeks.

Chayyei Olam: Everlasting (or Eternal) Life, the Life-type in *Elohiym*; made available to dwell in the bodies of all born again persons.

Dahm HaSeh: Blood of the Lamb; Blood of the Savior.

Elohiym: The first of all revealed appellations of the Creator of the Universe according to the Hebrew version of the *Holy Scriptures*. As can be seen in this book, the name ***"God"*** which is used by many Christian theologians and clergymen in reference to the Almighty, the Most High One, the Creator of the Universe, has been avoided.

In the author's view, names and titles of people and names of places must never be translated into other languages, but must always be transliterated. This author sees no difference in sound between ***"God"*** and ***"god"*** and as such, any of these may respond when called or even respond simultaneously.

This author believes that the name, ***"God"*** given by theologians and Christian clergymen to the Creator of the Universe, is highly derogarotory and preposterous, and puts Him in the class of gods—only that He is considered by them to be the biggest, greatest, wisest and most powerful of all gods!

Obviously, The Creator is not in the class of gods and the name ***"God"*** used in reference to Him must be stopped forthwith.

Gan Eden: Garden of Eden.

Gevurot MeyRuwakh HaKodesh: The *Acts of the Apostles* or *Acts.*

HaAdon: The Master, of every born again person who must be obeyed and followed; *Yahushua HaMashakhYahu.*

HaAv: The Father; the Good Father of *Yahushua HaMashakhYahu* and of all born again persons.

HaDavar HaEmes: The Word of Truth—*Elohiym's* Word.

HaDerekh: The Way.

HaMashakhYahu: A Hebrew title for *Yahushua*, the Savior. *HaMashakhYahu* means ***"The Anointed One of Yahuwah (Elohiym)***. Sadly, *"MashakhYahu"* has been corrupted to sound as "Messiah" in English, becoming of no value to *Elohiym* as a result.

HaSefer HaChayyim: The Book of Life in which the names of all humans saved or made to become the children of *Elohiym* in, by, and of the sacrifice of *Yahushua HaMashakhYahu* are recorded.

HaSeh HaElohiym: The Lamb of *Elohiym—Yahushua HaMashakhYahu.*

HaSheini HaShamayim: The Second Heaven

HaShlishi HaShamayim: The Third Heaven.

Holy Scriptures or Scriptures: This is the same in value and meaning as the Word of *Elohiym* revealed by Him and written by holy men in the Hebrew tongue. For the avoidance of doubt, the *Holy Scriptures* are the *Tanakh*—comprised of the *Torah* (Law of Moshe), the *Neviim* ("Prophets") and *Ketuvim* (the "prophetic" writings such as the *Psalms, Proverbs, Ecclesiastes,* etc.)—and the *Beyrit Chadasha* (the records and teachings of the New Covenant dispensation) put together.

Kapporah: Atonement.

Kehillah: Congregation or assembly of Believers in *Yahushua.*

Kes HaMisphat: Judgement Seat (of *Elohiym*).

Kohen Gadol: High Priest of *Yisroel;* also refers to the Savior.

Ma'asim: Same as the book of *Acts* or *Acts of the Apostles.*

Malchut HaElohiym: The Kingdom of *Elohiym.*

Navi: Prophet.

Neviim: Prophets.

Ohr HaAmitti: The True Light; the Savior—*Yahushua HaMashakhYahu.*

Parochet: Curtain, or partition in the *Yerushalayim* Temple of Old.

Pentecost: A word of Greek origin found in the *Greek New Testament* and carried wholesale by translators into the English version of *The Bible,* popularized by Christian theologians and clergymen in their recognition of a "Day of Pentecost" in reference to a so-called Feast of Pentecost.

To Christian clergymen, their so-called Feast of Pentecost is considered to fall on the fiftieth day after another, the so-called Easter Sunday, another Christian feast—wrongly considered to have replaced the Feast of *Pesach* that was established by *Elohiym* on the last night of *Yisroel* in *Mitzrayim* to be celebrated yearly by the house of *Yisroel* throughout all his generations.

The *Holy Scriptures* neither reveal the Day of Pentecost, nor issue instructions for the celebration of a so-called Feast of Pentecost! Because both the Day of Pentecost and Feast of Pentecost are nonscriptural, their observations by Christians are, therefore, sinful (*Romans* 14:23)!

The *Holy Scriptures*, however, reveal and instruct the celebration of *Shavuot* or the Feast of Weeks, meaning a Sabbath of Sabbaths—which falls on the seventh consecutive weekly Sabbath day that follows the first weekly Sabbath after the *Pesach* of every year.

As the Feast of Weeks must always fall exactly on the seventh weekly Sabbath after *Pesach*, it has to always fall on the forty-nineth day, and not on the fiftieth as is wrongly taught among Christians; and it must always be on a weekly Sabbath day and not on Sunday as is believed by Christians!

After the death of *Yahushua HaMashakhYahu*, whose burial-hour kick-started the celebration of *Pesach* in the year of his sacifice, the next scheduled feast of the Hebrew calendar was the seven-day-long Feast of Unleavened Bread which commences on the first day after *Pesach*. The count-down to the Feast of Weeks was anxiously and meticulously made from the seventh day Sabbath within the seven days of the Feast of Unleavened Bread, toward the forty-nineth day—seventh Sabbath or Sabbath of Sabbaths, Feast of Weeks—and not toward the fiftieth day (Pentecost).

What events recorded in the *Holy Scriptures* on the Outpouring of the *Ruwakh HaKodesh* upon the *talmidim* of *Yahushua HaMashakhYahu* who had gathered in the upper room in *Yerushalayim*, therefore, did not happen on a "pentecost" or fiftieth day, but one clear day before—the forty-nineth!

The word *"Pentecost"* has, therefore, no bearing to the faith of true followers of *Yahushua HaMashakhYahu*. In fact, the earliest followers of *Yahushua HaMashakhYahu* never even heard about this so-called Feast of Pentecost. The faith developed by Christians in this word, associating it to their beliefs and practices, is post- and anti-"apostolic", misplaced, and unprofitable in every way!

Perushim: Pharisees

Pesach Seder: *Pesach* (Passover?) lamb.

Ro'eh HaTov: The Good Shepherd.

Ruwakh HaKodesk: The Holy Spirit.

Ruwakh Kodesh: Holy Spirit.

S'air Azazel: Scapegoat (of Azazel).

Shabbat: Sabbath

Sha'arei HaShamayim: Gates of Heaven.

Shed: Demon

Shedim: Demons

Shliakh: Emissary, sent one, or "apostle" of the Savior.

Shlikhim: Emissaries, "apostles" of the Savior.

Shamayim: Heaven.

Shamayim HaRishonah: The First Heaven

Talmid: A follower, student, "disciple" of the Savior.

Talmidim: Followers of the Savior.

The Bible: Any one of the versions of the *Holy Scriptures* translated from Hebrew into any languages of the world. All these versions are made without the mandate of the Most High One and hence, all of these versions contain human errors, inaccuracies, and deceptive thought. *The Bible* must therefore be read with this in mind.

Word of Elohiym: This is generally considered by many salvation seekers to be the same as *The Bible.* In the author's view, however, this should not be so. The *Word of Elohiym* as used in this book is more about the spirit of *The Bible* and not just the letter of it. The *Word of Elohiym* is the unadulterated Hebrew version of the *Holy Scriptures* and not its translated versions.

This is because, the many versions and translations of *The Bible* by people of diverse standing in the Christian faith, cannot all be considered to be the pure Word of the Creator—as the letter of these versions stand.

The *Word of Elohiym* is the substance of these versions, which reveals the mind, wisdom and power of the Most High One, given only by *Ruwakh HaKodesh* to the salvation seeker. Please refer to the earlier definition on *Holy Scriptures or Scriptures* in this index for more information on this.

Torah: The *Law of Moshe* (Moses) or simply the *Law.*

Tzedukim: Sadducees.

Yahushua: This is the Hebrew name by which the Son of *Elohiym*— the Savior, the Anointed One of *Yahuwah,* the *Netzer* (Branch of king *Dovid*) of *Natzeret,* the Sin Bearer of Mankind—was called in his native land of *Yisroel* when he was on Earth. It is this name that a holy angel delivered from *Shamayim* to *Yosef* and the Virgin *Miryam* on two different occasions. *Yahushua* means "**Yahuwah gives Salvation**" or "**Yahuwah Is Salvation**"; the only appropriate name for the Savior of the world.

This author finds it unacceptable to have this name translated into English as "***Jesus***", on the basis that the names of all people and places can only be transliterated in order for them to continue to serve their intended purposes of identification across all races and cultures of people, and should thus never be translated.

The use of the name *Jesus* has been deliberately avoided in this book, except in the quotations taken from *The Bible,* simply because names must never be translated. In fact, a change from *Jesus* to **Yahushua** seems imperative now.

Just as *Tom* and *London* must remain same to all races and cultures, and throughout all times and seasons, so must *Yahushua* and *Natzeret* also forever be.

Elohiym has given a particular name to His Son, by which name alone sinners may be saved: That unique name with power to bring salvation to sinners is **Yahushua HaMashakhYahu**, and NOT "Jesus Christ"!

Yahuwah: Another Holy and Sacred Name of *Elohiym*.

Yom HaCheron: The Last Day.

Yom HaDin: Day of Judgment.

Yom Kippur: Day of Atonement.

Bibliography

Black, H. C. (1968). *Black's Law Dictionary: Definitions of the Terms and Phrases of American and English Jurisprudence, Ancient & Modern* (7thed.). St. Paul, MINN.: West PublishingCo.

Douglas, J. D. (Ed.) (1990). *The New Greek-English Interlinear New Testament* (UBS 4th ed., Nestle-Aland 27th ed.). USA: Tyndale House Publishers.

Garner, B. A. (Ed.) (1999). *Black's Law Dictionary* (8th ed.). USA: West Publishing Co.

Goble, P. E. (Ed.) (2011). *The Orthodox Jewish Bible.* New York, NY: AFI International Publishers.

Heward-Mills, D. (2005). *Born Again.* Ghana: Parchment House.

Kyle, R. (n. d.). Are You Walking in the Truth? *The Voice of Truth International, Vol. 53.*USA: Churches of Christ.

McCoy, V. G. *What is the "One Baptism"?* A Bible tract. YorbaLinda, CA: Gospel Tracts International.

Otabil, M. (2006). *How to be born again.* Ghana: Combert Publications.

Otabil, M. (2006). *How to be filled with the Holy Spirit.* Ghana: Combert Publications.

Rood, M. J. (2013). *The Chronological Gospels: The Life and Seventy Week Ministry of the Messiah.* Fort Mill, SC: Aviv Moon Publishing®

Strong, J. (Ed.) (2001). *The New Strong's Expanded Exhaustive Concordance of the Bible* (Red letter ed.). USA: Thomas Nelson Publishers.

Thompson, F. C. (Ed.) (1988). *Thompson Chain- Reference Bible (KJV)* (Improved 5th ed.). USA: Kirkbride Bible Company Inc.

Today's Parallel Bible (2000). USA: Zondervan.

www.quotationspage.com/quote/35298.html. (2013). Goebbels, J.

www.quotationspage.com/quote/39728.html. (2013). Churchill, W.

www.quotationspage.com/quote/1407.html. (2014). Toffler, A.

Index

C

D

E

G

H

I

M

N

Q

R

S

T

U

Z

About the Author

NngmingBongle Bapuohyele was born in one of the most deprived forest belt villages of *Sefwi* in the southwest area of pre-independence Ghana. At age ten, he was sent to live with an uncle and continued his primary education in the savanna grassland village of *Saa-Charikpong*, Upper West Region, Ghana, where his father hailed from.

He walked five kilometers to school daily, often staying without food, and walked back home to perform domestic chores. He survived a stressful and challenging childhood.

By Providence, he became the first from his village middle school to enter university, where he graduated with a Bachelor of Science (Hon) degree in Geology/Physics.

The author is a man of many parts: mineral explorer, businessman, and soul winner. Searching for Elohiym's salvation in *Yahushua HaMashakhYahu*, he came into contact with diverse faiths of denominations and fellowships, and revelations that form the subject of this book.

The author believes *Elohiym* delivered him from seven life-threatening encounters with snakes, sickness, motor accidents, and an unprovoked physical attack by a tribe of barbarous village folk, so that he could become Elohiym's teacher to the world today.

He is married to Esther, a midwife. They live in Accra, Ghana, with two of their five biological children, and one adopted child.

Lightning Source UK Ltd.
Milton Keynes UK
UKHW01f2242151018
330600UK00001B/66/P